David Dolan

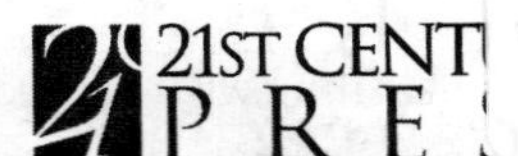

CHRISTIAN PUBLISHING WITH A PURPOSE
WWW.21STCENTURYPRESS.COM

Published by 21st Century Press
2131 W. Republic Road
PMB 41
Springfield, MO 65807

21st Century Press is an evangelical Christian publisher dedicated to serving the local church. We believe God's vision for Gospel Light is to provide church leaders with biblical, user-friendly materials that will help them evangelize, disciple and minister to children, youth and families.

It is our prayer that this book will help you discover biblical truth for your own life and help you meet the needs of others. May God richly bless you.

Printed in the United States of America

ISBN 0-9725719-3-0

Cover: Lee Fredrickson
Book Design: Lee Fredrickson and Terry White
Visit our web-site at: 21stcenturypress.com and 21stcenturybooks.com
For great childrens books visit: sonshipbooks.com

The apocalyptic novel you are holding in your hands was originally published in 1995. In this edition I have updated the original version to reflect international and Mideast developments since then. On top of that, some original material that was edited out of the first version to keep the manuscript a certain length has been incorporated into this edition.

Although The End of Days is "just a novel," many readers have told me that it is the most realistic end-time scenario that they have ever read. Possibly that is partly due to my intimate knowledge of Israel-having lived in the land that the prophets foretold would be at the center of the worldwide drama set to unfold in the biblical "end of days" since 1980. On top of that, I introduce what I believe is some largely overlooked biblical evidence for the identity of one of the "Two Witnesses" who were foretold to appear in the last days in Jerusalem. At the very least, this has added to the uniqueness of this work. The overall scenario that I unfold is based entirely on biblical scriptures, with many of them noted so that the reader may go to the source if so desired for further study.

One of the most controversial eschatological issues among Evangelicals is the timing of the "rapture"-the end-time supernatural gathering to the Lord of true believers from around the world, said to take place in the "twinkling of an eye." I have chosen to leave this out of my novel, since the Apostle Paul called it a "mystery" and its exact timing is hotly disputed. While I personally lean toward the "pre-wrath view" that believers will be caught away toward the end of the Antichrist's short reign, I do not hold this as an unassailable position. I therefore decided to leave the rapture out altogether so as not to distract from the main thrust of my novel-the centrality of Israel and Jewish believers in the prophesied End of Days.

I trust you will enjoy, and be blessed, by this novel. If anything, events here in Israel and around the world in recent years demand that we be as well informed as possible concerning what the Bible has to say about the end of this age. All signs are indicating that the prophesied events are about to unfold. So buckle up and enjoy the read!

David Dolan

Jerusalem

Contents

1

Awake in the Night

"Who in the world could be knocking at our door at this time of night?" asked Sarah as she shot up in bed. The clock read 2 A.M.

"I don't know, but they sure are persistent," replied Jonathan, scratching the day-old growth on his chin.

"I'm coming!" shouted the irritated American-born Israeli, pulling on a T-shirt.

"Honey, don't forget to take your—"

"I won't," said Jonathan, reaching for his loaded revolver on the top shelf of the clothes closet.

A husky voice called out his name as he switched on the front porch light of his southeast Jerusalem home. "Jonathan Goldman, this is Shimon Chai. I need to speak with you. It's urgent." Jonathan's heart sank. He already knew what his visitor, a forty-eight-year-old lawyer wearing army fatigues, was going to tell him.

"Shalom, Jonathan. Sorry to wake you in the middle of the night, but our unit is being called up immediately.

Throw some things in a bag. An army van will be by to pick you up in about an hour."

Sarah stood listening near the bedroom doorway. One hour! The words were bullets ricocheting in her head.

"Okay, Shimon, I'll be ready. Have any idea how many other units are being mobilized?"

"Not exactly, but I understand it's a large-scale call-up. See you in an hour. Shalom."

The thirty-four-year-old reserve soldier carefully locked the front door and retraced his steps to the bedroom. "Princess, it was Shimon Chai from my—"

"I heard," Sarah interrupted, not wanting to waste any of the precious moments she had left with her cherished partner. "I'll pack some things for you and then wake the children. They wouldn't forgive me if I let you go off without giving them hugs and saying good-bye."

Jonathan gently held his twenty-eight-year-old wife. She finally allowed herself to look into her husband's affectionate brown eyes. "The children love you so much, Jonathan, and so do I."

He softly kissed his petite partner and began stroking her long, silky, auburn hair. He was determined not to show the tinge of fear he was already feeling. Sarah could not hold back her tears. She knew the nighttime call-up meant the government anticipated war with Syria. She knew it might be the last time she would see her beloved Jonathan.

"Princess, before you wake the kids, let's spend a few more minutes alone." Quietly closing the bedroom door, Sarah placed her arms around the waist of the only man she had ever loved.

Prime Minister Yacov Nimrod had slept only one hour when Defense Minister Rafi Hochman phoned on the secure bedroom line of his official Jerusalem residence.

"Yacov, this is Rafi. I have extremely important news for you."

"Give me a minute to wake up." The groggy prime minister reached for his watch on his bedside table.

"Good grief, what time is it?" asked his slender wife as she rubbed her eyes.

"Okay, Rafi, shoot."

"It's the Syrians. I just received a call from Tom Roberts at the State Department."

"The Secretary for Near East Affairs called you at this time of night?" interrupted Nimrod.

Hochman, a former general in the Israeli army, glanced at his notes. "Roberts says the American embassy in Damascus is monitoring unusual troop movements on the outskirts of the city. And, more ominously, there seems to be a large-scale Syrian reserve call-up in progress."

The fifty-six-year-old prime minister looked again at the face of the watch that his father had given him when he finished his army duty.

"How long has this been going on?"

"The Americans began noticing it early yesterday morning. Roberts said they didn't want to inform us until they were completely sure."

The Israeli premier strapped his watch on his arm as he paused to gather his thoughts. "What do you advise, Rafi? Should we respond with a nationwide call-up?"

"I believe we have no choice, but I think we can get by with a partial mobilization at this point."

"Alright," responded Nimrod, rubbing his leathery eyelids. "We'll take another look at the situation in the morning. Phone Roberts back and express my appreciation for the tip. And try to get some sleep."

"I will, Yacov. Shalom."

The portly defense minister sighed as he hung up the phone, content with his decision to order a partial mobilization even before consulting his superior.

Esther Nimrod sat up and began gently rubbing the arched back of her husband. "The Americans must not be as angry at us as you thought, Yacov," the demure mother of two said as she pressed on the muscles near his lower spine. But her thoughts were actually focused elsewhere. *Wives and mothers around Israel will be bidding goodbyes to their men tonight. At least my Yacov will be here with me, even if he does have the weight of the nation on his shoulders.*

"I think the president is still a bit angry, Esther," Yacov replied as his wife massaged his neck. "But he certainly doesn't want to see the Syrians attack us. Cliff understands that a full-scale war would be devastating, to say the least, and not just for the Middle East."

Relations with the United States had been tense ever since Syrian/Israeli peace talks ground to a halt several months earlier. President Clifford Williams blamed both Mideast countries for the negotiating impasse. The assassination by Iranian-backed Muslim terrorists of Israel's United Nations ambassador in New York—coming on the heels of an upsurge of suicide bombing attacks against Israeli civilians—had made it impossible for Nimrod to make major concessions at the peace talks. The Israeli leader was unwilling or, more accurately, politically unable to agree to Halled Hasdar's unbending demand for a total Israeli abandonment of the strategic Golan Heights, captured from Syria in 1967. He also refused to link a withdrawal to a staged Israeli pullout from the eastern half of Jerusalem, as Hasdar had insisted.

On the other side, the Syrian leader refused to consider anything short of a total Israeli withdrawal from "every centimeter of the Golan Heights," as he often put it, and he demanded that Israel relinquish the vital plateau in a short period of time, not the three-year phased retreat proposed by Nimrod. He also resisted Nimrod's suggestion that an Israeli pullout be linked to a staged Syrian retreat from Lebanon, where over thirty thousand soldiers had been stationed since 1976.

"I cannot quickly evacuate the Golan and dismantle our settlements up there without raising complete havoc in my country," Nimrod had explained to President Williams as the talks bogged down. "The area is strategically too vital to abandon overnight, Cliff. We get much of our fresh water from there, and our electronic listening posts on top of Mount Hermon are virtually irreplaceable. Quite a few of your own generals acknowledge that it would be military suicide for us to withdraw entirely from the area, even if you send American troops to act as a peacekeeping buffer force. And for us, Jerusalem is . . . well, Jerusalem."

"But the alternative to peace will surely be war," replied the somber president. "Don't you trust us to keep Hasdar's forces away from the Golan ridges?"

"Of course we do, Cliff. But I cannot agree at the same time to begin a phased pullout from the eastern half of Jerusalem, the very heart of our Jewish state, the place where our ancient Temple once stood. Many of our citizens would go crazy at the prospect of abandoning David's ancient city. I would have civil war on my hands in no time.

"Besides, we already offered Hasdar a long-term phased withdrawal from the Golan Heights in good faith—a quite generous offer, I might add, in light of past Syrian attacks on us from there. Hasdar refused to compromise, so what can I do?"

"I realize the Syrians have been obstinate, Yacov, but the peace process must go on."

"We're ready for it to continue, Cliff, but only if the Arabs will meet us halfway. I can't yank thousands of Israeli Jews from their homes overnight on the Golan, and we will not turn over eastern Jerusalem to Arab control, period. The Arabs have Mecca. Jerusalem is our holiest city on earth. We will not cede control over any part of our capital city, even if Muslims around the region launch their threatened holy war."

"If my intelligence reports are accurate, they may be planning to do just that."

"That's a risk we'll have to take, Cliff. Israel has survived several wars already. We're not afraid."

Jonathan slipped on his fatigues as Sarah went to wake up Tali, nearly seven, and her brother, Benny, who had just turned four. "I used to fit into these with no problem," he mused, struggling to close his waist button.

"Tali, sweetheart, wake up," Sarah whispered as she reached down and gently shook her daughter.

"What's going on?" the sleepy girl inquired while rubbing her eyes.

"Abba has to go away for a little while," replied Sarah, pulling back strands of dark brown hair from the face of her firstborn child.

"Right now? But it's still dark outside."

"I know, sweetheart. Get up quickly or you might miss him."

"I'm up!" she announced, springing out of bed.

Rousing Benny proved more difficult, but soon he was in his Superman slippers and standing sleepily next to his sister in the living room.

Sarah felt a tinge of pride when her handsome beau emerged from the bedroom, smartly decked out in his recently pressed army uniform. While kneeling down to hug his two blurry-eyed darlings, Jonathan winked at her like some soldier at a Saturday night dance.

"You two are so special to me!" he said as he tucked the little ones under his arms. "I've got to go away for a few days, but Mama will be here with you." He glanced up at Sarah and managed to smile.

He's the most handsome man in the world, she thought as the soft light from a nearby lamp highlighted the touch of red in Jonathan's black hair.

"Abba, why are you wearing your uniform?" asked Tali, now fully awake. "Didn't you finish your army duty last month?"

"Yes, honey, I've already done my reserve time for this year. But something special is happening, and my friends need me to be with them."

"Is Uncle Eli going to be with you?" asked the freckle-nosed Benny.

"Of course, son, Uncle Eli and I are always together in the army," replied Jonathan, his face brightening at the mention of his best friend's name.

"Abba, is there going to be a war?" asked Benny as he rubbed his tired eyes.

How do kids today figure these things out at such a young age? Jonathan wondered, thinking back to his carefree childhood in Skokie, Illinois.

"No, little one, there is *not* going to be a war," Sarah answered emphatically with a certainty that surprised even her.

Jonathan gave his slender wife a reassuring look. "Abba will be alright," he told the kids.

"Yes, he will," affirmed Sarah. "Now you two give Daddy a big kiss and get back to bed."

After tucking the children back in bed, Sarah returned to find Jonathan sitting pensively on the living room sofa.

"The van should be here any moment," she sighed as she snuggled into his lap.

"Yeah, I need to get going."

Sarah stroked her husband's neck. Tears formed in her eyes. "Sweetheart, will I ever see you again?"

"Don't talk like that, princess," he scolded, forcing back his own tears. "Whatever happens, we'll spend eternity together with the Lord. Let's thank Him now while we're together for all He's done and is going to do.

"Abba," Jonathan prayed, "Sarah and I love You. And we trust You, no matter what the future holds. Lord, I cannot hide the fear that's inside me right now. But I can ask You to take it away and replace it with Your joy. Abba, please grant Your deepest peace to Sarah and the kids. I thank You so much for them.

"The Lord is my shepherd," began Jonathan as tears formed in his eyes. "I shall not want."

Sarah wiped Jonathan's cheeks as she joined him in reciting the Twenty-third Psalm.

"I better wait outside, love," he said after a few moments of silence.

Before the two got to the door, a horn sounded. The reserve soldier kissed his wife of nine years good-bye. "Princess, I love you."

"And I love you." Sarah put her arms around her husband's waist. "Be careful!" she urged as the night swallowed up her husband's fading form.

"I will, princess, and I'll phone as soon as I can."

"Shalom, brother!" exclaimed Jonathan as he squeezed in the waiting van next to his longtime buddy, Eli Ben-David. "Another stint in the army together!"

Eli laughed, placing his short, robust arm over Jonathan's broad shoulders. The Jerusalem-born Israeli was his usual cheerful self. "This time, Uncle Yacov is going to let us play with real ammunition!"

"I suspect you're right," opined Jonathan.

"How is Sarah taking this mysterious call-up?"

"It's not so easy for us American-born Jews to get used to all this war stuff, but she'll be okay."

"Do you think us Sabras ever get used to it, Yonni?" Eli asked, using his friend's Israeli nickname.

"I suppose not. But at least you don't have a wife and youngsters to worry about." Jonathan smiled at his swarthy friend. "But you have plenty of pretty females worrying about you—at least a fourth of our congregation, I suspect!"

Eli chuckled and abruptly changed the subject. "What do you suppose is going on?"

"I imagine it's the Syrians and the situation in Lebanon." Jonathan prided himself on being well-read when it came to the Middle East. "Old Hasdar has been beating the war drums lately. I suppose our prime minister feels we have to be ready for anything."

"But why a mobilization in the middle of the night, Yonni? Slightly overdramatic, don't you think?"

"Maybe, but don't forget that we shot down three Syrian jets over Lebanon this past week, after those missile attacks on our northern border by Hizbullah militiamen that left four Israelis dead. Who knows, maybe another missile has hit or another plane has gone down. The situation is not good."

"And the chaos in Jordan and Iraq isn't helping."

Eli's thoughts drifted to an old movie he had just seen on television. "Yonni, did you ever see that film *On the Beach,* about a nuclear war that destroys civilization in the northern hemisphere?"

"Yeah, centuries ago when I was still in the States."

"Well, I feel a little bit like the Australians in that film. They know death is coming, yet there is nothing they can do about it. Eventually the nuclear fallout reaches them, and—"

"Come on, Eli, don't be so morbid."

"Then I had this vivid dream the other night about nuclear war here in the Middle East. It was awful."

"Man, you've been staying up too late and watching too many old movies."

Despite his mild rebuke, Jonathan already thought that just such a disaster might in fact be looming.

"Yeah, I suppose you're right," said Eli as the van stopped to pick up another soldier. The crowded vehicle proceeded north past long city blocks filled with tall, white Jerusalem-stone apartment buildings. The pink streetlights made the buildings look so soft, Jonathan thought. Yet the white light shining out of many apartment windows gave a hint that this was not an ordinary spring night.

As the van neared the northern edge of the city, Jonathan's eyes caught a glimpse of the Dome of the Rock located on Jerusalem's ancient Temple Mount. Bright floodlights cast a pink hue on the Muslim shrine's golden dome.

"Do you think we'll ever see a Jewish temple up there again?" he whispered to his buddy.

"Only God knows," replied Eli, as he gazed back at the fading Jerusalem skyline.

Yacov Nimrod spent most of the night tossing in bed. As the sun began to rise behind the Mount of Olives, he got up and walked over to gaze out of his bedroom window. *That old, gnarled tree has survived many generations,* he thought as he focused his eyes on the twisted trunk of an olive tree in the yard. *And so have we.* Nimrod turned back toward the bed just as the phone rang.

"This is President Williams's office in Washington with a call for Prime Minister Yacov Nimrod," a female voice drawled in a southern accent.

"Speaking."

"Good morning, sir, I'll put the president on."

"Yacov, this is Cliff Williams. They tell me it's 5:30 in the morning there. Sorry to wake you so early."

"I wasn't sleeping, Cliff," Nimrod said as he sat down on the bed. "How are you and your wife and children?"

"Probably doing better than yours," responded the American leader. "Yacov, I'll get right to the point. We have word from our folks in Tel Aviv that you're mobilizing your reserves. Is that correct?"

They don't miss a thing, thought Nimrod.

"Yes, Cliff, but only partially at this stage. Our region has been tense since that dogfight with Syrian jets over Lebanon earlier this week. And the recent action in Iraq hasn't helped things either, nor the Palestinian terror attacks."

The president glanced at a situation report on his desk. "I understand why your pilots bombed those Hizbullah bases. Those Muslim fundamentalist fighters have been attacking your settlements across the border with increasing ferocity, haven't they?"

"They have. In the last week alone we've lost eight soldiers on the ground and four civilians along the border. By the way, thanks for the tip from Damascus. You understand we have to match Hasdar's call-up."

"I understand," Williams quickly replied. "And I have some related news for you. Our satellites show heavy Syrian troop movements toward your border. We've also spotted unusual activity in Lebanon and at Syrian air bases and at their Mediterranean port of Latakia."

He's forgotten we launched our own spy satellite last month, thought Nimrod.

"Thanks, Cliff. It confirms yesterday's pictures from our Ofec Seven satellite. I'm afraid Hasdar is serious about a showdown."

"I forgot about your Ofec, Yacov. Sorry," Williams responded, annoyed that his aides had not reminded him. "I think you may be right about Hasdar, and I want you to know that you have the full backing of the United States if Syria attacks. But," the president paused, "Congress and the American people may not understand if you make the first move. Things are pretty tough here right now, and taxpayers don't want to spend money helping anyone, not even Israel."

"I understand, Mr. President. But you understand, as a leader sworn to defend your own country, that I can't just sit back and let an enemy attack us. Shamir may have sat out Saddam's Scud strikes on our cities because America requested it, but Syria poses a far greater threat."

"I realize that, Yacov, and I think most Americans do, too. I'm not going to sit here in Washington and try to quarterback your present situation. I'm only urging caution and restraint. We both know how ugly this thing could turn out to be."

"All I can promise you," said a grave Nimrod, "is that we'll do our best to avoid conflict. War is the last thing we want—or need."

The two leaders said good-bye, and Nimrod phoned his cabinet secretary. "Pinkas, this is Yacov. Arrange a top-secret cabinet meeting for eight o'clock this morning," he directed. "We have some urgent business to discuss."

2

The Gathering Storm

The twenty-one government ministers met as directed in the cabinet room located on the fifth floor of the government office building in the center of Jerusalem. Despite the departure of many men during the night, rush hour traffic passed by noisily on nearby Ruppin Boulevard.

"Ladies and gentlemen, we are facing an extremely grave situation in the north." The age lines in the prime minister's face stood out this morning. "I'm sure you have heard the media reports that Syrian troops are moving toward our Golan Heights border and our border with Lebanon."

Most of them nodded.

"Ofec Seven spotted this movement yesterday afternoon. Around 2:00 A.M., the Americans confirmed that Hasdar is calling up his civilian army reserves. Rafi Hochman and I discussed Syria's mobilization last night, and I ordered an immediate call-up of our reserves."

"All of them?" asked the finance minister, Amnon Zahav, clutching his somewhat generous belly. "That will cripple our economy!"

Nimrod glared at him. "No, not a complete call-up, at least not yet."

"How many men can the Syrians mobilize?" inquired the housing minister, thinking about his son on his way up to the Golan border.

"They can muster a reserve force of around one million men to back up their regular army of some four hundred thousand soldiers," replied Hochman.

Foreign Minister Yudah Sephres was Nimrod's political rival within their Likud party. He nervously fingered a pencil as he spoke up. "Do the Americans know about our mobilization? How have they responded?"

Yudah will be angry about this, thought Nimrod before he answered. "President Williams and I spoke at 5:30 this morning."

Sephres, sporting a full head of gray-white hair at sixty-three, was also the leader of the peace camp within the Likud party. *That's the first time he's spoken to you since your paranoid views contributed to the collapse of the peace talks with Syria,* he thought.

Nimrod went on. "The president had already heard about our call-up from Ambassador Norton in Tel Aviv. He pledged to support us if we are attacked by Syria. However—"

"Not if we hit them first!" interrupted Edna Satori, the social welfare minister from the small, centrist Immigrants Rights party—a pivotal part of Nimrod's coalition government.

"Cliff didn't exactly say that, Edna. But he did indicate that his own deepening economic troubles would make it difficult to raise congressional support if we appear to be the aggressor."

"Will we launch a preemptive strike?" asked environment minister Yossi Ritzar, a member of Satori's party.

"There's a good chance," defense minister Hochman answered with his usual disdain for his leftist cabinet colleagues. "You know that we've collectively vowed never to allow another Masada. If we have good reason to believe we might be attacked, we must consider striking first."

"Rafi, the Syrians aren't the Romans," retorted Satori, whose blond hair was showing more than a touch of gray. "They don't have the power to destroy us."

"We don't know that for sure," piped in the prime minister, who also mistrusted some of the aims of his Peace and Welfare ministers. "The Americans didn't realize how far along Saddam's nuclear program was before the Gulf War. Neither did the British or French, and we only suspected it. And who really anticipated Al-Qaida's initial terror strikes in America? We can never be certain what a Muslim dictator like Hasdar is up to."

The Israeli premier raised his pen in the air as if pointing to a chart. "We know Syria has an advanced chemical and biological weapons program. We believe Hasdar has around two dozen Soviet-built SS–21 missile launchers. They took delivery of many advanced Scud–C launchers from North Korea and are now building the missiles themselves in Syria. Scud–Cs are far more accurate than the missiles fired at us by Iraq."

"And Scud–Cs have a range of over three hundred miles," added Hochman, who possessed a keen mind at fifty-seven. "So they can easily strike our population centers from deep inside Syria."

"Hasdar also has the older Scud–Bs, with a range of 180 miles," Nimrod continued, "and other missiles he can fire from submarines in the Mediterranean. The Russians and others have been supplying him with all kinds of sophisticated weapons over the past few years."

Hochman took up the argument. "Don't forget that Syria's closest ally is Iran, and Iran has advanced warplanes that could be added to Syria's arsenal, not to mention their North Korean and Chinese-built missiles."

"So, how is our partial mobilization going to stop Hasdar from firing these deadly missiles?" asked immigrant absorption minister Rivlin, worried that the unfolding drama might make his job superfluous.

"It's not," sighed Nimrod. "But it could make him realize we won't sit passively by and let ourselves be attacked."

Again the tall, lean defense minister chimed in, "Our call-up might at least help deflect a ground assault. As I pointed out, the Syrians have a standing army of over four hundred thousand men, almost three times the size of ours! They have eleven crack divisions, five fully armored, and they've got five mechanized infantry, plus a command division. Their ground forces remain a threat."

"Realize that they have double our tanks—over four thousand, and many of them are advanced Russian T–72s," added Nimrod, an army general before he entered politics. "And their air force! Hasdar's father was air force chief when Syria lost the Golan to us during the Six Day War in '67. I believe he wants Syria's jets to play a big role in getting it back. He's also been taking delivery of more Sukoi–24 long-range bombers from Russia and MIG–29 jets!"

Dressed in her usual flamboyant style, Mrs. Satori fingered an enormous string of pearls that hung around her neck. "Let's not forget we have a very good army and air force," she declared, "and nuclear weapons. Around three hundred isn't it, Yacov? Let's not forget that!"

No one said a word for at least fifteen seconds. Nimrod

cleared his throat. "The North Koreans may have sold nuclear weapons to Syria, and Hasdar has strong ties to Russia, Iran and Al-Qaida. In fact, Iran may have already acquired a few nuclear weapons from the former Soviet Union. And Russian military advisors have been spotted with Syrian forces in Lebanon, just like before the Soviet collapse."

Sephres scowled and pounded his fist on the arm of his chair. "Yacov, the Russians are preoccupied with their internal problems right now, especially their economy."

"True, responded Nimrod, but so is our ally America. Things can change fast in this world. We can't take anything for granted, not when our very existence could be at stake."

Just then, the prime minister's advisor on Arab Affairs, Simcha Levy, opened the door and entered the cabinet room. He headed straight for his boss, bent down, and whispered into Nimrod's ear.

"Friends, Hasdar is about to address his nation on Syrian state radio. You understand Arabic, don't you, Yisrael?" He directed his question at Yisrael Chofi, the Moroccan-born transport minister. "Aiwa," Chofi replied. "It's my mother tongue."

"Good," said Nimrod, while loosening his beige silk tie. "Let's listen."

The Arab affairs advisor, also fluent in Arabic, tuned in Radio Damascus. As the static filtered out, the Syrian national anthem filtered in. Then, the familiar voice of the notorious ruler of Syria came across the airwaves.

"Hasdar is beginning in the name of Allah, the usual salutation about his being merciful," reported Chofi. "Now he's talking about what a great nation Syria is." The wiry minister paused. "He has just mentioned Israel." The other ministers had already noticed.

"He's talking about Syria's supposed victory over us in the '73 Yom Kippur War—what the Arabs call the 'Ramadan War.' He says Allah helped Syria deliver a decisive blow to the Jewish infidel state."

"I didn't think Hasdar used such religious terms," said Satori, the only atheist in Nimrod's cabinet.

"He normally doesn't," responded Amos Shimshon, the religious affairs minister, who was clad in his usual black garb. "But most Arab leaders, whatever their convictions, use Islamic terms before going to war, just like Saddam did."

Chofi continued. "He says another glorious victory is near, and he claims he tried to get back, peacefully, the sacred land stolen from Syria during the Six Day War."

"We did not steal the Golan!" Hochman protested. "Moshe Dayan had no other military option than to take the strategic Heights!"

The transport minister leaned forward. "Calm down, Rafi, I'm just reporting what Hasdar is saying. He is maintaining that world leaders understand he has done all he could for peace and that he has no other choice now but to take up the sword. He says Libya, Sudan, Iraq, Yemen, and Jordan back him, along with Iran."

"I don't think King Abdul supports him," interjected the foreign minister, who was taking meticulous notes.

"That may be, Yudah, but does Abdul really control Jordan?" Hochman asked rhetorically. "Our latest intelligence indicates that the Palestinian fundamentalists and leftist insurgents fighting against his forces in the eastern Jordanian desert will probably prevail. If so, we'll have a solid wall of enemies to the north and east of us."

Nimrod stared at the radio on a table to his right. "And even if Abdul comes out on top, Syria could force Jordan into supporting military action against us, like they did in '67 and '73."

"Hasdar is going on about Iran," reported Chofi, having some trouble listening over the talking ministers. "He claims the Iranian people fully support the Arab struggle against Israel even though they're Persians. He says that Iranian Shiite Muslims have vowed to spill every ounce of blood in order to liberate holy Jerusalem."

"What does that mean?" Satori looked worried for the first time.

Hochman answered her. "Probably that Iran is planning to send men to fight alongside the Syrians, or at least to unleash Hizbullah forces against us." The defense minister knew that the Ofec satellite had already detected increased cargo flights between Tehran and Damascus over the past week. He and Nimrod suspected these jumbo jets were carrying men, as well as arms, to Syria.

"But Iran is a nation of around sixty million people!" exclaimed Satori. "We are less than six million Jews. Why don't they leave us alone!"

"You don't understand how these Muslim fundamentalists feel about us, do you, Edna?" Hochman sneered with contempt.

"I'm not so sure I want to."

Chofi wiped beads of sweat from his brow with a white handkerchief. "Hasdar is going for the jugular now! He's vowing to liberate the Golan Heights and Jerusalem from the 'tyranny of Zionist occupation.' He says the Syrian people must be ready to lay down their lives for this sacred cause, just as he himself is."

The sound of the Syrian national anthem filled the room again. Chofi angrily switched off the radio and returned to his cabinet seat.

Nimrod finally broke the silence. "I don't want any statements to the press," he ordered, looking directly at Sephres. "I'm declaring a full military alert. I want each of you to stay in Jerusalem in case we need to hold another emergency session."

"May the God of Israel help us all!" declared Rabbi Amos Shimshon.

Even Edna Satori nodded her head in agreement with the religious affairs minister's cry.

"Shimon Chai."

"Here."

"Boaz Feinberg."

"Here."

"Jonathan Goldman."

Jonathan sat cleaning his rifle. "I'm here."

The unit commander, Uzi Bilam, continued. "Moshe Salam."

"Yes, sir."

"And our medic, Eli Ben-David, are you here?"

"He's gone over there to get some things," answered Jonathan, pointing to a nearby supply truck.

"Good!" replied Bilam as he lowered his clipboard. "Now, men, our current position is five miles back from our Golan border with Syria. We'll stay put here until further notice. I know you guys hardly got any sleep last night, so you may return to your tents for a short while. Feinberg, take the first guard duty. We'll hold firing exercises in two hours."

The late morning sun was hot. Jonathan unbuttoned his army shirt as he walked toward the supply truck. He was hoping he could use its portable telephone to call home.

"I hope we won't need all this stuff." Eli appeared from behind the truck with his arms full of medical supplies.

"You and me both. We already signed in. I told them you were getting some things over here."

"Thanks, brother. We're in this together, hey?"

"Yeah."

Although born on different continents, the two men had become good friends eight years ago after they met at congregation Beit Yisrael in Jerusalem. Jonathan was only a couple years out of college and had just quit his job as an accountant and moved to Israel with Sarah, his bride. Eli was working as a grade school teacher in north Jerusalem. He offered private Hebrew lessons to the new immigrant couple to supplement what they were learning at the government absorption center where they lived. After one year in Israel, Jonathan began his fulltime army service and was later assigned to the same reserve unit as Eli. The new friends considered this an act of God.

"Bilam says we can't use our cell phones, but we can make one call on the portable phone. Do you know where it is?" Jonathan inquired.

"It's over there next to the jeep."

"I want to call home and then get a few winks of sleep."

Eli smiled. "Tell her 'shalom' from me."

After ten minutes, the soldier got a line into Jerusalem. "Hi, Sarah."

"Oh, Jonathan, it's so good to hear your voice!"

"It's taken awhile to get through. Everyone and their mother must be on the phone."

"Where are you?"

"I can't tell you, princess. Let's just say close enough to the enemy but not too close. How are the kids?"

"They miss you, but they're fine. Still fairly oblivious to it all. I'm not so sure about their mother though! That reminds me; your parents phoned. So did mine."

Jonathan looked at his watch. "But it's the middle of the night in the States."

"You know Daddy! He heard about the call-up on the midnight news. He immediately called me and then phoned back east to your folks in Skokie. Then they called here."

"Are they all okay?"

"Daddy is mad at Hasdar. Mom is fine but worried. Your folks sounded calm, but I could tell they are worried."

"A natural reaction, I guess. If they phone again, tell them I love them."

"You know they will. I'll tell them. You don't think Ma Bell is behind all this war talk, do you? It sure increases her business!"

"Could be," laughed Jonathan. "Did you tell my boss where I am?"

"Yes, I phoned him around 9:30. He said another bank accountant was missing too, apparently called up like you. Sweetheart, we're having a special prayer meeting at the congregation at 7:30 this evening. Two of the elders have been mobilized and eight other members besides you."

"Tell everyone 'hello' for me."

"I will. I'll be praying for you, honey."

Jonathan wiped the sweat running down his temple. "Thanks. I'd better go, princess. I love you."

"Don't forget, the Lord is our shepherd! Shalom, love."

"Shalom."

After Jonathan put back the portable phone, he pulled out a piece of Passover matzah bread from his pack. A mental picture of the Lord's Last Supper flashed through his mind. "This is my body," he said softly, "broken for you."

3

In the Shelter

The orange rays of the setting sun shone through Nimrod's office window as he quietly digested the latest intelligence information. The secure telephone rang.

"Yes, Ora?"

"An urgent call from the defense minister, sir."

"Put him on."

"Yacov, the Syrians are arming their missiles!" Hochman exclaimed frantically. "Ofec and our high altitude reconnaissance flights confirm it, without a doubt!"

"Get over here right away. Bring Chief of Staff Bar-Am with you, and Yudah."

Five minutes later, Nimrod's two senior ministers entered his office, followed by the armed forces commander.

Hochman somberly laid out eight enlarged photos on Nimrod's desk. "You may flip when you see these! General Bar-Am, please."

The armed forces chief approached the large oak desk. "This is clear photographic evidence Hasdar is arming his Scud–C and SS–21 missiles. We have not spotted any Scud–B or Frog missiles yet, but we assume some are being fitted."

"Fitted with what?" Sephres asked as he leaned closer to view the pictures.

"It appears to our experts that chemical warheads are being placed on the Scud–Cs, and possibly on the SS–21s as well."

Nimrod pivoted his chair around to gaze out his window at the modern city of Jerusalem below. The buildings glowed in the late afternoon sun. He looked at several nearby hotels. He was glad that they were hosting few tourists, due to the escalating Mideast crisis. He sighed as he thought of the possible fate that awaited them.

The moment that had given him occasional nightmares since he became prime minister had arrived. His tiny nation stood on the brink of a nonconventional missile attack. The consequences were almost unimaginable. "So Hasdar's going to try and fulfill Saddam's threat to wipe out half of Israel with chemical weapons," he said aloud as he swung back around.

"Yes, sir, it looks that way," General Bar-Am replied.

"How much damage could a first strike do?" inquired Sephres.

"Plenty," Hochman replied as he folded his arms across his chest. "We believe the Scud–Cs can deliver substantial amounts of chemicals or even biological weapons, like anthrax and VX nerve gas."

"What's the latest estimate of Syrian nonconventional warheads, Rafi?" Nimrod asked.

"We estimate Hasdar has at least one hundred ballistic warheads, plus thousands of chemical artillery shells."

"Which he'd use in the local theater of fighting," added Sephres.

"Exactly," confirmed General Bar-Am.

Nimrod sighed. "How old are these photos, Rafi?"

"The satellite shots—these here—were taken less than forty-five minutes ago. The high altitude airplane photos are roughly two hours old."

"So a first strike could come at any time."

Hochman nodded. "I'm afraid so, I'm afraid so," he heard himself say twice.

"Rafi, I'm ordering a total mobilization of our reserve forces. Would you see to it?"

"Yes, sir, right away."

Nimrod pressed his inter-office intercom.

"Ora, arrange a meeting of the security cabinet for one hour from now. Tell everyone to meet in the pool hall."

"The what, sir?"

"It's a code word, Ora. The pool hall."

"We're having a deadly game of billiards," added Sephres, turning to leave the room.

It was an unusually hot day in May, due to dry winds blowing southwest from the Syrian desert. Jonathan Goldman and Eli Ben-David sat next to each other on the thick grass, facing east toward Syria. To the north lay the snow-covered peaks of towering Mount Hermon, the 9,200-foot mountain that provides much of the water for the Jordan River. The two buddies could barely hear the birds chirping in the apple trees around them above the noise of distant Israeli tanks engaged in target practice. The sound of exploding shells echoed into the lush Hula Valley below the Golan Heights, where fields of cotton basked in the fading sunlight.

"What do you think is going to happen, Yonni?" Eli asked as the two men relaxed together.

"I'm not sure, but I keep thinking about that prophecy in Isaiah 17."

"The one about Damascus being destroyed?"

"Yes. If we take it literally—and I take Scripture literally—then it hasn't been fulfilled."

"But hasn't Damascus been destroyed several times in history?"

Jonathan had taken a number of courses at a small Bible college near Los Angeles. He pulled out his pocket Bible from his army pack. "It has been conquered many times, Eli, but never totally destroyed. I remember reading that Damascus is one of the oldest continuously inhabited cities on earth." He flipped open his Bible. "It says here in Isaiah 17:1 that Damascus will be 'removed from being a city, and it will become a fallen ruin.' Verse 3 says sovereignty will disappear from Damascus. I think the King James says something like the kingdom will cease from Damascus. Syria's capital has been overrun many times, but it's still a vibrant city. This prophecy seems to be talking about a complete and lasting destruction."

Another tank blast echoed through the nearby foothills of Mount Hermon.

"Sounds like my dream—or should I say nightmare—might have been prophetic after all," sighed Eli. "But what about us? In the dream I saw thousands dying—here in Israel."

"If this really is the time for Isaiah 17 to be fulfilled, then it's bad news for us."

"Why do you say that?" Eli reached into his pack to pull out a water bottle and take a swig.

"In verse 3, Isaiah says that 'the fortified city will disappear from Ephraim' along with sovereignty from Damascus."

Eli sat up straight, nearly ripping the seams of his army shirt that fit too snugly on his stocky frame. "Isn't Ephraim the biblical name for the hills of Samaria north of Jerusalem, where my Uncle Yuval lives?"

"That's right. In ancient days, Ephraim was another name for the entire northern kingdom of Israel. Ephraim was its largest tribe. Actually, this part of Isaiah's prophecy might mean that armed fortifications won't be needed anymore in the north because of the destruction of Damascus, which is good news. But here comes the bad news."

"I'm all ears, Yonni."

"Here's verse 4: 'Now it will come about in that day that the glory of Jacob will fade, and the fatness of his flesh will become lean.' Isaiah writes that Israel will be shaken like an olive tree but that some fruit will remain. In chapter 24 he uses the same analogy of an olive tree being shaken, but there it refers to the final judgment of the whole earth. So, the Bible seems to indicate we are going to suffer when this Damascus prophecy is fulfilled, but we won't be destroyed."

"Thank God," replied Eli, thinking about his large family scattered across Israel, a tiny country less than fifty miles wide and only two hundred fifty-six miles from the northern Lebanon border to the southern port of Eilat.

The two men sat quietly for a few moments, their backs warmed by the setting sun's rays.

"So Yonni, we might be in for some real shaking, if that word is for now."

"The prophecy ends by stating that the nations will be in an uproar, possibly because of something Israel does to Damascus. They will rush together against us like a noisy sea.

"But, the really good news is that God himself will rebuke them. Verse 7 of Isaiah 17 reads, 'In that day man will have regard for his Maker, and his eyes will look to the Holy One of Israel.' That's another reason I think this is an end-time prophecy—it's connected to others that talk about a great revival among our people in the last days."

"A real turning toward God could follow this war?"

"Yes. A serious spiritual awakening could begin. Verse 3 says that the remnant of Syria will 'be like the glory of the sons of Israel'! Think of that—an awakening in Hasdar's own country!"

Eli picked up the barrel of his Galil rifle. "Maybe, Yonni, but right now the remnant of Syria is facing us with very real, and very deadly, weapons. Can I tell you something?" Eli set his weapon on the ground.

"Of course you can, brother, what is it?"

Eli collected a few blades of grass and began to play with them between his fingers. Jonathan waited.

"Do you remember how Sarah joked after we became close friends that she would have to change her name to Bathsheba because now her Jonathan had found a David?"

"Sure," Jonathan smiled. "I told her she had it all backwards. You are a Ben-David, a son of David, and Saul's son Jonathan didn't marry Bathsheba, King David did!"

"Right. Well, I've often thought about that, because in many ways you really are like a Jonathan to me. I feel a closeness to you that I don't even feel with my four brothers." The Israeli paused to gaze at the majestic peaks of the nearby mountain range, painted amber by the setting sun.

Jonathan grinned. "I appreciate that. I feel a special kinship with you too."

Eli glanced down at the wild red tulips clustered just beyond the toes of his black army boots.

"Like I told Sarah this morning, Eli, whatever happens, we have eternity ahead of us."

Jonathan quietly began to sing a Scripture song in Hebrew from Psalm 84. His buddy quickly joined in.

"Shemesh ooh magen, Adonai Elohim. Ashrei adam botayach bach." A sun and shield is the Lord God. Blessed is the man who trusts in him.

The ten-member security cabinet was comprised of two ministers from the Holy Torah Orthodox party, two from the Immigrants Rights party, and six from Prime Minister Nimrod's Likud party. They met in the "pool hall," which was not a game room but a reinforced nuclear-proof bomb shelter located under the main government office building in west Jerusalem. A large slate pool table occupied one corner of the shelter's main room. "The boys need something to do if we get stuck down here," Prime Minister Golda Meir had explained when she ordered the pool table brought into the newly built shelter during the 1973 Yom Kippur War.

"Good evening, lady and gentlemen," said Nimrod, smiling politely at Edna Satori as he opened up his black briefcase and began passing out the top-secret aerial photos. "Rafi will explain to you what these are."

Hochman waited until everyone had a copy. "These pictures, some from Ofec and some by our high-altitude jets, reveal that Syria is arming its Scud–C and SS–21 missiles. They were taken this afternoon. Our experts believe that nonconventional chemical warheads are probably being fitted onto the missiles."

"Chemical warheads! How can you tell?" asked a shaken Satori.

"Well, Edna, I'm no expert but our military analysts say the dimensions of these warheads are different than standard conventional ones, meaning they're probably chemical."

The ministers sat in silence for a few seconds, letting the awful significance of the news sink in.

"What can we do?" finance minister Zahav asked, with a slight tremor in his voice.

"I only see two options: We either sit back and do nothing, hoping that Hasdar isn't willing to absorb the political and military consequences of a first strike, or we order our bombers to destroy these missiles before they can be fired at us."

The foreign minister leaned forward. "If we take the missiles out now, our European and American friends won't lift a finger to help us in any ensuing war. And the Russians and Chinese will scream to high heaven!"

"True, Yudah, there are unpleasant political consequences from a preemptive strike," replied the Israeli leader in his usual low-keyed manner. "But at least we will not be poisoned by the Syrians." Nimrod slowly scanned the table. "Two weeks ago we observed Holocaust Memorial Day. Do any of you want to be responsible for allowing some of the survivors of Auschwitz to be gassed by Halled Hasdar?"

"Yacov, get ahold of yourself," scolded Satori. "I think you're afraid of a public witch hunt like the one following the Yom Kippur surprise attack on us by the Egyptians and Syrians."

"I'm not advocating a first strike to make up for our past errors" replied Nimrod with irritation. "This time we have irrefutable evidence of an imminent attack—one that will be far more devastating than the surprise assault on Yom Kippur. We have no choice but to act!"

Yudah Sephres slowly pushed back his chair, letting its legs scrape loudly across the concrete floor. "Well, Yacov, you are the commander in chief, as the Americans say. "But I think it is ironic that Yitzhak Shamir could restrain himself in the face of Saddam's scuds, while you are apparently planning to start a war that could end in God knows where!"

What would Yudah say if he knew that Rafi and I have already decided to go ahead and prepare our own chemical warheads? "This situation is quite different from the Gulf War," Nimrod replied. "For one thing, we're facing more accurate missiles that can carry far greater payloads. They're located much closer to our homeland. Our soldiers are face-to-face with an enemy who possesses chemical artillery shells. And despite your concerns, Yudah, there is no one pressuring us to stay out of this conflict, like there was during the '91 war."

Nimrod slowly turned his head to gaze at each minister at the emergency cabinet table. "It's time for a vote," he announced. "All those in favor of a preemptive air strike, raise your hands."

"Excuse me, Yacov. There is one more thing we should make clear to our colleagues." Hochman waited for the nod. "Our warplanes can't spot and strike the missile launchers with enough accuracy at night. In other words, we have to wait until dawn."

The defense minister detected frowns of disapproval. "There may be hundreds of them, and many are mobile. We must wait until dawn."

"This will make for a peaceful night," quipped Rabbi Amos Shimshon.

"Surely the fact we are meeting here means you are afraid Hasdar may shoot his missiles any time!" protested Satori, her voice rising higher with each word.

"It's a standard precaution," replied Nimrod. "Now, let's get on with the vote. All those in favor of a preemptive air strike, raise your hands."

Everyone but Sephres and Satori raised their hands in the air.

"And all those of sanity who want to avoid World War Three, put up their hands!" barked Sephres, looking his longtime rival directly in the eyes.

Nimrod turned to Hochman. "The vote is affirmative, Rafi, although I wish it had been unanimous. Prepare for a dawn strike on Hasdar's missile launchers.

"The meeting is adjourned. Please remain in Jerusalem. Some of you may want to stay down here. There are private bedrooms in the living section. Rafi and I will be here."

The ministers ignored Nimrod's suggestion and got up to leave. As they were walking past the steel-reinforced door, the premier's cellular phone began to beep. Everyone froze, realizing that only a call of the highest importance would be made over the leader's personal line.

"I sure hope it's only Esther wanting to know why Yacov is late for dinner," joked Satori as she placed her leather pocketbook back on the table.

"Mr. Prime Minister, General Bar-Am. Our radar has just picked up what we believe to be a massive Syrian missile launch. Heat sensors on Ofec confirm that a large-scale firing has just occurred."

"Friends," relayed the tired Israeli leader as he held his hand over the phone's mouthpiece, "please sit down."

4

Chemical Warheads

The warm breezes blowing gently across the Golan Heights carried the soothing evening sounds of chirping crickets. The strategic plateau had been quiet since the cessation of firing practice at dusk. Jonathan sat alone on a rock while he guarded his makeshift camp. Eli was inside his tent sorting out bandages and other medical supplies. His turn for guard duty would come up at midnight.

Although all Golan commanders, medics, and guards had been ordered to put on their protective gear, the order was optional for everyone else.

"We can't make them sleep wearing gas masks!" protested northern army commander General Motti Silvan when Chief of Staff Bar-Am had phoned him just after sunset and ordered all frontline soldiers into their anti-chemical equipment. "And even if I give the order, many men will disobey it, especially on such a warm night."

"All right," replied the armed forces chief. "But order all commanders and medics to put on their protective suits. And command everyone else to keep them on at all times when not sleeping. Trouble is brewing."

Jonathan had taken off his gas mask because of the heat and set it down on the ground near his right boot. He stared intently at the bright stars in the eastern sky and felt a deep peace inside. *Does it really take untold centuries for the light of some of those distant orbs to reach us?* he mused. *Only a powerful creator could put together such a universe.*

Jonathan closed his eyes to pray. "How many are Your wonders, O Lord, who can know them? Yeshua, if You take me in the coming days, please be with my family in a special way and reveal Yourself to my parents, especially Dad. He's still hurting so much from his childhood in Europe. Help him remember all that I've shared with him. I love You, Lord."

As Jonathan sat thinking, a sharp distant noise startled him. It sounded like fireworks exploding across a lake on Independence Day. Within seconds, a barrage of artillery shells began raining down on the Golan Heights, sending fiery shrapnel everywhere. One landed twenty yards from Jonathan as he threw down his rifle to grab his mask. But it was too late. Poisonous fumes were already infiltrating his lungs.

Eli darted out of his tent to witness fires flaring up everywhere, illuminating the spring night. When he spotted his buddy he rushed over and knelt down. Quickly, he pulled a syringe out of his medical kit and filled it with anti-chemical medicine to give Jonathan a shot. But he knew it was futile. "Oh Yonni, my precious brother, Yonni!" Eli cried as tears flooded his tightly fitted mask. "Your beauty, O Israel, is slain on your high places! How the mighty have fallen in the midst of battle! Jonathan is slain on your high places!"

The young medic clutched the body of his dear friend to his breast and sobbed.

Eighteen believers huddled close together in the main meeting room at congregation Beit Yisrael to pray. Perched in front of an open window, an electric fan blew evening air into the hot room and caused the large red and gold banner, which contained the seals of Israel's twelve tribes, to sway back and forth behind the podium. The group could hear the roar of city buses passing by on nearby Hebron Road.

As founding elder and pastor Yoseph Steinberg ended his opening prayer, sirens began to wail across the City of Peace. Everyone knew what to do. They dashed toward the back stairs leading to the basement. Sarah grabbed Benny from the small nursery. Tali was at home with Sarah's younger sister, Donna, who had moved to Israel only three months before.

Yoseph, a former teacher from Brooklyn, grabbed his desktop radio as he passed his office. *I'm glad I put those new batteries in this afternoon,* the fifty-two-year-old pastor thought to himself.

Several people had gas masks, including Sarah. She had brought a special children's mask for Benny.

"Mommy, what's going on?" asked her frightened son as the loud sirens wailed on.

"We have to go downstairs for awhile, little one. And guess what?" Sarah showed Benny his mask. "You get to put on your special Purim mask!"

"All right!" whooped the excited youngster, momentarily forgetting his fear.

After everyone had safely gotten to the small basement storeroom, Yoseph switched on the radio. The announcer's voice blared in Hebrew, "Get to your emergency shelters with gas masks on!"

Sarah adjusted Benny's mask over his small chin. "I wonder where your abba is," she said quietly. Trying to steady her hands, she prayed silently. *O Lord, keep Jonathan safe.*

Stacy Pearlman, Sarah's best friend, helped her strap on her mask. Sarah smiled through the clear plastic. She cherished Stacy's keen wit and sincere faith but loved her compassionate heart even more. Sarah knew it had come from her friend's long experience of taking care of her alcoholic mother in Manhattan until her death in 1998. Stacy had dreamed of being an actress off-Broadway, but never had a chance to achieve her goal.

"Do you want to wear this?" Sarah offered, since Stacy did not have a mask.

The New Yorker answered in her usual nasal accent. "Don't be ridiculous! You're a mother, remember?"

"I haven't forgotten," she said somberly, thinking about Tali at home with her new-immigrant sister.

The twenty-six year old, slightly plump Stacy sat down on the wooden bench. "Sarah, I know you're worried about Jonathan. I am too, and I'm afraid for Eli."

Sarah smiled into her friend's big brown eyes. "We all know how you feel about Eli, Stacy."

"I only wish he felt the same way about me," she sighed. "What is the radio saying? I wish I understood more Hebrew!"

"They're warning everyone to go to their emergency rooms and put on gas masks."

"But how many people have special sealed rooms?" interjected Craig Eagleman, a husky twenty-nine-year-old Gentile from Oklahoma who was finishing his doctoral degree in Semitic languages at Jerusalem's Hebrew University.

"Not many," responded Yoseph, nearly shouting so he could be heard through his mask. "It's been a few years

since Saddam sent us his Scuds. I'm sure most people h
forgotten about sealed rooms."

Sarah spoke up as she tightened her mask. "Don't you think some people prepared sealed-off areas today, with the partial call-up and all?"

Yoseph's wife, Cindy, a fit jogger and accomplished violinist, pulled her gas mask up over her forehead. "I suppose a few people besides you may have prepared sealed rooms today. Most didn't. I didn't have a moment all day."

Tel Aviv–born Miri Doron nodded in agreement. "I think you're right, Cindy. Most Israelis get so used to war talk that we tend to ignore it."

Stacy frowned at Miri, her main rival for Eli's affection.

"Oh, no!" shouted the twenty-four-year-old Sabra.

"What's wrong?" exclaimed Stacy, startled by Miri's sudden outburst.

Deep wrinkles appeared in Yoseph's brow as he turned up the radio. "They've just announced that missiles are striking parts of our country."

The overhead light flickered and went out.

"Mommy!" cried Benny, now certain that this was not a Purim party.

Prime Minister Nimrod removed his tailored suit coat and carefully placed it on the metal table. "I could use a stiff drink," he muttered to himself. Rafi Hochman and Yudah Sephres sat next to him staring at the large computer monitor being run by an emergency generator. A detailed map of Israel and Syria covered the screen.

General Bar-Am's staff was feeding on-line information from the army's fortified underground command center, located just outside of Jerusalem. Suddenly, orange dots appeared.

"Oh no, they've hit Tel Aviv!" the defense minister shouted.

"And Haifa and Tiberias," added Sephres, pointing to the screen with his narrow index finger.

"They're targeting our military bases as well," Nimrod sighed loudly. "I just hope our Patriot and Arrow missiles are intercepting some of the incoming warheads."

"This is outrageous! How long can we wait?" asked Hochman.

"Until we're sure they're firing chemical-tipped missiles," replied the Israeli leader.

The prime minister's emergency phone beeped. "Sir, General Bar-Am. We have confirmed reports of chemical hits on several cities and on eighteen military targets. Also, General Silvan has just informed me that chemical artillery shells are landing on the Golan."

Nimrod shuddered. "How are the Arrows doing?"

"They're intercepting some missiles. But as you know, sir, this is a relatively new weapon that has never been tested in actual combat. The Syrians have fired dozens of missiles at us, many armed with multiple warheads."

"Some of the orange spots on our computer map are changing to red. Are those confirmed chemical strikes?"

"I'm afraid so."

"Thank you, General. We'll get right back to you."

The three aging politicians watched the monitor in horrified silence as the orange dots took on the color of blood.

How many lives do each of these red dots represent? wondered Rafi Hochman, holding back tears as he thought about his wife in their home just north of Tel Aviv.

Nimrod's emergency phone beeped again. The leader was glad to hear his wife's voice.

"Yacov, it's me! I'm safe in the shelter under our home. The security people let me phone you on this line. Hannah Sephres is here with me. Are you alright?"

"As well as possible under the circumstances," replied Nimrod. "Esther, Hasdar is using chemical weapons, but so far nothing around Jerusalem. Don't leave the shelter."

I've got to go Esther. Shalom." Yacov put the phone back into its cradle. "Good news, Yudah. Your wife is safe underground with Esther.

"Now, gentlemen, I think an immediate chemical missile strike on Hasdar's military bases is in order. I'm sure General Silvan is already using chemical shells in the local theater. He has standing orders to do so if attacked with nonconventional weapons."

"I agree," said Hochman.

"You have my support," confirmed Sephres, relieved that Nimrod was not considering a nuclear strike. "But we better get to it before we hear from President Williams."

"We'll wait for a fuller assessment of casualties and damage before considering any additional retaliation," added the prime minister.

Within minutes, Israeli chemical and conventional ballistic warheads were blasting military targets throughout Syria, causing substantial damage. Two Jericho missiles struck the Soviet-built naval and submarine port at Latakia, on the Syrian Mediterranean coast north of Lebanon. Seventy-four Russian officers and sailors were among the casualties.

Syrian armored brigades began pushing past United Nations buffer forces stationed along the Golan Heights border. By midnight Hasdar's juggernaut had punched five holes through frontline Israeli positions. In several places Syrian tanks ran over the bodies of gassed Jewish soldiers. They rapidly advanced past Israeli fortifications south of the border with Lebanon. Israeli chemical artillery shells seemed to be having little effect since both the Syrians and their Lebanese Muslim allies, aided by Iranian volunteers, were wearing protective gear.

When Syrian armored vehicles reached Eli's unit, only fifteen reserve soldiers remained alive. As the enemy ground forces approached, Eli prayed for mercy while wrapping the shrapnel wounds of a fellow soldier. "Father, I'm ready to join Yonni, if that's Your will."

"Here goes another one!" exclaimed a snarling Syrian soldier as he fired a tank shell directly at Eli's tent. The searing shell ripped through the top of the tent and landed at the foot of one of the cots.

"What the—did you see that?!" shouted the astounded patient, who was lying nearby.

Eli grabbed his medical bag. "We better get out of here. It could be a delayed-reaction bomb!"

"No, I mean did you see that—there was something in here. A ghost-like being! It fell down on top of that shell and then vanished!"

"Let's still get out of here, but remind me to talk to you later."

Israeli forces were besieged from every direction. More than three thousand men were killed in the initial chemical artillery strike. The Scud attacks on military bases deeper inside Israel left many dead and wounded. Powerful conventional warheads had landed on most major roads, cutting off supply lines to the Galilee. More than two dozen Israeli warplanes had been destroyed on the ground. Fortunately most of the jets were already airborne when the Scuds and SS–21s struck; they were soon engaged in fierce aerial combat over the Golan Heights.

By 2:00 A.M. Syrian armor had successfully broken through Israeli defenses in the southern Golan plateau. Troops poured into the Hula Valley below the Heights. Syrian and Lebanese Shiite forces, supported by Iraqi and Iranian units, steamrolled through southern Lebanon toward Israel's panhandle border. The combined Muslim forces easily penetrated the flimsy border fence and fought their way in from the west. By 5:00 in the morning they had joined up with the advancing juggernaut from the Golan and effectively cut off the panhandle, trapping tens of thousands of Israeli civilians and soldiers behind Syrian lines.

During the night, Nimrod received telephone calls from several world leaders. The prime minister of Spain, whose country held the six-month rotating leadership of the European Union, called after the Israeli reprisal missile strike and urged Nimrod to refrain from any further launchings against Syria. "Several Arab leaders have already threatened to impose an oil embargo against any European nation that aids you," he informed him.

Russian President Yuli Greskin said that, while his country no longer considered Israel an enemy, it regarded Syria as a close friend. Several hard-line generals, who never really accepted the harsh reality that the Soviet Union had fallen apart in the early 1990's, were extremely angry about the Latakia bombing. Supported by ultranationalists in Parliament, they were urging Greskin to come to Syria's aid. Muslim militants in the former southern Soviet republics were also agitating for intervention. Greskin warned that any further Israeli reprisal attacks would be followed by a sharp increase in pro-Syrian sentiments.

President Williams phoned Nimrod twice during the night. He was on the line just ten minutes after the Syrian missile barrage promising that American drones carrying anti-missile, air-to-air rockets would immediately be made available to Israel.

"I pledge our total support, Yacov. I won't ask you not to respond, but I urge you to think carefully before you do."

"Thank you, Mr. President. This is the most difficult moment I have ever faced."

"You have my prayers."

A second call came twenty minutes after Israeli Jericho missiles hit Syrian military targets. Williams reported that the already battered New York Stock Exchange had fallen sharply after the surprise attack on Israel and had to be shut down altogether when news came of the reprisal strike against Syria. He said he was calling an emergency meeting of his National Security Council. He would order American forces to be put on full alert throughout the Middle East.

At 4:20 that morning, Hasdar ordered a second ballistic missile strike, mostly on Israeli civilian centers. Still, no Syrian Scuds were directed at Jerusalem because of its large Arab population.

Alone in his small shelter cubicle, Nimrod made his decision. The second Syrian missile blitz was causing chaos in his cities, and enemy forces were choking off the Galilee panhandle. He knew the time had arrived to use his ultimate weapon.

5

Nuclear Warheads

Eli stared at the green plastic body bag containing Jonathan's corpse and tried to hold back his tears. He was glad it was dark in the back of the Syrian army truck, meaning few of his compatriots could tell he was weeping.

However, one fellow prisoner did notice since he was handcuffed to Eli's left wrist. It was his buddy, Moshe Salam. "You really loved Goldman, didn't you," Moshe whispered, motioning with his head toward the front of the truck where the body bags were piled together.

"He was my closest friend: closer than a brother."

"I hate to say it but maybe he's better off dead," replied Moshe. I've heard that the Syrians don't exactly roll out the red carpet for Israeli prisoners of war."

"Yonni *is* better off," murmured Eli. "I know that for a fact."

Moshe was surprised by this change of tone. "What do you mean?"

"I might as well tell you, but you probably won't like it. Yonni and I are—I mean he was—" Eli straightened up and pressed his aching back against the side of the truck. "I believe that Yeshua is the Messiah, the Son of Man, and the King of Israel, Moshe. Yonni believed in Him, too. I've only followed Him since last year."

"Followed Him? You talk like He is still alive! Yeshu may have been the most famous Jew that ever lived, but He's been dead for almost two thousand years!"

Eli grinned. "You're wrong, Moshe. Yeshua—that is His full given name, not Yeshu—is still alive. And He is the King described in Daniel, chapter 7."

"You're out of your mind!" Moshe blurted as he turned his eyes back toward the pile of body bags, shifting as the truck bounced along the potholed road.

Eli changed the subject. "I hope they're not taking us to Damascus."

"Why?"

"Well, just yesterday Yonni was explaining a biblical prophecy to me about Damascus being destroyed. He thought it might be fulfilled during this war."

"A prophecy from your still-alive Yeshua?"

"I thought you were raised in a traditional Sephardic home, Moshe. Don't you know your Bible?"

"Actually, I'm not even sure I believe in God anymore." Moshe had questioned the existence of God ever since his father's accidental death.

"Well, the prophecy about Damascus is found in Isaiah—Isaiah 17. That's where the destruction is prophesied and also great trouble for Israel."

The dark-skinned Israeli slowly panned the shaded, yet clearly sad faces of his fellow prisoners of war. "It seems the last part is already being fulfilled. I suppose half our Golan army has already been captured or killed. Who knows what has happened to our cities or our families."

"God knows, Moshe, and He will ultimately be the one to respond."

Yacov Nimrod poured hot steaming coffee from a metal pitcher. It was 7:30 A.M.

"One sugar or two, Edna?"

"None, Yacov, thank you."

"Rabbi Shimshon?"

The Holy Torah party leader leaned forward. "Two, please."

"Rafi? Yudah?"

"One is fine. Thanks, Yacov," Hochman answered. Sephres shook his head.

The five senior Israeli officials had not slept much during the night. Fresh information constantly streamed in describing the horrendous damage caused by the Syrian blitz. An estimated sixty thousand Israeli soldiers and civilians had perished, the majority from poison gas during the initial attack. Hochman received frequent battlefront updates from General Bar-Am at underground army headquarters. Every half hour he briefed his fellow leaders on the latest news, which was mostly bleak. Yudah Sephres kept in contact with the State Department in Washington, and with the Russian, Chinese, British, and French foreign ministries.

Playing nervously with his pen, Nimrod prepared to make his announcement. "Friends, we have just passed through the worst night in our modern history," he began. "More people are dead than in all our previous wars combined. Missiles were deliberately directed at our civilian centers. Our forces are being pushed back in fierce combat in the north." Nimrod paused and examined the tired faces of his cabinet colleagues. "There is only one way to prevent further attacks on our cities. Hasdar must realize he cannot kill tens of thousands of Israelis without paying a heavy price. I have decided to order a nuclear strike on Damascus."

Sephres bolted out of his chair. "That will set the whole world against us!" he screamed. "Many nations already blame us for starting the war. They believe Hasdar's claims that he hit us first to preempt a surprise attack against him."

Nimrod put his pen next to the clipboard full of notes in front of him and focused on his foreign minister's agitated face. "We can't worry about what others think right now, Yudah. We have our own agenda, and it's the survival of our country."

"Well we'd better worry about the Russians! They still have nuclear missiles, you know. Greskin has warned me his generals are livid over our strike on Latakia. Are we Jews, the main victims of Hitler's hideous holocaust, going to be the ones to unleash the powerful nuclear genie bottled up for over half a century?"

"I see no other way to put a quick end to this war," said Nimrod as he rose to his feet. "Our forces are under tremendous pressure in the Galilee. Tiberias is under siege even as we speak. Two thousand of our soldiers have already been captured, and tens of thousands of our citizens are trapped behind Syrian lines in the Galilee panhandle. God only knows how many have been gassed to death! It's enough!"

Rafi Hochman stood up and placed his hand on Nimrod's shoulder. He then turned toward Sephres. "Most Arab countries are expressing support for Syria. Several are beginning to send men and equipment. Fighting could break out any time along the Jordanian front. Iran, Afghanistan, and several former Soviet Muslim republics are sending in men. Even Saudi Arabia is supporting them. I agree with Yacov. Using nuclear weapons is our only hope of ending this war before it gets totally out of hand."

"How can we be sure this will stop it?" Satori demanded nervously. "What if Iran or our other enemies have nuclear bombs themselves, as you suggested yesterday, Yacov? How can we act like our enemy and kill thousands—probably hundreds of thousands—of innocent civilians?"

"And what if some of our captured soldiers are in Damascus?" interjected an irate Sephres. "They'll be radiated as well!"

"I doubt they've taken hundreds of Israeli prisoners into their crowded capital city," replied the sullen Israeli premier. "In fact, the Mossad has told me that our captured soldiers have been transported to southeastern Syria, near the Jordanian border."

"What about nuclear fallout?" asked Rabbi Shimshon as he scratched his long, peppery beard. "Our northern border is not very far from Damascus."

"We'll use low-yield atomic bombs dropped from high altitude jets, not one of our Jericho warheads. This should produce minimal fallout. The weather reports this morning show the prevailing winds shifting toward the northeast, meaning that any fallout should blow into lightly populated desert areas."

"How good of Mother Nature to cooperate," snarled Satori. "Yacov, Damascus is a city with over a million human beings. What about them?"

"We'll issue a warning to the Syrian public to evacuate, and then give them ten hours to get out."

"But that will alert Hasdar that a nuclear strike is imminent!" protested Hochman, a former Northern Command general. "Won't that leave us dangerously exposed?"

"I don't think so, Rafi. In fact, it may bring Hasdar to his senses. Let's pray to God it does. If he asks for a ceasefire, then I won't drop the bomb."

Satori sensed that Nimrod had already made up his mind, rendering the whole conversation useless. "Why are you telling us all this if we don't have a say in it?"

"I want your support," he replied. "Let's vote. All who favor my proposal, raise your hands."

The defense minister's hand shot up along with Nimrod's. Sephres and Satori kept theirs in their laps. Rabbi Shimshon hesitated a moment then slowly raised his.

"The majority have voted affirmatively," announced Nimrod. "The plan to bomb Damascus will be executed, unless Hasdar calls off his attack."

"This is exactly what I feared!" shouted Cliff Williams, responding to the late-night television bulletin.

"Turn up the volume, Pete," the president instructed his White House chief of staff.

World News Network anchorman, Thad Crocker, was speaking. "Sheila Watson in Jerusalem: Can you tell us what is going on?"

"Well, Thad, just a few minutes ago, Israel's Arabic radio service began its 7:00 A.M. morning newscast with a warning for everyone in Damascus to immediately leave the city. Analysts here say the warning can only mean one thing—an Israeli nuclear strike is being planned against the Syrian capital."

"Couldn't Israeli leaders just be bluffing, Sheila, perhaps to get Syrian President Halled Hasdar to call off his military offensive?"

"That might be the case, Thad. But what we have here this morning is a badly wounded Israel, apparently fearing for its very survival. Anything can happen under these circumstances. Israeli military analysts note that the rapid Syrian advance in the north is being cheered on by much of the Muslim world. Volunteer fighters are on their way from Iraq, Sudan, Libya, and other countries. And the

Iranians, who already have thousands of warriors in the battle, particularly in south Lebanon, have announced this morning that millions of men will be sent to join what they are calling a 'holy war for the liberation of Jerusalem.'"

Watson dropped her microphone to her side and quickly cleared her throat as file pictures of Iranian Revolutionary Guards pulsed across the viewing screen. "The Israelis seem genuinely scared, Thad. Analysts say Prime Minister Nimrod fears that nuclear weapons—believed to be in Iran's arsenal—could soon be deployed in this conflict. Apparently he wants to get in the first strike."

Crocker gasped. "It almost sounds like a recipe for World War Three." He tried to keep the quiver out of his voice.

"Indeed it does!" barked President Williams as he slammed his fist down on his Oval Office desk. "Get Nimrod on the phone. Immediately!"

Donna Hazan was almost hysterical by the time Sarah and Benny Goldman walked through the front door.

Tali had been holding down the fort all night. Although she was not yet born when gas masks were widely used in Israel during the Gulf War, she had calmly slipped into her special child-size gear when the sirens went off. Her Aunt Donna had left her adult mask—issued to all new immigrants upon arrival at Ben Gurion airport—at her north Jerusalem apartment. The thought of donning such a thing had so revolted Sarah's stylish sister that she had immediately stuffed it away in her closet, vowing she would never wear it.

After putting the kids down for a much-needed morning nap, Sarah went to her bedroom. She knew she really should take the children down with her to the basement shelter, but she could not force herself to leave the room where she had spent so many precious hours with her husband. As she sat down at her cosmetics bureau, her light brown eyes caught the mirrored reflection of a pair of Jonathan's tennis shoes, tucked halfway under the bed. *They're empty. Jonathan's shoes are empty,* she thought as tears filled her eyes. Though irrational, the jarring thought would not leave her.

The young woman kept the bedside portable radio on all morning. Israeli army announcements were bare, offering scanty information about fighting on the Golan Heights. The fact that the Syrians had already captured the strategic area and cut off the Galilee panhandle was never disclosed. In an effort to boost morale, the extent of civilian casualties from the chemical blasts was also played down. At one point, Sarah was tempted to tune in to BBC broadcasts from nearby Cyprus, but she decided against it. She was not yet ready to know everything that might be going on.

Yacov Nimrod wiped the misplaced graying hair from his forehead and pushed the speakerphone button in front of him so his four senior cabinet colleagues could hear the American president.

"I guess it isn't a very good morning for you, is it, Yacov?"

"No, Cliff, it isn't. You are also speaking, sir, to my foreign minister, to Defense Minister Rafael Hochman, and to the leaders of my two government coalition partners, Edna Satori and Rabbi Amos Shimshon."

"Shalom to you all. I won't waste any words, Yacov. I've just heard on WNN that you're advising the Syrian people to evacuate their capital."

"Intelligence travels fast these days."

"This can only mean one thing."

"If you mean, am I planning a nuclear strike on Damascus, the answer is affirmative."

The U.S. leader was startled by Nimrod's bluntness. After clearing his throat, he continued. "Are you really intending to blast one of the largest Arab cities into smithereens with nuclear weapons?"

"Cliff, we're in deep trouble. Three hours ago we were hit with a second barrage of Syrian missiles. Tens of thousands of our civilians are dead. We just learned that some of your own embassy personnel in Tel Aviv were gassed in last evening's attack, along with other foreign nationals."

"I know. But, Yacov, I've told you I've placed our forces on full alert to aid you. A nuclear response is a very drastic one."

Edna Satori could not help herself. "Indeed it is!"

Nimrod ignored her. "Frankly, Mr. President, we're hoping to avoid dropping any bombs. It's my prayer Hasdar will order a halt to his offensive, now that we have issued this warning. However—with all due respect—if Hasdar does not stop, I will use this weapon, just as Truman did in Japan."

The president paused and then resumed somberly. "Let me be frank. My advisors tell me that, in light of your announcement, a full-scale financial panic is expected in Europe, and here in the States when the markets open up. The Tokyo exchange has already fallen drastically. The dollar is under intense pressure there. And I've received messages from the leaders of several Arab Gulf states. They've threatened to shut off oil supplies to us, like they did in '73, if we make any overt moves to support you."

The religious affairs minister leaned forward toward Nimrod, who nodded at him. "Mr. President, Rabbi Amos Shimshon. You mean the countries you saved from Saddam are now threatening you?" Shimshon was not surprised to hear this.

"Well, one Gulf leader told me he wasn't really planning to shut down the pipeline. But he said Islamic fundamentalists were demanding action in support of Syria, so he would have to make a public gesture of some kind. I told him the threat of an oil embargo could cause financial havoc. Yacov, I want to help you, but I can't if you drop a nuclear device on Damascus!"

The Israeli leader spoke slowly. "Mr. President, I realize you were already facing severe economic trials before this. We felt the ripples here when State Bank, your largest financial institution, collapsed last September and brought down many of your smaller banks with it. I know your economic crisis has led to sharp cutbacks in your overseas military commitments. Those recent base closures in Turkey have hurt your Mideast readiness."

"That's true, but we're still willing to help you despite our problems."

"Thank you, but I'm not asking you to intervene. Harry Truman saw no other way to end the war with Japan than to drop atomic bombs on Hiroshima and Nagasaki. If we don't stop Syria's offensive now, it will soon involve other nations. You yourself told me that Kazakhstan and other former Soviet republics are threatening to join Hasdar's declaration of war against us, as Iran, Iraq, Sudan, Algeria, and Libya already have. They must all see—and soon—that our failure to respond to Saddam's Scuds was an aberration. There is no other realistic option for Israel now."

"The United Nations is meeting to discuss this. Maybe Hasdar will agree to a ceasefire?"

"I hope so. But he must know—and your people can let him know if you wish—that we are dead serious. He should act today or be responsible for the destruction of his capital city."

"May God help us all," said the president. "Let's talk again before you give any actual orders."

"We will, Cliff. Shalom."

Late that morning an irascible Halled Hasdar concluded that Nimrod would not dare risk the wrath of the United States and Russia by dropping nuclear bombs on one of the world's oldest and greatest cities, not to mention an historic Islamic center. Besides, Syrian troops, bolstered by forces from around the region, were performing too well to call off his offensive.

Since he could not prevent his frightened people from evacuating his capital, the Syrian dictator decided to help them get out in an orderly manner. By 1:00 P.M. almost half the population had left. As the crowds of frenzied people grew, so did the resulting chaos in the streets. Finally, Hasdar put a stop to the evacuation at 3:30, and rioting resulted when the police blocked the major thoroughfares out of the city.

The sun was sinking low in the western sky, although Hasdar could not see it from his underground mountain bunker. He did, however, hear the deafening roar and feel the powerful jolt at 5:42 that evening when Damascus was leveled to the ground.

6

The Valley of Tears

The Syrians held Eli Ben-David and his companions in a newly constructed camp near the small town of Salkhad, sixty-five miles southeast of Damascus.

The heartbroken Israeli medic was so distressed over Jonathan's death, and so physically spent that he wanted to pray the Lord would take him home. Instead, he decided to pray for his friend's family.

"Lord, please give Sarah and the children your strength."

"Who?" Moshe asked, almost sitting on top of Eli in the cramped prison cell.

"Sorry. I didn't realize I was speaking out loud. I was praying for Yonni's family."

"Good. Send up a prayer for me, too."

Suddenly a bright light flashed through the small window above Eli. He instantly thought of the apostle Paul's encounter with the Lord on the road to Damascus.

"Maybe Yeshua is coming to get me," he whispered under his breath. But the cell walls shook violently and the prisoner realized something else was going on. The boom that followed was so loud he cupped his hands around his ears.

"We've nuked Damascus!" he shouted to the others.

Three low-yield nuclear bombs had been dropped on the Syrian capital city. One landed on the ancient bazaar in the southern part of Damascus. Another leveled the main business district in the northwest section, and the third destroyed Syrian government buildings as well as surrounding neighborhoods. Nearly three hundred thousand people were instantly incinerated.

The bombs ignited huge fires in many parts of the decimated city. Mushroom clouds of radiating particles soon drifted toward the northeast, and fallout rained to earth over the sparsely populated Syrian Desert. Some later fell on northern Iraq and Iran and even on the southern republics of the former Soviet Union. The prison camp southeast of the city was not in the path of the deadly fallout.

Another type of fallout—panic—swept through the major world financial centers. The New York Stock Exchange shut down shortly after the nuclear explosions, having tumbled the maximum allowed in one day. Frightened Americans flocked to their banks after hearing of a virtual free fall of the dollar in Europe. Most banks closed early rather than risk a run on their assets. Rioting broke out in more than a dozen American cities. Jewish neighborhoods were targeted; Arab areas were also attacked by angry mobs upset over reports of a second Arab oil embargo against the U.S.

President Williams refused to phone Nimrod because he had failed to keep his promise to consult with him before dropping the bombs.

"Just when my economic recovery was beginning to take off, this had to happen!" He almost yelled at Hugh

Clayton, his secretary of state. "Let them all just rot in their own stinking juices! I've had it with the Middle East! Those Jews and Arabs are living in a time warp. We have far too many problems to deal with here without getting any more of their smelly camel dung in our hair!"

"There are still many Jewish voters in our country who strongly support Israel, along with millions of evangelical Christians," protested Clayton, who had never seen his boss quite this upset. "And our reliance on Arab oil has been increasing in recent years. We can't simply write off the Middle East, especially now!"

"We'll still buy their oil, but the days are over for America to police the region. The Europeans are doing better economically than we are, despite the worldwide recession, and they need the oil even more than we do. Let them patrol that rotten part of the globe!"

The attitude in Russia was markedly different. Despite the internal problems following the 1991 collapse of the Soviet Union, many leaders of the hard-line National Recovery Front, an alliance of right-wing, nationalist and Communist parties, saw a golden opportunity. Meeting in emergency session, they agreed that Russia now had a chance to become a major world power again. Their path to restored greatness passed directly through the Middle East.

Halled Hasdar was devastated. His first response to the destruction of his capital was to try to convince Iran to avenge the Israeli attack by hitting Tel Aviv with nonconventional warheads. But Iranian leaders were horrified by Russian satellite pictures of the annihilated city and decided that Tehran would undoubtedly be Israel's next target if Iranian missiles were deployed. The Syrian dictator then attempted to convince Russia and China to come to his rescue. Both nations expressed shock at the Israeli action and vowed to sponsor harsh UN economic sanctions against the Jewish state, but neither would do anything else for the Syrians. Pakistani nuclear missiles were located quite a distance from Israel, rendering their threatened use pointless. Hasdar, therefore, sued for peace. The United Nations arranged a cease-fire, which went into effect seventeen hours after Damascus was destroyed.

"Eli, are you asleep?" Moshe asked softly.

"I don't think anyone is in this packed, sweltering cell," came the reply.

"Would you mind telling me some more about that prophecy in Isaiah, then, and about your faith in this Yeshua? If your faith can clue you in to something as important as the nuking of Damascus, then I'm ready to hear more."

For over an hour, Eli shared his convictions with Moshe. Deciding that he had nothing to lose and everything to gain, the twenty-six-year-old plumber from Ashkelon committed his life to the Lord.

The next morning Eli smiled as his new brother shared his faith with a Syrian guard. He listened to Moshe's first evangelistic effort while doing situps in the exercise yard. Twenty minutes later, the young Syrian guard asked the Lord into his life.

"I told him everything that you told me about Isaiah's prophecy," Moshe reported afterwards. "These guys are scared. Syria may be ripe for the gospel message you shared with me."

"Well, you certainly didn't waste any time!" observed Eli.

With a look of concern, Moshe replied, "If everything that's occurred over the past two days is pointing to the end of the age, we'd better get going, right?"

"Right," replied Eli, a little ashamed that he had not been more bold about his faith.

Yacov Nimrod convened a special meeting of his cabinet just before the cease-fire with Syria went into effect at 11:00 A.M. The ministers were weary but relieved the intense war with Syria was over. Like everyone they were grieving over the deaths of relatives and friends. The Prime Minister was shaken by the loss of his first cousin, a close childhood friend, who commanded a Golan tank battalion. Edna Satori had just gotten off the phone with her closest friend, whose son had died when a missile struck his army base near Haifa. Defense minister Hochman's wife survived the gassing of north Tel Aviv, but one of his teenage nieces had perished while buying last minute supplies at a grocery story in Netanya.

Nimrod cleared his throat and gazed at the sorrowful faces around the large cabinet table.

"Friends, the state of Israel has survived another attempt to destroy it. We are all thankful. Unfortunately, around fifty thousand Israeli civilians were murdered in the Syrian gas attack."

Several of the ministers gasped.

Nimrod continued, "Thousands of our soldiers have also perished. Conventional warheads caused both civilian and military casualties. Altogether we now estimate our death toll at more than seventy thousand. The bombs also left many roads in complete shambles, along with several of our military bases and industrial centers. Electricity supplies have been disrupted because of the destruction of our main power plant near the town of Hadera. On top of this, we've been forced to unleash the deadly atomic bomb, but it brought the desired result—a quick end to the war."

The premier paused to take a sip of strong, black coffee. "There is some good news though. Our last powerful neighbor has been effectively neutralized. The United Nations is already talking about destroying Syria's remaining military infrastructure, like it did Iraq's. I believe this will bring in a new era of peace, with open borders all around. We can direct our remaining financial resources toward rebuilding our country."

"Excuse me, Yacov," interrupted Rabbi Shimshon, who was never one to leave things alone too long. "Aren't you ignoring the renewed military threats being directed at us? The Muslim world is seething over our use of nuclear weapons. The Iranians and others are calling for an even greater holy war to destroy us."

"And," added Hochman, "the Russians and Chinese are condemning our action in the strongest language possible. Both powers say they'll sponsor severe UN economic sanctions against us. Several European nations are signaling that they may support such a move."

Nimrod took off his glasses and placed them next to his coffee cup. "I expect our demonstration of a willingness to defend ourselves with nuclear weapons will leave a deep and lasting impression on any potential enemy. Everyone knows that we have much more powerful warheads on our Jericho long-range missiles than the ones we dropped. I hope that a real and lasting peace has finally arrived in our region. As for economic sanctions, we'll deal with that when we have to."

"I pray you're right about peace, Yacov," replied the anxious rabbi. "But somehow, I don't think so. I fear we've only seen the beginning of a full-scale Muslim jihad."

"Mommy, a man in army clothes is walking up to our front door!" shouted Benny as he ran to the kitchen to fetch his mother.

It was the moment Sarah Goldman had been increasingly dreading since the cease-fire was announced the night before. Thousands of women were beginning to get telephone calls from their husbands and sons up north. She waited for hers, but it never came.

"Mrs. Goldman?" the officer said politely as she opened the front door. "I have some official news for you from the army command's northern office."

Benny peeked around his mother's denim skirt. "Benny, go to your bedroom and play for a few minutes. Mommy will come and get you when lunch is ready." The youngster reluctantly obeyed and scampered down the hall. Sarah braced herself.

"Jonathan's unit was captured in the early hours of fighting. The men are being held in southern Syria. We don't know if your husband is dead or alive, but we should receive a list of Israeli prisoners of war later today or tomorrow."

Sarah's heart leaped with hope.

"Just before dark, UW personnel will be allowed into the camp where most of our soldiers are being held. The camp was not in the path of the nuclear fallout. We'll notify you as soon as we have any firm news about your husband."

Sarah immediately telephoned her best friend. "Stace, the army says Jonathan and Eli's unit was taken prisoner by the Syrians, but they don't know yet who's alive. The men are being held in southern Syria, so they weren't harmed by the nuclear fallout!"

"Oh Sarah, there's hope! When will we know for sure?"

"United Nations forces will go into the prison camp later today, and then I'll be informed. Can you come over and pray?"

"I'm on my way."

Sarah hung up the phone and called Tali and Benny, who were playing in Tali's bedroom.

"Children, I have some news about Abba. His unit was captured by the Syrians, but we think he's alright. The man from the army promised to tell us more later today or tomorrow."

"Who are the 'earians,' Mom?"

"Syrians, Benny. They were our enemies in this war. But it's all over now. You two must stay indoors today. The government has ordered that all children remain at home. Maybe you can watch a Bible video if the electricity comes back on. Stacy's coming over in a few minutes to pray with me, but we'll go into my bedroom, so we won't disturb you."

"Mom, are you sure Daddy is okay?" asked Tali as she sat on the floor with her arms wrapped around her knees.

"No—not really, baby. War is terrible, and many bad things can happen. For now, all we can do is pray, hope, and wait."

Early the next day Sarah and Stacy were sipping coffee in front of Sarah's living room bay window. Stacy had spent the night with her friend after Tali and Benny were driven to Donna's apartment following the partial lifting of the government-imposed curfew. Sarah had decided that if the news about Jonathan was bad, she wanted to absorb it before telling the children.

Their small talk turned to silence when they noticed a man in army fatigues heading toward the front door. Sarah tried to steady herself while opening the door. She studied the messenger's face.

"Good morning, Mrs. Goldman."

"Good morning, sir. Won't you come in?"

"I can only stay a moment. Mrs. Goldman, the army has received information about your husband, Jonathan. I'm afraid I have to tell you that your husband is dead."

Sarah fell backwards toward Stacy, who was standing directly behind her.

The courier continued, "I'm so sorry, Mrs. Goldman. We expect that all of the Israeli prisoners will be released in about two days. The United Nations will then turn over the bodies of our fallen soldiers. Once a positive identification is made, we'll immediately inform you. Of course, we will hold military funerals for all our departed men. Your husband died for his people, ma'am."

Sarah turned and buried her face in Stacy's shoulder. Stacy spoke for her, "Thank you. We know he died honorably, doing his duty to our Jewish people. We know he is with the Lord."

As the courier nodded politely, Stacy asked with some hesitation, "Is there any news about another member of Jonathan's unit, Eli Ben-David?"

"Are you a relative of his?"

"No, but he was Jonathan's best friend."

"Let me check my list of names. Ben-David. Yes, here it is. He is alive and in good condition."

"Praise God!" Stacy exclaimed before feeling guilty over her sudden joy in the face of Sarah's grief.

"Oh, Stacy, Jonathan is gone!" The bereaved widow flopped down on the sofa and wept. She felt like someone had punctured her heart with a sharp bayonet and left her to slowly die. After weeping together for several minutes, the two friends joined hands and prayed for Eli's quick release.

"I loved him so, so much. I never even thought about any other man after I met him." Sarah did not know if she could stand the pain. "What will I do without him? He was the warmest, gentlest human being I have ever known."

Stacy listened quietly.

"I have to tell the children. Oh, Stacy, will you help me? I don't know what to say."

Stacy drove her grieving friend to Donna's apartment as Sarah pondered how she was going to break the tragic news to her children.

"Hi, Mom! We're watching a Bible video," announced Benny as Sarah entered the front door. She sat down between her children on Donna's beige couch, clutching their hands in hers.

"Tali, Benny, I have some sad news about Abba. The Lord has taken him home to heaven."

The children said nothing. They just curled themselves around their mother. Donna and Stacy sat down with the three of them, and the couch was soon bathed in tears.

Eli asked the army van driver to drop him off at Jonathan's house so he could see Sarah first, before spending the night with his parents.

Sarah opened her front door. "Oh, Eli!" she exclaimed as she flung her arms around his neck. The two friends wept together on the front steps.

"Our unit was stationed in an area known to Golan Heights residents as the Valley of Tears," he later explained. "Today there is a beautiful vineyard and some apple orchards, but in '73 it was the site of a major tank battle during the Yom Kippur War. It was later called the Valley of Tears because so many of our men died there. I was holding Yonni when he slipped away, Sarah. His face was peaceful. I know he is with the Lord."

"I know it too, Eli. I'm glad you were there. We're holding the funeral tomorrow morning at 10:00."

The fallen soldier's interment took place in bright sunshine at the Mount Herzl military cemetery in Jerusalem. Eli, Stacy, and Donna stood with Sarah and her children. Moshe and several other members of Jonathan's unit were there as well.

Abraham and Rebecca Goldman had barely been able to arrange a flight in time to attend their eldest son's funeral. The El Al jet from Chicago was mostly filled with weeping passengers on similar journeys of pain.

Abe Goldman recited Kaddish—the Jewish prayer for the departed—for his beloved son. Tears flooded his eyes as he recalled the last time he said the special prayer, which combines sorrowful mourning with praise of God. It was in September 1945 in the British city of Leeds when news arrived that his father, Benjamin, had perished at the Auschwitz Nazi concentration camp.

Jonathan's father began to wail as he completed the Kaddish. "God of Israel, why? My father and my son, both gassed to death by hate-filled madmen!"

7

Out the Door

President Williams reluctantly agreed to co-sponsor a new Mideast peace conference along with Russian President Yuli Greskin. Both thought a formal resolution of the Arab/Israeli conflict might put an end to calls from hard-liners in Moscow for a military response to Israel's destruction of Damascus.

The peace conference opened in Rome in early July. Most of the Arab nations showed up for the negotiations, even though they were still bristling over Syria's humiliation. Several Arab countries, including Iraq, Libya, and Sudan, boycotted the conference. Although invited, Iran also failed to show up, vowing to continue the holy war against Israel until Jerusalem was once again in Islamic hands.

President Williams flew to the Italian capital city to deliver the opening speech. "Why should the cradle of civilization, of three great religions, continue to be torn apart by war?" he asked. "We in America pledge to do everything in our power to help bring a permanent end to this most bitter of struggles, so that all the children in your region can grow up in an atmosphere of peace and tranquillity."

He paused for dramatic effect. "The time for a permanent Mideast peace has finally come."

Greskin was equally sanguine in his remarks. "The world is yearning for a just and lasting peace in the Middle East. Like America, we also believe that the moment for such a peace has arrived. This horrible cycle of violence must end. Russia will do everything possible to help establish a durable peace in your region."

The opening conference lasted four days, but President Greskin was not able to stay until the end. Late on the third day, he was called out of an early evening negotiating session to take an urgent call from his vice president. He put down the receiver and wiped his furrowed brow. Then he quickly ordered his foreign minister to arrange a private meeting with President Williams in Greskin's suite.

Within an hour a shaken Greskin greeted the U.S. president and his secretary of state. "Thank you for coming so quickly. Mr. President, I must fly back to Moscow immediately. I've just been informed that the National Recovery Front is attempting to stage a coup against me!"

"You mean Vladimir Konstantine, the leader of the reactionary block in your Parliament?"

"Yes, he and several others. Armed units loyal to them have surrounded the Parliament building and are attempting to capture several government office centers. They already control state television."

"Is actual street fighting going on?"

"Fierce fighting, I'm afraid. Several army brigades are now completely under Konstantine's control. It seems he has carefully plotted this attempt to seize power. It was probably a mistake to co-sponsor this conference. He and his backers—including former KGB leaders, I suspect—have strongly condemned me for not doing anything to aid Syria."

President Williams was deeply concerned. "But why have they moved now?"

"Our economy is on the verge of collapse. Several local wars are being fought along my borders. They realized that my grip on power has been slipping away."

Vladimir Konstantine wasted no time in ousting Greskin and taking over the reins of power in Russia. The charismatic leader, known for his often outrageous remarks about anyone or anything not distinctly Russian, promised to devote all of his attention to rebuilding the shattered economy and making Russia a great world power again.

What most Russians did not know was that Konstantine and his conspirators had already put together a master plan for economic recovery. In order to create jobs and employ the millions of demobilized soldiers, the new regime decided to use an old tactic—send the boys to war and employ others to support them.

The news of the coup in Russia sent renewed shock waves through world financial centers. The American dollar, already battered by Islamic terror attacks in America and natural disasters, had lost nearly 40 percent of its value against other major currencies since the Mideast war in May. Now it plunged still further. Finance ministers from the European Union met to discuss new regulations for their united currency, the Euro, which was quickly replacing the sagging dollar as the international reserve currency.

Despite the global unrest, Mideast peace talks continued. By late August, a tentative peace plan was beginning to take shape. Featuring open borders between Israel and all its neighbors, the plan called for a comprehensive peace that included the formation of trade and tourism links where they did not already exist. Israel would retain control over most of the Golan Heights. United Nations forces would be stationed in Syria until all weapons of mass destruction were eliminated. The World Bank would aid Syria in rehousing displaced residents of Damascus and in building a new capital ninety miles to the north. Palestinian autonomous zones would be linked to Jordan. The question of the ultimate status of Jerusalem remained unresolved.

Israel hailed the initial agreements as an achievement of immense proportions. The prime minister proudly announced that the long war between Arabs and Jews had finally come to an end.

Sarah Goldman spent the summer months at home. One night in mid-August, she had a dream that snapped her out of the inertia that gripped her following Jonathan's death. A young girl was appealing to her for help. The girl wore a large Star of David on her arm and was running up a set of stairs. She appeared frightened. Something was chasing her, but Sarah could not tell what it was. Sarah was sweating when she awoke, prematurely ending the dream.

The young widow contemplated her dream over a glass of milk in the kitchen. *Many people in Israel are needy and scared right now,* she thought. Sarah glanced up at a family picture taped to the refrigerator and scolded herself out loud. "Here I am, staying at home sulking, when I could be out helping others. That's what Jonathan would have wanted. It's time to stop grieving now, Sarah Goldman. It's time to help those who cannot help themselves."

Sarah was aware of the deep needs in her country. No one was personally untouched by the short war. Whole families, even whole neighborhoods, had perished in the chemical attack. She knew that as viral diseases like pneumonia spread, many survivors would discover their immune systems had been harmed by the poison gas. An epidemic of suicides was gripping the land. Over 20 percent of workers were without jobs because so many factories, stores, and office buildings had been damaged or destroyed by the Syrian missile blitz.

Sarah also realized that many Israelis were turning to God in the wake of the war. Some had even professed faith in Yeshua as Israel's Messiah, mainly as a result of street evangelism by the believers. The bereaved widow chose a quieter mode of witness. She volunteered at Jerusalem's Hadassah Hospital, located on a hill overlooking the south Jerusalem village of Ein Kerem, where Mary had greeted the pregnant Elizabeth centuries before.

The modern health complex was overflowing with sick and wounded. Sarah's assignment was a simple one: to help feed those who were unable to feed themselves.

One elderly patient, a World War II Holocaust survivor, grew particularly fond of her. Yitzhak Solstein had no relatives, and Sarah quickly realized he was more in need of companionship than food. She fed him regularly on Mondays and Thursdays and would often stop by to visit after her volunteer shift was over. The eighty-two-year-old man was delighted. There was something about this young Jewish girl, and he greatly enjoyed the extra attention.

One evening, Sarah came to Yitzhak in the room he shared with three other patients. "I've really been dominating our conversations these past weeks," he told her apologetically as she cranked up his hospital bed.

"No, Yitzhak, you have not. I've enjoyed listening to you, even though some of your experiences have been tragic." She glanced at the concentration camp number tattooed on his left forearm.

"Well, it's time for me to hear about you. Tell me about your life."

Sarah spent the next several visits painting a picture of her adolescent years in a comfortable suburb north of Los Angeles. Yitzhak realized that her childhood in America had been worlds apart from his own in pre-war Germany. She told him about her wealthy Jewish parents, who were almost divorced when she was twelve, and about her younger sister and brother. And she detailed how she became interested in the Jewish state while dating an Israeli who attended her local Reform synagogue.

"And how did you meet your Jonathan?"

Sarah hesitated. She had been debating for several days whether or not to share her faith with her aged friend. She wondered how she could explain how she met Jonathan without bringing in her beliefs. "I met Jonathan at a singles retreat in Pennsylvania. He was actually one of the counselors at the retreat. I went to him for advice. I think I fell in love with him the moment I laid eyes on him."

"From the pictures you showed me, I can see why. He was very handsome, wasn't he?"

"Yes, but that wasn't what initially attracted me to him."

"Oh? And what else could capture the heart of a pretty young woman like you?" Yitzhak's blue eyes sparkled under his white bushy eyebrows.

"It was his gentle spirit," she replied as she poured them both a glass of water. "And his strong faith in God."

"Was it a religious singles retreat?"

Sarah swallowed some water before continuing. "It was a Messianic youth retreat. Most of us were Jews, but all of us were believers in Yeshua, or Jesus, as his name is translated in Greek. You see, Yitzhak, I believe that Yeshua is the Messiah of Israel, the Son of God."

"You're not serious!" protested the Hadassah patient as he sat up straight in his bed. "Our people have suffered immensely from the church over the centuries. A Jew does not believe in that man. It's against our religion!"

"I'll admit that Christianity has often appeared to be the enemy of our people. Frankly, that's why we Jewish believers use the name 'Messianics,' which is the anglicized version of the original Hebrew word for followers of Messiah. The word 'Christian' comes from the Greek translation of the same word. Although the church has departed from its Jewish roots, Yeshua was entirely a Jew, an Israeli—in fact, a Galilean."

"He may have been born a Jew, but He died a rebel and an apostate!"

"That's how most of the Jewish leaders at the time viewed Him. The Romans just saw Him as a rabble-rouser. But the Scriptures say that the common people, our Jewish ancestors, saw Him as a great prophet, a teacher, and a healer. In fact, much evidence has been unveiled recently showing that the number of ancient Israelis who believed in Yeshua was far greater than earlier thought."

"People could be wrong." Yitzhak grimaced at Sarah. "I may have abandoned my belief in God after the Holocaust, but I still know it's idolatry to worship that man, or any other. Our Scriptures make that clear."

Sarah nodded her head. "Yes, Yitzhak, it's idolatrous to worship anyone other than God alone. But what if God takes on the form of a man? Numbers 12 says that Moses beheld the form of God, that God spoke to him face-to-face. And do you remember the verses at the beginning of Ezekiel where the prophet sees a glorious throne and someone with the appearance of a man seated on it?"

"Yes, I studied the Bible intensely as a boy in Hamburg."

"Ezekiel calls Him 'the Lord,' the same term used elsewhere for Israel's God. Isaiah also saw a vision of the Lord seated upon a throne, with angels worshipping Him. Yitzhak, what if Messiah is more than most of our sages expected? What if He is actually God Himself in human form? Is it beyond the power of God to manifest Himself in bodily flesh to His earthly creation?"

Yitzhak hesitated. His nearly bald head revealed the beads of perspiration between the strands of wispy gray hair. "I suppose not. The Bible does make it clear that the Messiah will just be a man. Listen to me! I almost sound as if I believe in all this nonsense!"

"It's not nonsense, Yitzhak. In fact, there are several Scriptures that seem to reveal the divine nature of the Messiah. One is Daniel, chapter 7, where the prophet sees a vision of someone he calls the 'Son of Man,' who comes with the clouds of heaven. He is given glory and dominion over an eternal kingdom by another called the 'Ancient of Days.' Scripture tells us in many places that only God is worthy of such honor, that only God will reign in glory forever."

"It sounds like God is sharing His glory with this Son of Man."

"He is, Yitzhak. What if this 'Son of Man' is also the Son of God—of the same substance and nature as the Father? This is exactly what Yeshua claimed to be. Wouldn't that make Him divine enough to worship?"

"Maybe so, but if this Son of Man is also divine, then that makes two gods, doesn't it?" Yitzhak scratched his head. "Don't Christians believe in three gods?"

Sarah sat back in her chair and smoothed the wrinkles in her tan cotton skirt. "No, although some Christians seem to think so. I believe the confusion stems from poor phrasing of an ancient church creed. The New Testament teaches that the one eternal God is manifested in three forms: the invisible Father, the visible Son, and the Holy Spirit, who convicts humanity of sin and leads us to the Savior, Yeshua."

"But why bother with all these manifestations? It seems to be so . . . untidy."

Sarah giggled at her friend's remark. "Dear Yitzhak, you are something! The Bible says God fills the universe, He is everywhere at all times. But before He began to create, He focused Himself in the Son—the Son of God. The Son has actually always existed, since His essence is from the Father. Yet He has a separate existence—He is physically either here or there at any one time, not everywhere, as the Father is. The Father then poured Himself through the Son when He created the angels and the universe. This manifestation is called the Holy Spirit. The Spirit's function is specific—to point sinful humans to the Son, but the Spirit is of the same essence as the Father and the Son."

Yitzhak sat back against his pillow, his arms falling at his sides. "Sarah, this is getting too complex for my simple brain!" he sighed heavily.

"And *why* should the creator and sustainer of our vast universe be so easy for us mere mortals to understand?" she retorted. "Sweet Yitzhak, I knew that you wouldn't like what I had to say."

"No, I don't, but I wanted you to be honest so I guess I can't complain."

Sarah picked up her leather bag from the bedside table. "I better be on my way and let you rest. I'll see you again after the Sabbath. Eat well in the meantime!" She leaned over and kissed her friend on the forehead. His heart warmed from the touch.

"Until then!" Yitzhak said as she left the room, thinking as he often did how much she reminded him of his sister.

8

Rumblings from the North

By early September Russia was aiming fiery war rhetoric at Israel. Neither Yacov Nimrod nor Yudah Sephres seemed overly concerned. Only Rafi Hochman felt there might actually be something behind Vladimir Konstantine's threats to avenge Syria's humiliation.

"We'd better take him seriously!" The defense minister was angry with his senior colleagues, especially Nimrod. He was sitting in the cabinet meeting room at 8:30 in the morning, and no one would listen to reason. What good was a defense minister when no one would listen!

"Yacov, as commander in chief, you are ultimately responsible for the welfare of our small country, but I am defense minister. And I say we must place our forces on full alert in response to Konstantine's threats, if only to show him that we won't be bullied around!" He gripped his pen so tightly his knuckles began to turn white.

The prime minister liked Hochman and valued his opinion. On most matters, they agreed; however, this time the highly educated premier happened to side with his two rivals. "Rafi, I agree with Yudah and Edna that the Russian leader is only bluffing. Many of Konstantine's strongest supporters are Muslims from his southern republics. They want us to cave in to the Arab demands at the peace talks in Rome. It's a well-worn negotiating tactic and I'm not impressed."

Foreign minister Sephres nodded in agreement. "Konstantine thinks he can force us to withdraw from east Jerusalem by holding this threat of invasion over us. It won't work. We must stay put as we've already made clear, and I recommend that we issue a new statement saying so. We must not panic."

The security cabinet voted eight to two against their colleague's proposal to place the army on full alert. Although deeply insulted, the defense minister decided not to resign, at least for the time being.

Four days later the security cabinet was called into another emergency session. Nimrod had received American intelligence reports that dozens of Russian transport jets loaded with troops and equipment were headed toward Syria. Other aircraft had been spotted flying toward northern Syria from Iran and Libya.

This time there was no debate. The senior cabinet ministers voted unanimously to place all Israeli forces on heightened alert. Hochman congratulated himself as he prepared a statement warning Konstantine that Israel would defend herself, even from a powerful Russian-led assault.

However, the warning did not faze Vladimir Konstantine, who continued to amass military forces in the eastern Syrian Desert. He also ignored American pleas to call back his men or risk confrontation with the West.

At Russia's suggestion, Muslim leaders in Iran, Sudan, Libya, Lebanon, Pakistan, Afghanistan, Indonesia, and several former Soviet republics signed up thousands of volunteer fighters for a jihad against the Zionist state. Iraq, Yemen, and other countries stepped up their anti-Zionist rhetoric. Muslim militants rioted in parts of Saudi Arabia, demanding the overthrow of the pro-American government. Fundamentalists in Egypt staged anti-Israel marches. The crowds were so large the Egyptian police refused to carry out government orders to break up the demonstrations.

One month after Russian forces began arriving in Syria, Nimrod decided to arm twelve underground Jericho missiles with nuclear warheads. The unprecedented move came after U.S. President Williams confirmed Israeli intelligence reports that more than three hundred thousand Russian soldiers had either flown into the northern part of the Syrian Desert or traveled overland through Iran and northern Iraq. These troops had been reinforced by Iranian and Iraqi soldiers, along with volunteers form Sudan, Libya and Afghanistan. A few thousand of Halled Hasdar's remaining Syrian soldiers were also assembling in the staging area under the waning October sun. The combined military forces had begun coordinated exercises under Russian command.

Eli playfully tossed Benny high into the warm autumn air. The excited child squealed with delight. "Now you really do look like Batman!" Eli laughed, swinging the youngster to the ground.

Jonathan's friend was spending a lot of time with Benny and Tali these days. Sarah lounged on the soft grass next to her daughter and smiled broadly. Stacy, who had moved into the Goldmans' small home to be with her friend and to look after the children when their mother was volunteering at Hadassah Hospital, found herself having to fight feelings of jealousy as she watched Eli with Sarah and the children. She scolded herself. *It's good for Eli to be here and spend quality time with the children. You must get rid of these feelings.*

Just then, the front doorbell rang. Glad for a diversion, Stacy sprang up to answer it. Benny took off after her. Eli sat down on a nearby chair exhausted but exhilarated. His eyes noticed Sarah as she soaked up the rays of warmth from the afternoon sun. *Sarah really looks pretty in that yellow dress,* he mused.

"Look who's here and with more food!" exclaimed Stacy, who was now escorting several guests into the backyard. Yoseph Steinberg and his wife, Cindy, carried four large soft drink bottles while Craig Eagleman trailed behind with two large homemade pizzas covered with foil. Miri Doron had brought plastic cups and plates. Moshe Salam, now living in Jerusalem with his buddy Eli, toted a huge chocolate cake.

Sarah rose to her feet to hug Cindy. "You shouldn't have!"

"Our pleasure," Yoseph responded as he plopped down next to Stacy.

"You have all been so good to me these past few months," gushed Sarah, looking around at her very unexpected guests. "I can't begin to tell you what it's meant to me and the children. I realize food isn't plentiful these days, and the cost of most things is horrendous, yet you've gone out of your way to see we always have enough to eat."

Cindy set the plastic bottles on the round patio table and took the chocolate cake from Moshe. Two pairs of anxious little eyes followed her every move. "Miri got hold of some chocolate while visiting her folks in Tel Aviv, and she made this beautiful cake. And I finally found some mushrooms for my pizzas, although it took some doing!"

"And cheese!" Craig added excitedly, remembering the last pizza made with sour cream. "The government may be rationing cheese along with almost everything else, but at least some is available again."

"And pop! Can you believe that Yoseph and I found some at that wholesale shop near Jaffa Road? Still no tomato sauce though," sighed Cindy when she handed Benny a slice of warm pizza. "Who could have believed that Israel would ever run out of tomato sauce?"

Yoseph put his arm around the waist of his childhood sweetheart. She was dressed in faded blue jeans and a red cotton blouse. "It shouldn't take too long for the government to get the agricultural system back to normal. It's only been a month since they repaired the national water carrier from the Sea of Galilee. With fresh water flowing again, it won't be long before more irrigated vegetables hit the market." Yoseph gave Cindy a tight hug.

"But industry is another matter," commented Craig, accepting a piece of Cindy's pizza. "I hear it will probably be later this fall before we have regular electricity supplies. The Syrians really did a number on the Hadera power plant."

"At least we have juice for most of the day now," added Stacy. "It sure feels good to take a hot shower again, even if we have to ration our water use."

Once again the doorbell sounded and in walked Sarah's sister, Donna, who quickly discovered the picnic brewing in her sister's small backyard. "Shalom, y'all," she proclaimed in American slang while proceeding down the back steps to the yard.

"Can we have some cake now?" pleaded Benny, his eyes wide with anticipation. This would be his first real dessert since before the late spring war. The only other sweet he had consumed was a piece of a small pound cake that had mysteriously appeared on the front doorstep on Tali's birthday in June. The Steinbergs felt that their wheat ration had gone to a worthy cause that week.

"Yes, you can," Sarah replied as she scraped some cheese off Cindy's large kitchen knife. "Then it's off to your naps, you two."

Tali protested, "Oh, Mom, I'm too old for that. Can't I stay out here with the grown-ups?"

"Me, too!" her brother pleaded.

Eli picked up Benny and swung him back and forth. "Here, catch a chocolate kid!" he boomed to Craig, who had just finished his pizza. Blond and blue-eyed Craig was another favorite of Benny's. In fact, all the children at Beit Yisrael liked the laid-back graduate student, who helped Cindy supervise the children's ministry.

Sarah sensed that some of the adults wanted to discuss the latest news. "Tali, you didn't sleep well last night, so I want you to take a short nap after you finish your dessert." She bent down to clean some chocolate off Benny's face. "The same goes for you, fatman—I mean, Batman!"

Soon after the children left, Moshe looked grimly at Yoseph seated in the shade opposite him.

"Do you think the Russians will really lead an attack against us?" he inquired.

"It's very possible," the congregational leader replied. "I don't think Konstantine would have made that announcement this morning if he didn't plan to do something."

"But isn't he afraid of the Americans?" asked Donna as she helped Sarah pass out the dessert plates.

"President Williams has his hands full after that terrible earthquake in the Midwest last month," interjected Craig, sitting under an olive tree next to Yoseph. "He's had to call in some regular soldiers to supplement the National Guard. My cousin, stationed in Georgia, is one of them. It's going to take weeks, if not months, before Williams can get the looting under control and clean up the mess."

Yoseph, who had not lived in the U.S. for more than twenty years, nodded. Plus, there's the continuing threat of more Muslim terror attacks. People have already suffered so much because of them. I don't think the Americans are in any position to help us right now, nor am I sure they really want to."

As the men talked, Eli quietly contemplated the horrific possibility of a Russian attack on Israel. He turned to Yoseph to ask a question that had been stirring in his mind all day. "What is the biblical significance of all this, Yoseph? Is more prophecy about to be fulfilled?"

"Could be, Eli." The well-read congregational leader set his plate down and wiped the crumbs from his mustache. "Many Bible teachers believe that Moscow will lead an end-time invasion into Israel. In fact, quite a few books have been written about it over the years."

"Where is this prophecy?" Moshe asked eagerly.

"In the Book of Ezekiel, chapters 38 and 39."

"It's Gog and Magog," added Sarah as she pulled up a chair next to Eli. "Jonathan used to talk about that prophecy all the time."

"There you go again!" Donna exploded as she sat down close to Craig. "Always trying to link current events to these supposed prophecies, Sarah. You yourself told me that many Christians thought this Gog thing was going to be fulfilled when the Soviets invaded Afghanistan. And that was back in the '70s! I just can't buy any of this prophecy stuff."

"But, Donna, don't forget that Yonni was right about Damascus," replied Eli gingerly.

"Look, everyone in Israel knew that war was possible after the peace talks with Syria broke down!" Donna argued, a bit more quietly this time. "My brother-in-law was bright, but it was just an educated guess that Damascus would be bombed."

Moshe gently took Donna's hand and held it, diverting his eyes from her tight halter top in the process. "I want to know what Ezekiel's prophecy has to say. Please go on, Yoseph."

"Well, it speaks of a war launched by a coalition of nations, led by a great power located to the far north of Israel. This alliance comes to destroy us and capture our goods."

"And Moscow is north of Israel—dead on," noted Craig matter-of-factly.

Yoseph nodded and continued. "This great power, Gog, will have several other northern countries with it, along with a few from our region. Scholars are not sure of the identity of some of the northern nations. The Mideast ones are easier to pick out; they're located east, south, and west of us."

"Is Syria among them?" inquired Moshe, who had dropped out of high school at sixteen.

"Interestingly enough, no. But other countries allied with it in the last war are named: Persia, which is of course Iran; Cush, the area due south of us in Africa where Sudan and Ethiopia are today; and Put, to the west of Israel, which they say was the ancient name for the area that is now Libya. Oh, the scholars also think that Persia could also include Iraq, since it was once part of the Persian Empire."

Eli squirmed in his chair as vivid pictures of the surprise Syrian artillery attack on the Golan flashed through his mind. "Iran was Syria's closest backer in the war, along with Libya and fundamentalist Sudan," he stated pensively.

"Indeed they were, Eli," confirmed Yoseph. "And all three are the fiercest opponents of the current peace talks."

"And they're all three vowing to avenge Syria's defeat, along with Russia," Craig added quickly.

"Exactly. So I think we could be seeing the pieces falling into place for the fulfillment of Ezekiel's prophecy. He said we'd be at peace and living securely in our own land when this invasion occurred. Israel may not be without enemies, but at least all of our neighboring enemies have been virtually neutralized."

Pulling a small Bible out of his jeans pocket, Craig began to recall what a college professor in Dallas had taught concerning Ezekiel's prophecy. "Yoseph, when we studied this section in Bible college, my prof thought it would probably be fulfilled at the end of the millennium. He cited Revelation 20:8 where it says that Satan will 'deceive the nations which are in the four corners of the earth, Gog and Magog, to gather them together for the war.'"

"Many think Ezekiel's prophecy will only be fulfilled at the end of the thousand-year reign of Yeshua on earth, Craig. But very sound arguments can be made that the prophecy will be fulfilled before the end of this age."

Yoseph's eyes scanned his small, captive audience as he solemnly continued. "Many scholars say that the apostle John was using the names Gog and Magog in a broader sense in that Scripture, to describe the rebellious forces from all over the globe who rise up at the end of the millennium. In other words, the final revolt described in Revelation 20 will echo an earlier invasion occurring before Messiah's thousand-year reign begins in Jerusalem."

"Is that what you believe?" asked Moshe, who still found the Bible a bit of a puzzle.

Craig handed his Bible to Yoseph, who answered, "Yes, it is, Moshe. Ezekiel 38 and 39 describe a massive attack against a restored, peaceful Israel. One of the verses—yes, here it is, chapter 38, verse 8—says that our people will have returned to the mountains of Israel from all over the world before this attack occurs. The end of chapter 39, though, tells us that a still fuller ingathering occurs after this great war, when the people of Israel fully recognize and worship their God."

"So, many Jews, but not all, are living here in the land when Ezekiel's invasion takes place?" Sarah asked as she rose to collect the dessert plates.

"Correct, although most apparently do not profess deep faith in the God of Israel before the war occurs. In fact, God makes Himself known to all the nations on earth during the war by miraculously delivering Israel from the powerful attacking armies."

"Praise the Lord!" exclaimed Moshe.

"Amen, brother," agreed Yoseph as he handed the Bible back to Craig. "I just can't believe that Ezekiel is speaking here about a war at the end of the thousand-year messianic reign, Craig. That would mean the Israeli people do not even realize that the Lord is ruling in their midst during the millennium! Verse 7 of chapter 39 implies that Israel will be profaning the name of God before this huge attack occurs. Yet, many other prophecies make it clear that our country will be a holy nation during the thousand-year reign of Yeshua."

Yoseph took a sip from the glass of soda pop sitting by his foot. "The war in Revelation 20 is a rebellion against Israel and the Messiah. It occurs at the end of the millennial reign. Ezekiel's prophecy describes an invasion that occurs when most people, including most of our countrymen, aren't even sure about the existence of God."

"That certainly sounds like now," observed Miri, who typically had not said much, "although many people *are* returning to synagogue in the wake of the war with Syria."

Yoseph liked the shy Israeli woman, who had grown up in a wealthy suburb of Tel Aviv. "You're right, Miri. I think we'll probably see Ezekiel 38 and 39 fulfilled sometime in the near future, sometime before the end of this age."

"Do you mean—soon?" Donna's brown eyes opened as wide as buttons. She was deeply frightened by the prospect of another Mideast war.

"Could be, Donna. But many think this prophecy will only be fulfilled at the end of what we know as the Great Tribulation, when the Antichrist is defeated by God."

"Now don't start with that Antichrist business!" she protested in a stronger voice as she got up to help Sarah.

"I won't," chuckled Yoseph. *But others will,* he thought to himself.

On October 14 the Israeli government issued another warning to Konstantine: *The leaders of Israel will not sit back and permit you to attack our country. Do not forget the lesson we taught the Syrians and their allies. We have demonstrated our ability to adequately take care of ourselves. The Jewish state of Israel will survive.*

Two days later, the massive Russian-led military machine moved southwest toward the Golan Heights and into northwestern Jordan.

Israel's security cabinet voted unanimously to launch three nuclear-tipped Jericho missiles at Konstantine's juggernaut. The ballistic missiles, carrying warheads far more powerful than the bombs that leveled Damascus, were directed at the rear of the advancing forces. The prudent prime minister did not want to take any chances that nuclear fallout might gravitate back on his tiny nation.

The Israeli leader informed President Williams as soon as the Jerichos were airborne.

"I realize that you've been calling for restraint from both sides, Cliff. But the Russians are apparently willing to risk a global war in order to wipe us out. We see no other way to defend our small country. We've just fired three of our nuclear warheads at the rear of the advancing troops."

"You did what?! Isn't Konstantine likely to send nuclear missiles back against you in response? This time we really are looking at World War Three!"

"I don't think he'll do that, Cliff. Tens of thousands of Russian soldiers are already close to our Golan border, or along the Jordanian border to our east. The prevailing winds blow east. Konstantine's men will perish with us if he uses his long-range missiles. So will millions of the very Arabs he is claiming to defend."

While the Israeli and American leaders spoke, several underground silos blasted open in central Russia. Bewildered farmers raced outdoors and watched as four giant, nuclear-tipped missiles hurled headlong into the night sky.

9

Sudden Death

For almost a month Sarah had been storing food, water, blankets, and other supplies in her basement shelter. Eli had given her some medical items. Not having a personal shelter, Donna had left a suitcase filled with clothes in anticipation of the expected Russian-led assault on Israel.

Stacy was on her way home from the bakery on the number seven city bus. It was just after 8:00 P.M. on October 17. The former New Yorker gazed wistfully at the few Jerusalem passengers riding with her and was glad the driver was in a hurry to finish his run.

"Oh no!" An elderly woman holding two shopping bags screamed as a sonorous wail saturated the air. "The siren. The siren. What'll we do?"

Two minutes later, the fast-moving bus turned on to Beitar Street just as Donna was pulling into the driveway.

"Look's like we made it just in time," Donna shouted as Stacy scrambled off the bus. The mournful wail of sirens all over Jerusalem pierced their ears and wounded their hearts. "Let's get inside quickly."

Sarah met them at the door, and the three women hastened down the stairs.

A worried Eli was pacing back and forth inside the shelter when the women entered.

"Let's get this door sealed," he shouted to Moshe, who immediately jumped up to help. Stacy and Sarah plopped down on a bench as the men sealed the steel door with masking tape.

Eli, whose unit was not called up due to its heavy losses in the spring war, distributed gas masks to the five adults and two children. "Put them on," he ordered. Next he switched on a portable radio to receive instructions but kept the volume low so that the children would not become any more frightened than they already were.

The apprehensive Israelis made themselves as comfortable as possible in the small basement shelter. Tali clutched her Raggedy Ann while Benny laid his head on Eli's lap.

"Do you think this is it?" asked Moshe of no one in particular.

"Ezekiel's thing? Might be," offered Eli, trying to sound nonchalant so he would not scare the children. "Or it could be just one of the many wars Yeshua said would occur prior to his return."

"Now where does it say that?" Donna asked with a bit of mocking in her voice.

"In the Gospel of Matthew, chapter 24, among other places."

Donna shook her head. This prophecy thing was not going away, and it was making her increasingly uncomfortable.

"At least we've got enough food down here to last for a few weeks," noted Sarah as she scooted Tali over on her lap.

"But you weren't expecting us hungry men to be here with you," quipped Moshe, who had dropped by with Eli after supper to check on Sarah and the children.

"You're wrong," said Stacy with a tinge of jealousy in her voice. "Sarah's been praying for weeks that you two would be here with us when the war came."

Sarah blushed. "You agreed with me, Stace, that it would be good for us all to be together if— " Sarah glanced up at Jonathan's handgun, resting on a nearby shelf. "It's not so bad to have some men around if, God forbid, we should have any trouble around here."

Feeling somewhat guilty that he was not with the front-line troops, Eli spoke to the group. "Let's take time to pray for ourselves and our country. I hope you don't mind, Donna, but this is important right now."

"With the Russians and their allies storming our way, I should object to some prayer?"

Eli clasped Benny's little hands and bowed his head. "God of our fathers, God of Israel, we need Your protection now more than ever! Please shine forth for us in our hour of need!"

"Amen," affirmed the adult voices, including Donna's.

Eli then quoted the opening section of Psalm 91 from memory. It was one of his favorites.

> He who dwells in the shelter of the Most High will abide in the shadow of the Almighty. I will say to the Lord, "My refuge and my fortress, my God, in whom I trust!" For it is He who delivers you from the snare of the trapper, and from the deadly pestilence. He will cover you with His pinions, and under His wings you may seek refuge.

"Lord, deadly pestilence could be heading in the direction of our tiny country even now. On behalf of our people, we beg you for mercy. Remember Your ancient covenant with our forefathers and deliver us from all evil. Show Yourself mighty in Your deliverance, for the sake of Your great name! We ask these things in the name of our Messiah, Yeshua."

"Amen," responded everyone, except Donna.

The elite Israeli missile crews sweated profusely even though the air conditioners were working as usual inside their underground silos. If they failed to shoot their anti-missile Arrows at exactly the right moment, the computers might not be able to guide them toward their targets. Anything less than exact precision could spell the end of their beloved homeland.

Konstantine's intercontinental ballistic missiles were just descending into the lower atmosphere when the three Israeli nuclear warheads exploded over the Syrian Desert. Instantly, nearly a quarter of a million soldiers were wiped out. Large mushroom clouds of radioactive sand ascended high into the evening sky. The fallout, which would kill many thousands of people and leave millions sick, slowly floated northeast toward Iraq, Iran, and the Muslim republics of the former Soviet Union.

The Israeli anti-missile crews did their best, and their best was good enough. Four Arrow explosives hit their marks (later strategic analysts would find this miraculous since the targets were so high up in the atmosphere). The Russian ballistic missiles were completely destroyed as they descended toward the Holy Land. The lessons learned during the Syrian Scud and SS–21 strikes had paid off. Only one Israeli was killed when metal debris from a Soviet-era missile fell to earth. God was watching over Israel.

Within an hour, an astounded Vladimir Konstantine called off his offensive. With half of his force wiped out, he had lost the war even before it began. The enraged

Russian leader vowed never to forget his humiliation. "I will destroy Israel one day!" he promised his closest comrades. "And I won't wait long to do it!"

At their next meeting, Beit Yisrael leader Yoseph Steinberg explained to his congregants how he personally viewed the brief but intense conflict. "Brothers and sisters, this short war was not the one prophesied by Ezekiel. It was one of the many conflicts Yeshua said would break out in the last days, before the time of Jacob's trouble spoken of by Jeremiah, a time also known as the Great Tribulation. It was another birth pang of the coming kingdom of God. The recent Russian attempt to invade us was, I think, a warning from God that the end of the age is truly upon us.

"We are drawing close to the time when the prophesied false messiah, the Antichrist, should appear on the world stage. The Scriptures say he will claim to be acting on behalf of God and eventually even claim to be God! But he will be a liar who is actually working in the power of the father of lies, Satan. We must watch world events carefully."

Yoseph looked around at the faces in his congregation. Several displayed more than a touch of anxiety. "The attempted Russian-led invasion was a prototype of Ezekiel's prophecy. I believe the massive Gog and Magog attack against Israel will not occur until the time of the final battle of Armageddon, described in Revelation 16. The time of the Lord's return is drawing very close, so let's get ready and get to work!"

The Mideast atomic explosions led to further panic in the world's money markets. Stocks everywhere plunged to new lows. Banks collapsed, particularly in North America.

If anyone doubted that a full-scale economic depression was descending on the world, they doubted no longer.

Israel's economy, however, stayed afloat. Repair of the country's heavily damaged industrial and transportation infrastructure provided many new jobs. Thousands of American Jews had started to transfer money to Israel after the May war with Syria. The trend accelerated after the Russian defeat.

Many Americans blamed Israel for their growing economic woes, with some politicians and commentators openly calling for the U.S. to halt all financial, political and military support for the isolated Jewish State. The huge wave of anti-Semitism sweeping across America was leading many Jews to conclude that Israel was where they needed to be.

The flow of dollars into Israel became so substantial that President Williams ordered a $10,000 limit on the amount of personal capital Americans could send abroad.

Russia erupted in chaos after the failed invasion. Street fighting between supporters and opponents of the government engulfed all major cities. The ruble plunged to new lows. Grieving parents and wives blamed Vladimir Konstantine for dragging their country into an unnecessary war. Yet the ruthless dictator, using old-style Communist and Fascist methods, maintained his iron grip on power. He severely rationed food to the general public while providing amply for his soldiers and government workers. Demonstrations against his rule were broken up swiftly and violently. Within a month, the fifty-eight-year-old ruler had crushed all dissent.

Realizing that the Americans were preoccupied with internal matters and buoyed by the rapidly strengthening Euro currency, European Union leaders decided to sponsor a renewed Middle East peace conference as well. It got underway on December 18. The European Union chose the Spanish capital of Madrid as the venue since the original Arab/Israeli talks had been launched there back in October 1991.

The ornate central hall in the Madrid Royal Palace was filled with leaders, diplomats, and journalists from around the world. Now without an army, Halled Hasdar sat meekly at the far end of the long negotiating table. Yacov Nimrod sat close to the front podium.

Crown Prince Andre represented the European Union. A man in his early thirties who was an athletic sports enthusiast, the prince had been chosen for this task because of his rising popularity in Europe. The charismatic prince had an opportunity to prove his skills in the maze-like Mideast arena. Europe's royal houses, linked together through centuries of intermarriage, were certain he was up to the task.

The tall, broad-shouldered prince slowly approached a podium at the head of the large oak table.

"Ladies and gentlemen, welcome to this august hall. We have gathered here today to bring a permanent end to the awful conflict between your countries. The European Union is determined to extend its hand to you to help you overcome this bitter struggle.

"We join with you to bring an end to war in the Middle East. Arabs and Jews are both physical descendants of Abraham, that great spiritual father of all humanity. The Middle East is the center of the world and the cradle of civilization. Together we can succeed in lighting a torch of peace to brighten the entire earth. We Europeans pledge to help you work earnestly toward this goal."

The World News Network carried the opening speech into homes around the globe. Yoseph and Cindy Steinberg sat in front of the small television on their kitchen counter. "His English is very good," Cindy observed.

"I've read that he is fluent in most European languages."

"He certainly is handsome," said Cindy as she munched on some celery. "I love his long, arched eyebrows and dark, wavy hair. You had that same deep brown color ten years ago, love. Do you know if he's married?"

"Why? Are you ready to dump me?" quipped Yoseph as he turned up the volume.

The Steinbergs listened as television commentators analyzed the speech. The cameras followed the tall young man as he left the podium and walked around the table. He first shook hands with a proud Yacov Nimrod. The Israeli leader felt drawn to the dynamic prince and realized he was on his way up in world politics.

Nobody noticed the thin man dressed in a loose sports jacket standing among the media reporters. He wore a press badge and appeared to be taking notes. As Andre moved closer, he slowly placed his right hand on his belt near his pants pocket.

Suddenly he screamed *"Allahu akbar!"* and propelled himself through the reporters, lunging toward the surprised prince standing only a few feet away. The dark-skinned assailant pulled out a razor-sharp knife and plunged its blade into the right temple of the astonished prince. Andre collapsed to the marble floor as blood gushed from his head.

World News cameraman Ken Preston raced forward to get as close to the dying prince as possible. He was almost knocked down as three security guards rushed in and fell on the attacker. Preston's camera followed their every move.

Cindy and Yoseph stared at their television screen in horror, barely daring to breathe.

Along with millions of others, they watched as the guards forced the assassin to the floor. By this time, the conference hall was in a state of mass confusion. Someone screamed, "Is there a doctor anywhere? Can someone get a doctor?"

Andre's aides knelt beside the wounded prince. He lay on the floor, blood pouring from around the knife, still embedded in his temple.

A doctor quickly appeared clutching a black medical bag. Preston's camera recorded every movement. The hall fell deathly quiet.

The doctor felt for Andre's pulse. He dared not remove the wood-handled knife for fear the young prince would bleed to death. He began to administer CPR. Once. Twice. A third time. But there was no response.

Finally the doctor stood to his feet. "I'm afraid that Crown Prince Andre is dead," he announced to the stunned crowd.

At that moment, it seemed as if the whole world had died with him.

10

MAN OF SIN

The Spanish royal palace hall became a raging sea of jostling bodies as news spread that Crown Prince Andre had been pronounced dead. There was no need, however, for reporters to rush off and phone their editors around the world with the tragic news. The popular prince had been murdered on worldwide television.

Ken Preston moved his portable camera closer to the victim. The sight was gruesome, yet he had no choice but to focus his lens on Andre's bleeding head. WNN reporter Carl Wilson, standing next to him, recapped what had just occurred. "We are in the main hall of the royal palace in Madrid where renewed Mideast peace talks are being held. Crown Prince Andre, representing the European Union, had just completed his opening speech and was moving through this crowd when a man suddenly lunged at him and stabbed him in the head. As you can see, the young prince has been mortally wounded."

Cindy Steinberg turned down the television volume as the commentary continued along with an instant replay of the terrible attack.

Yoseph reached for her trembling hand. "I think this might even be worse than it seems," he said as he wrapped his fingers around hers.

"What do you mean?"

"I've been reading lots lately about Prince Andre. It was almost supernatural the way he so quickly rose to prominence right after those terror attacks in London and Rome. It has occurred to me that he might be more than just a popular European prince."

The Beit Yisrael leader was about to elaborate when something on the TV screen caught his eye. "Cindy, please hit the volume button."

Wilson spoke solemnly into his microphone. "Something unusual is happening here. In case our camera is not picking it up clearly, let me describe what I am seeing. An odd light is emanating from Andre's face. It is as if someone has turned on floodlights, but that is not the case. I really don't know what to make of this."

The slain prince suddenly opened his hazel eyes. The crowd of onlookers gasped in complete astonishment. Preston tightened his camera shot, focusing sharply on Andre's glowing face.

As if in some medieval fairy tale, the handsome prince sat up and pulled the knife out of his bleeding temple. The crimson flow immediately ceased. As several billion people watched worldwide, the laceration closed up. Within seconds, not even a trace of the wound remained.

The astonished crowd gasped collectively as Andre rose to his feet and lifted his arms high in a gesture of triumph. People in the hall began clapping and then cheering. Some were smiling, others weeping. No one was quite sure what had just occurred, but everyone was thrilled just the same.

A number of world leaders, including Nimrod, rushed up to shake the prince's hand. Journalists charged up to thrust their microphones under Andre's square-jawed face as he spoke.

"Fellow citizens of our great world, on this historic day, I stand before you born again!"

The crowd exploded in applause. Andre motioned for silence.

"A prophecy given to me as a young boy has come true! I have been chosen by the master of our universe to bring healing to a hurting world, to save our planet in this critical hour, when nuclear destruction threatens us all! A new age is dawning, an age of universal brotherhood and harmony, peace, and tranquillity! Wars shall cease, and nations will beat their weapons of death into instruments of life!"

Preston shook his head in disbelief. He had just witnessed a miracle. A dead man had risen back to life. Although the American cameraman's religious convictions were few, he had to admit that something higher and more powerful than himself had done this. It must have been God, or at least a god. Preston was not alone. Similar thoughts filled the minds of everyone in the Spanish hall and all around the globe.

Yoseph Steinberg turned down the volume.

"It's him!" he announced dramatically as Cindy clutched the edge of the table. "It's Revelation 13."

He held his face in both hands. "And it happened just like the apostle John wrote." He opened his Bible. "Andre had a wound to his head and it seemed fatal, but the wound was healed."

"Doesn't Daniel refer to the Antichrist as a prince?" Cindy asked as she tried to absorb the significance of her husband's words.

"Yes. And he said this prince, the Antichrist, will rise up and lead a confederacy springing out of the old world empires, especially the Roman Empire. Decades ago Christian teachers thought the European Economic Community might become the base for this final empire. Apparently they were right."

Yoseph sighed as he turned the sound back up.

"Thank you, ladies and gentlemen, thank you. I know you're excited for me, but be excited for yourselves. My resurrection is a gift from the Supreme Being to each one of you. I will reveal more about his glorious plans for us in the coming days."

The prince exited the hall followed by a retinue of eager admirers. As he passed through the arched doorway, his weeping parents embraced him. King Dan and Queen Dorothea had witnessed the horrible slaying from their balcony seats. Their grief had turned to ecstatic joy as they saw their eldest son rise from the dead. They accompanied the regal prince as he proceeded through the front rotunda with camera lenses and reporters monitoring his every move.

The celebration of Andre's resurrection quickly spread to all parts of the globe. From Rome to Rio, from Tokyo to Toronto, from Delhi to Dallas, people danced in the streets with delight. A new age had arrived! Miracles were happening. Perhaps this did mean world peace at last. Perhaps this man was the savior of the world.

However, the reaction was not so positive in the Mideast. Many Muslims, especially in fundamentalist countries like Iran, and Orthodox Jews were not dancing. How could a prince from a Christian country be the savior of the world? Many evangelical Christians were also abstaining from the global bash. The Chinese leader,

Quay Chin, and Vladimir Konstantine of Russia were not celebrating either.

Privately, the European prince exploded in anger when told about these negative reactions to his supernatural resurrection. He would deal with these opponents soon enough. For now, the public party had to go on.

Moshe Salam was confused. "How can you be so sure that this guy is evil?" he demanded, rising up demonstratively from his seat. "Prime Minister Nimrod claims he is a man of peace. The same thing is being said by many religious leaders here and abroad. I know I'm a new believer, but I think you all might be jumping the gun a little bit."

Yoseph, who founded Beit Yisrael in 1987 along with two other Israeli believers, responded from the pulpit. "I'm sorry, brother. All of us in this room want peace for our country, as do most of our Arab brethren. But Andre has all of the hallmarks of the prophesied world leader known as the Man of Sin.

"The Bible says this ruler will come as an angel of light, Moshe. He'll deceive the world into believing he is good, but he'll be a man of lawlessness. In 2 Thessalonians Paul says that many professing Christians will even be taken in by this man. Ultimately, he'll be able to convince mankind that he is divine because he'll be given extraordinary powers by Satan."

Moshe sat down and frowned. Yoseph continued: "Look, friends, I won't stand up here and pretend that the immediate future is full of fun and cheer. But we must remember that our God, the God of Israel, has not suddenly gone on vacation. Our Messiah still reigns at the right hand of power! So cheer up! He has given us His perfect love to cast out all fear. These recent world events really point to the nearness of our final redemption, and that of our nation. More than ever, it's time to praise Him and earnestly seek His face!"

The doctoral student at Hebrew University, Craig Eagleman, picked up the acoustic guitar leaning against the wall beside him and began strumming on the strings. The believers jumped to their feet. Within seconds, most were smiling and clapping as they sang in Hebrew, "Rejoice, daughter of Zion! Shout in triumph, Jerusalem! For the Lord is in your midst, a victorious warrior!"

But just outside the congregation's rear window, a United Nations soldier stationed in Jerusalem was clandestinely taping every sound.

European Union leaders held their economic summit in early January and decided to recommend to their respective parliaments that Andre be crowned emperor of the union. Andre's dynamic Christmas Eve speech, detailing the desire of a "Creative Force" to make Europe the center of a new world order, had added to growing calls for such a move. The leaders saw in this vibrant young man, who was already being proclaimed as god by many around the globe, a powerful tool to achieve their dream of total world domination—a dream that had captivated European leaders since the fall of the Roman Empire.

Within just three weeks, all parliaments in the Union had voted to crown Andre emperor. The move won unanimous approval at the European Parliament in Strasbourg, France, and a committee was set up to organize a coronation ceremony for late April in Rome.

In the meantime, the Middle East peace talks rapidly progressed in Madrid under Andre's magnetic guidance. By late February, a comprehensive peace treaty was ready to be signed.

Israel would be granted full recognition by Syria, Lebanon, and Iraq and would have permanent, open borders with all of its immediate neighbors, including the two that had earlier signed peace treaties with it, Egypt and Jordan. Tourism and free trade could now flow in all directions. The five Arab countries and Israel agreed to reduce their armed forces and stop purchasing foreign weapons. Palestinian refugees living in the Arab states would not be allowed back into Israel or the Palestinian autonomous zones, but would receive substantial economic compensation from a fund set up jointly by the EU, the UN, and the World Bank.

Syria reluctantly agreed to cede the strategic Golan Heights to Israel. For all practical purposes, Syria would cease to be a sovereign nation, coming under the direct control of the United Nations. A UN governor would run the ravished country until a new, stable government could be established. A similar UN-run government would be set up in neighboring Iraq. The Syrian army would be cut down to a token force. All Syrian troops would be withdrawn from Lebanon.

Under the new peace accord, Jordan would officially be declared a Palestinian state, and its name changed to Palestine. King Abdul, who had barely survived a Palestinian fundamentalist-led rebellion and two assassination attempts before he was forced to join Syria and Iraq in their war with Israel, agreed to abdicate his battered throne and turn the country over to the PLO.

Arab residents of the Gaza Strip and the area formerly known as the West Bank would now be free to become citizens of the new state of Palestine. Palestinian refugee camps in the territories would be dismantled and their residents moved to new, internationally financed housing projects. Most Jewish settlements in the areas would remain intact under Israeli control, although those in the

Gaza Strip would be abandoned along with several dozen in the hills of Judea and Samaria.

As expected, the status of Jerusalem was the thorniest issue at the talks. At the insistence of Egypt, the PLO, and the Vatican, Israeli leaders reluctantly agreed to allow UN forces to be stationed in the eastern parts of the city to insure Arab access to Muslim and Christian holy sites. UN troops would also be deployed in areas surrounding the holy city, particularly in Bethlehem to the south and Ramallah to the north.

By far, the most controversial part of the treaty dealt with the ancient Temple Mount located in Jerusalem's walled Old City. Fundamentalist Muslim groups insisted that Islam be accorded permanent control over the entire Mount. Orthodox Jews in Israel and some Christians argued that such a move would violate Judaism's most sacred hopes and dreams.

After two weeks of tough negotiations, Prince Andre pushed through a compromise solution. He did so by threatening to cut off European monetary aid and trade to any country that resisted his proposal. Islam would maintain control over its two venerated shrines on the Mount, with Israel recognizing permanent Muslim sovereignty around them. In return, Israel would be granted sovereignty over the empty northern third of the Mount, where it could rebuild the ancient Jewish temple. A stone wall would be constructed between the Dome of the Rock Muslim shrine and the designated Jewish zone.

The compromise solution caused tremendous consternation in Israel and the Arab world. Nimrod came under enormous pressure to desist from signing the treaty unless the section splitting control on the Mount was reworked. Most Orthodox Jews were now openly calling Andre a false messiah and were appalled at the idea that their prime minister would sign a document affirming permanent

Muslim sovereignty over most of their sacred Mount. A holy Jewish temple could never be constructed next to profane Islamic shrines, they avowed. Fundamentalist Muslims worldwide were equally repulsed by the idea of a blasphemous Jewish temple next to their holy monuments.

In mid-March Andre went on worldwide television to make a direct appeal to religious Muslims and Jews. As he spoke, he pointed to a large mural hanging next to his desk. It pictured a majestic temple, rising several hundred feet into the air and situated just north of the gold-roofed Dome of the Rock. A large, white stone wall with an open gate could be seen between the two grand edifices.

"To achieve lasting peace, followers of all religions must recognize the reality of one supreme being. It was he who raised me from the dead to be your champion and savior. If peace is to be achieved in the Middle East and throughout the earth, everyone must recognize and accept my divine appointment as his authoritative voice and his channel for peace to the world."

Andre, wearing a light green suit, which nicely set off his clean-shaven face, leaned forward as he continued. "The supreme force has revealed a wonderful truth to me. All nations will soon go up to Jerusalem to worship him on the Temple Mount, or Haram al-Sharif as you Muslims call it. They will pass through the golden gate pictured here and will be able to worship in both sacred places."

The animated prince looked straight into the lens of the television camera. His penetrating eyes sparkled as a slight smile crossed his lips. "The great Jerusalem temple will be rebuilt. The Universal Force has so decreed. Work must begin soon. It will be a magnificent temple, constructed with the help of funds donated from many of you. It will be a place of worship for all of humanity—a house of prayer for all nations.

"Religious rites practiced in the ancient Jerusalem temples such as animal and grain sacrifices are part of the passing era of darkness. The Great Force declares that they have been abolished forever. Our new temple will be dedicated to the powerful Universal Force, the god of all nations and people."

Eli sighed as he turned his gaze away from Sarah's television set toward Benny, snoring happily in his lap.

"A new temple—built by the Antichrist. Many in our Orthodox Jewish community are not going to like this, nor his prohibition against animal and grain sacrifices," he said as Sarah handed him the bowl of grapes.

Craig sat in the recliner near the window. "Doesn't Daniel chapter 12 say that the regular sacrifice will be abolished before the abomination of desolation is set up in the temple? We all know that several Orthodox groups here in Jerusalem are ready to reinstitute the sacrificial system. They won't be happy about this at all."

"And the European nations plan to make him emperor," observed Sarah. "Then he'll gain control of the whole world, including Jerusalem! May God help us all!"

"He will," Eli assured her. "Our God is the Rock of Israel, our fortress in times like these. We have to let others know who this Andre really is. It's time to proclaim that Yeshua is our true Lord and Messiah."

The Jewish believers were beginning to realize that the growing Orthodox antagonism toward Andre afforded a good opportunity to present their beliefs. It was time to hit the streets.

Prime Minister Nimrod signed the peace treaty hammered out by Prince Andre and the Israeli Knesset approved it in late March. In addition to the prime minister, Foreign Minister Sephres and Welfare Minister

Satori were the strongest government advocates of the accord. Even though she was an atheist and he an agnostic, both were skeptical about Andre's claim to be in direct contact with a higher being.

Rafi Hochman and Rabbi Amos Shimshon had grave reservations about the peace accord. The defense minister felt that ceding sovereignty over part of the Old City might simply be a prelude to further territorial concessions in the future. The religious affairs minister knew that his Orthodox voters would balk at the idea of a temple constructed by a European Gentile. Both men were seriously concerned over threats by Jewish and Muslim religious groups to disrupt any attempt to build a new temple next to the Muslim shrines.

After prolonged Knesset debate, Rabbi Shimshon abstained while Hochman reluctantly voted in favor. They decided that a negative vote would do no good. It was impossible to resist the will of the increasingly popular and powerful European prince.

11

Beloved Apostles

The photograph hung on the bulletin board over his bed. Today, the fourth of April, would have been Yonni's thirty-fifth birthday, Eli realized soon after waking up. Taken at a surprise party Sarah had thrown for her husband one year before, the picture showed Jonathan with his left arm flung over his buddy's shoulders. Eli smiled as he recalled how Jonathan had let out a whoop when the lights were switched on and how everyone had yelled out "surprise!" "Just one month later, you were gone," he whispered as he touched the cherished picture.

Soon after waking up, Sarah placed a rose-colored ribbon around a portrait of Jonathan displayed on a shelf above the living room sofa. Her thoughts drifted back to the last moments they had spent together. She had loved him so. She still did. Sometimes she felt like she would die from the weight of the grief, but other times she knew she could go on—that she had to go on because that is what Jonathan would have wanted.

Sarah intended to remind Tali and Benny during breakfast that it was their late father's birthday. But Jonathan's little girl beat her to it. As Sarah was arranging the ribbon, Tali appeared carrying a box neatly wrapped in blue and white paper. "It's a present for Abba," she announced, handing the small gift to her mother. "God told me to buy it and give it to you to keep for him. One day, Abba is coming back to Jerusalem with Yeshua." Sarah squeezed her daughter in a loving hug.

"Oh darling, it's beautiful!" she exclaimed to Tali's delight after unwrapping the precious gift. "It's a copy of the seven-branched silver menorah that God instructed our ancestors to make and place in the holy temple. Let's put it right here next to Abba's picture."

Eli intended to phone Sarah but decided to visit her instead. He knew that she would be feeling extra lonely today, just as he was.

"Where did you get that? It sure is a nice one!" Eli remarked when he saw Tali's present.

"It was a birthday gift from Tali for her father. Eli, she remembered his birthday all by herself!" Sarah sat down on one side of the sofa as she spoke. "She said God told her to buy a menorah and give it to me to keep for Jonathan. She knows that one day he'll be coming back to Jerusalem with the Lord. She must have saved up all of her allowance money for some time. Is my daughter a little doll or what?"

"And a little prophetess," Eli commented, sitting down next to Sarah.

Sarah looked puzzled. "What do you mean?"

"Well, I never told you because . . . because it was too sad. Sarah, the day he died, Yonni bought a silver menorah for Tali—almost exactly like this one—when we stopped to use the facilities at a restaurant gift shop on our way up to the Golan Heights. He told me it was for her birthday in June. 'Seven branches for my seven-year-old little girl,' he said."

Sarah grasped Eli's hands, tears flowing down her cheeks.

"Yonni had it in his army jacket when the artillery shells landed. I could feel it when I lifted him up on my lap. I've kicked myself many times for not putting it in my pocket because it wasn't with his personal items when we were released. But here it is!"

"Oh, this *is* from God!" exclaimed Sarah as she leaned over to hug Jonathan's dear friend. "And a very loving one, a *very* loving one."

Eli picked up a plastic bag sitting on the coffee table. "I bought a few groceries for the Passover meal. I hope you can use them."

Sarah's heart sank—her first Passover without Jonathan in nine years. "Of course I can," she responded, "but the seder meal is still four days away. You stopped by because it was Jonathan's birthday, didn't you, Eli?"

"Yeah, I did," he replied somewhat sheepishly. "I guess I just wanted to see how you were doing—and to give you this." Eli pulled a long-stemmed pink rose from the plastic bag.

"Oh, Eli, how thoughtful! Fresh flowers are still so hard to come by." She leaned over and gave the native Israeli a peck on the cheek.

"It was really nothing," he said, blushing.

Sarah had begun to notice a definite pattern to Eli's visits. Increasingly, he chose to drop by in the middle of the day before her children had returned home from school. And he always seemed to come by on those days Stacy was working part-time as a secretary at Beit Yisrael.

"Eli, thank you. You really are wonderful."

"Oh, I'm not so great. In fact, I was a real jerk before Yeshua got hold of me."

"Maybe so. But you've let the Lord change you into a really fine man."

"Well, you're pretty nice yourself—nice and pretty!" chuckled Eli, effortlessly hoisting the heavy sack of food onto the kitchen table. "Gotta go. Say shalom to big Benny and Tali for me."

"Thanks, Eli. See you on Passover Eve." Sarah smiled at him as she closed the door. Eli had become such a good friend to her, as he had been to Jonathan. But she was beginning to wonder if he had something more than friendship in mind.

Sarah spent the next few days thoroughly cleaning her home in preparation for the Jewish holiday. She kept finding personal items belonging to Jonathan or things that reminded her of good times they had shared. She crumbled on the sofa and wept when she discovered his gold Star of David tie clasp in the lining behind one of the davenport cushions. It had been his fifth wedding anniversary gift from her. When he lost it some months later, Jonathan had told her, "I know it's around here somewhere, princess. When I find it, I'll take you out to dinner to celebrate—just like we did on our fifth!" That promise had never been fulfilled.

The Goldman house was spotless when the Passover guests arrived late in the afternoon. In addition to Eli, Sarah had invited Donna, Moshe, Craig, and the Steinbergs. Everyone except Eli arrived on time for the feast. The friends chatted amiably. But when more than a half hour had passed, Sarah found herself worrying.

"If we wait any longer, Benny won't make it through the seder," she told Stacy, who was chewing contentedly on a carrot stick.

"Where do you think he is?"

"I haven't a clue, but I'm beginning to get really worried. It's just not like him to not show up—especially for a meal!"

Twenty minutes before he was supposed to arrive at Sarah's home, Eli Ben-David had been sidetracked as he made his way through the Old City. A friend from another congregation spotted him as he hurried along.

"Eli, you won't believe it! You must come and see!" The friend ran up and grabbed his arm.

"Shalom, Zev. Come and see what?" Eli said impatiently. "I'm in a hurry."

"You must follow me. You must see!"

Zev literally dragged Eli with him through the narrow streets of the restored Jewish quarter. The white Jerusalem-stone buildings reflected the yellow and orange hues of the late afternoon sun. The aroma of roasting lambs wafted down from open windows above the stone paths. Eli could hear the chiming of church bells and Muslim minaret prayer calls floating in over the warm breeze from other parts of the ancient walled city.

Within minutes the two men were bolting toward the Western Wall of the Temple Mount in the southeast corner of the Old City. As they drew close, Eli detected a strange noise. It was decidedly different from the usual sound of soulful Jewish prayer that had given the site its popular nickname, the Wailing Wall. He wondered what it could be. The two believers quickly swept down the wide steps leading to the expansive stone plaza in front of the venerated wall. Eli soon found himself mingling with a crowd of several hundred jostling Israelis gathered around two odd-looking men.

"Prepare the way of the Lord! Make ready a highway for our God! For the Day of the Lord is at hand."

Eli recognized the Scripture from the prophet Isaiah. But who were these two gray-bearded men? He looked closer.

The speaker had tanned leathery skin set off by thick, white eyebrows and a long, salt-and-pepper beard. The crown of his head was entirely bald. The second man, standing silently nearby, had dark brown eyes that revealed a burning fire deep inside. Both men looked like they had popped out of the pages of a book on Bible history. Each wore a garment of coarse camel hair.

"Behold, I am coming quickly," the elderly Jew exclaimed in Hebrew. "And My reward is with Me, to give to every man according to what he has done!"

Now Eli was becoming excited. "This guy is quoting the Lord's last spoken words, recorded in the Book of Revelation!" he whispered to Zev. "They must be believers in Yeshua!"

The setting sun cast a gentle golden pale on the ancient wall as the crowd listened intently.

The second man's voice was not as strong as the first, but his words were equally as powerful. "Blessed are those who wash their robes that they might have the right to the tree of life and may enter by the gates into the city."

"What on earth are they talking about?" asked a frowning Hassidic Jew, dressed in black and standing on tiptoes next to Eli. "And what's with those weird clothes?"

"Those are passages from . . . from the Book of Revelation in the New Testament," he replied with some hesitation.

"The Christian Bible? But these two seem to be Israeli Jews—they're speaking flawless Hebrew. Why would any of our people be quoting words from the Christian book?"

Eli thought he knew the answer but decided not to share it. "I'm not sure. The one who spoke before certainly has a powerful voice, doesn't he?"

"They better shut up if they're mixing things from the Christian writings with our Jewish prophets!"

Several people in the crowd began hurling verbal abuses at the two aged Jews.

"Get out of here, you traitors!"

"Leave us alone! This is holy ground!"

A young bystander pulled several fist-sized stones from his jacket and heaved them at the two furrowed men. "Take a hike, old men!" the assailant screamed while others roared their approval.

With calm deliberation the more prominent speaker raised his right hand into the air. Without warning, a ring of bright orange flames materialized directly above the assembled throng and swirled ominously overhead. Screams rose from the crowd as people charged into each other trying to get away.

Zev darted off like a fox to the far corner of the wall. But Eli stood still, completely transfixed. The fire evaporated as quickly as it had appeared, and Eli determined to find out who these men were. Standing alone in the center of the Western Wall plaza, he felt a tinge of fear mixed with expectancy.

"Shalom, young man. I believe your name is Eli Ben-David?" The first speaker began walking in his direction, followed by his partner.

Eli nodded in astonished affirmation.

"It is a good name, meaning 'My God, Son of David.' You understand that Yeshua, the Son of David, was the face of God in human form, do you not?"

The young Israeli stood dumfounded. His mouth dropped open.

"My name is Yochanan. This is Natan-el." The two antique-looking elders greeted Eli with rough, rutty, wrinkled hands.

"Very pleased to meet you," stuttered Eli, questions somersaulting in his head like circus acrobats.

"You are wondering who we are, I am sure." Yochanan's deep set eyes shone with a kindness Eli had not seen in a long time. "We are prophets of the most high God sent to Israel and the world in these last days before our Lord returns to Jerusalem. We are witnesses to Him—the two who are written about in the Book of Revelation."

Eli gasped. Yochanan held the arm of his elderly companion. "We have been sent to warn humanity about the judgment to come and to assist Yeshua's earthly body in the coming difficult days before He returns to His beloved city."

Eli felt like he was dreaming. Shadows of dusk now enveloped the nearby Western Wall. In quiet deliberation, Yochanan turned toward Natan-el. The second prophet then began to speak. "You, my young friend, have been chosen as one who will accompany us on our mission."

The robust Israeli felt the blood drain from his face. "But I am just an ordinary man. There is nothing special about me."

"I said that when the Lord first approached me," recalled the portly Natan-el with a slight chuckle. His round cheeks turned pink as he thought back over the centuries. "I was a firm skeptic, and yet He chose me."

"Think about the apostle Paul," added Yochanan, who was several inches taller than his companion. "He was a persecutor of Yeshua's followers and yet chosen by Him to be the main writer of the New Testament. God is no respecter of persons, Eli Ben-David. He chooses whomever He chooses."

Eli quickly caught up. "I've always heard that the two witnesses in Revelation would be our great sage, Moshe, who led our people out of Egypt and passed on to us God's Ten Commandments, and Elijah, the mighty prophet who ascended to heaven in a chariot of fire. Others think they'll be Moshe and Enoch. But you said your names are Yochanan and Natan-el?"

"Yochanan Ben-Zevedee is my full name."

Eli's eyes lit up. "But that was the name of the apostle Yochanan, or John, as my English-speaking friends say. He was the one who actually wrote about the two witnesses in the Book of Revelation. He was on an island called Patmos."

"A terribly hot place in the summer."

"You mean . . . you mean you are Yeshua's most beloved apostle?" Eli stared intensely at his strange new friend. Could this be?

"Greetings, brother Eli."

"But, didn't you die? I mean, didn't Yochanan die almost two thousand years ago?"

"My young friend, did Moshe not die too? Yet we saw him on Mount Hermon when Yeshua was transfigured before our eyes. You yourself said that many expect Moshe to be one of the two witnesses."

"Hmm . . . I didn't think about that. But Elijah and Enoch were taken to heaven alive; they never died, according to Scripture."

"And neither did we," added Natan-el matter-of-factly. Eli's mouth fell open once again. "Do you think, young man, that such a miracle could only take place in the days before our Lord was born? Yochanan and I were taken up alive to heaven after completing our earlier missions on earth. I am Natan-el, the disciple Philip found under the fig tree."

The Israeli's heart was pounding in his chest. He was becoming more excited with each passing moment. "Yes, and Yeshua said that you would see the heavens opened, and the angels of God ascending and descending on the Son of Man!"

Yochanan patted the broad back of his aged companion. "I should point out that Natan-el was later himself known as an apostle, like Paul. He planted many churches, especially in Mesopotamia. Well, enough about us. I believe that we are detaining you from an important Passover meal. We'll meet with you here at noon tomorrow. Several others will be joining us, including your friend over there." Yochanan pointed toward Zev, who was still cowering with several dozen Jewish men at the base of the forty-foot-high wall.

"This is Passover Eve!" Eli suddenly remembered. "You must eat the Passover seder. Please come with me to my friend's house. I'm sure there will be more than enough food to go around."

The venerable elders paused to consider. Natan-el smiled warmly and replied, "They should have at least one extra place set."

"Yes, we would be honored to join you," added Yochanan, securing the wrap over his slightly bent shoulders.

The three Jews slowly headed out of the Old City's Dung Gate, just south of the Western Wall plaza. As they proceeded toward Sarah's home, Eli's hand inadvertently rubbed against the stiff brown sackcloth Yochanan was wearing. The sandpaper roughness helped him overcome any lingering thought that he might be in the middle of a dream.

The warm evening air in Jerusalem was vibrant and clear. The soft light of candles flickered through apartment windows as Jewish voices sang the traditional Passover songs.

This is no dream! he thought excitedly. *But can this be happening to me? These sorts of things only occurred in the old days.*

Two prophets walking with me in Jerusalem on Passover Eve? The closest apostle of the Lord? Chosen to be part of some end-time drama? Wow!

Sarah's frantic greeting snatched Eli from the depths of his thoughts. "Eli Ben-David! Where in the world have you been? We were so worried!"

Eli walked across the threshold with a dazed look in his eyes. "I'm not sure I've even been in the world."

"What?"

"You'll find out." Eli softened his voice as he motioned toward the elderly men waiting on the sidewalk. "I've taken the liberty of inviting two friends of mine to join us for the Passover seder. I hope you don't mind. I know you have the one extra place we always set for Elijah at our Passover tables. Is it alright?"

"Oh, Eli," Sarah whispered under her breath. She strained to peek around him and get a look at the two men.

Great, he has brought two freaked-out weirdos, thought Sarah before she replied, "I'll set another place."

Eli and his new friends made their way across to the dining room table. A cold silence filled the air. Moshe finally broke the thick ice. "Where have you been?" he asked his flatmate, who took the empty chair next to his.

The young Sabra had a sudden brainstorm. "We don't want to interrupt the seder," he said in English, mainly for Donna's benefit. Then he added in Hebrew, "Atem midabrim angleet?"

"Yes, we speak and understand English," replied Yochanan in lightly accented English.

"I thought you might," chuckled Eli.

"Well, at least introduce them!" chided Sarah, as she again found her place at the table.

"Oh, I'm sorry. This is Yochanan and his friend Natanel. Gentlemen, these are my good friends, our hostess, Sarah Goldman, and big Benny and Tali, her children."

Benny eagerly thrust a sticky hand out toward Yochanan. The youngster was thinking how neat it was to have strange-looking guests show up unexpectedly for their holiday meal.

After the introductions were completed, Sarah made a place for Natan-el and directed Yochanan to the empty seat traditionally left for Elijah.

At the usual point in the Jewish celebration of freedom, Benny opened the front door just in case the ancient prophet was outside and wanted to come in. This part of the seder is based on the age-old Jewish expectation that Elijah will one day return to Jerusalem during Passover to herald the coming of the Messiah.

"Nope! Elijah's not out there!" the youngster announced while sliding in next to Yochanan.

The elderly visitors smiled.

Two hours later, the believers finished the last of the four traditional cups of blessing. Sarah motioned for Eli to pour a fifth cup of wine for her guests. "This one is the cup of Elijah, and we pour it especially if we have unexpected guests," she explained. Yochanan thought about his last shared cup with the Lord in Jerusalem and pronounced "la chaim" as glasses were raised in the air.

After the celebration, Sarah put her two sleepy offspring to bed while Stacy, Donna, Moshe, and Craig did the dishes. Yochanan, Natan-el, and Eli moved to the living room. The anxious Sabra waited for the others to return so he could tell his incredible story. He had been mentally rehearsing his lines all evening.

When everyone was back in the living room, Eli leaned forward on the couch. "I have something important to tell you all. It's the reason I was so late. In a nutshell, I have had the most blessed experience of my life!"

Eli proceeded to relate the amazing events in detail. When he came to the swirling ring of fire, Moshe exclaimed, "Wow! This is too much!"

"Indeed!" Donna's arms crossed her chest as she smirked. "And to think all this occurred before you drank the four cups of wine."

Eli frowned at the new immigrant. "These elderly men later introduced themselves to me as Yochanan and Natan-el. They then informed me that," Eli paused to swallow before he proceeded, "that they are the two witnesses of the Book of Revelation."

Sarah and Stacy gasped. Donna let out an overdone sigh. Moshe raised his hands to his cheeks as Cindy immediately reached into her purse for her pocket Bible. Yoseph exchanged skeptical glances with Craig, and then whispered in his ear, "Another pair of kooks who think they're the two witnesses!"

"You're entitled to be skeptical, Yoseph," said Yochanan, although he could not possibly have heard the private remark. "You're thinking you have counseled many like us before, and so you have, but not quite like us. Time will confirm that."

Yoseph frowned.

"Yochanan told me my full name before I could even introduce myself," Eli informed the skeptical congregational leader. "And then he told me his full name." Eli stopped and caught his breath. "It is Yochanan Ben-Zevedee."

"That rings a bell," said Stacy.

"Wasn't that the name of Yeshua's closest disciple, John, the beloved apostle?" Cindy asked incredulously.

Yoseph interrupted. "You mean to tell us you are not only one of the two witnesses of Revelation but also the man who wrote down the apocalyptic vision, along with a Gospel and several letters in our Bible?"

"Greetings, brother Yoseph," beamed Yochanan.

"And Natan-el is the disciple whom the Lord spotted under the fig tree in Galilee!" added Eli excitedly, almost jumping off the couch.

"Can any good thing come out of Galilee?" piped in a skeptical Craig.

Natan-el took the cue, "You will see, friends."

Donna could not help herself, "And when does the good fairy appear?"

"Donna!" scolded Sarah. "These are my guests!"

"Don't be too hard on your sister," advised Natan-el. "I was a skeptic myself about the things of God; that is, before Yeshua revealed himself to me."

In usual form, Yoseph probed the startling claims of the two visitors. "Almost all of our best evangelical scholars have taught that the two witnesses of Revelation 11 will undoubtedly be Moses and Elijah. Even Orthodox Jews believe Elijah will return to earth."

Natan-el tugged at his long gray beard and responded to the challenge. "It's true that the prophet Malachi wrote that Elijah will return before the great and terrible Day of the Lord. Yet Yeshua Himself said that John the Baptist—not the actual Elijah—had partially fulfilled the prophecy by heralding the Lord's first advent. Yeshua's cousin came in the spirit and power of Elijah. Why couldn't the second and final prophesied appearance of Elijah be in the form of another John—our brother Yochanan—manifesting the same spirit and power as Elijah?"

"Most interesting," Yoseph almost sang his words. "Can you give us any biblical evidence that two of the Lord's apostles would be the two witnesses?"

Yochanan arranged his sackcloth tunic about his knees. "There are several strong inferences in the New Testament," he replied, "but most people have missed them. The first is recorded in the Gospel of Matthew, chapter

16. Yeshua had just spoken about His second coming with His holy angels. He said there were some of us standing with Him that day in the northern Galilee town of Caesarea Philippi who would not taste death until we saw His glorious return to earth."

Yoseph scratched his forehead. "But that is usually thought to refer to the Lord's transfiguration six days later, when Moses and Elijah—our usual candidates for the two witnesses—appeared to Him. Some people think it refers to the outpouring of the Holy Spirit a few months later on Pentecost."

"Natan-el and I are aware of that," replied Yochanan. "But none of us with the Lord on that day died the following week, or even during the following year, except Judas. The Lord was talking about His actual return, Yoseph.

"For many centuries now everyone who was present on that day has been dead—except Natan-el and myself. We were taken up alive to heaven just like Elijah, although at separate times and places."

Everyone including Donna listened intently to the dialogue. Yoseph carefully pondered Yochanan's words. "That prophecy of Yeshua's does pose a problem for many scholars. If you and Natan-el are who you say you are, it would solve that problem. I have read that many in the early centuries of the church believed the apostle Yochanan remained alive beyond his natural years."

"Wasn't that based on something Yeshua said to you—I mean to John at the end of his Gospel?" inquired Craig, revealing his rapidly changing opinion.

"Exactly," responded Yochanan with certainty. "I deliberately included Yeshua's prophecy about my death in my Gospel account, even though many have missed its significance."

"Which verses?" asked a fascinated Moshe, reaching for a Bible lying on the coffee table.

"John 21, from verse 18," answered Yochanan.

"Here it is," said Cindy excitedly. "Yeshua prophesies about Peter's last years on earth and then about his death. Next Peter asks the Lord to reveal something about Yochanan's death. Yeshua replies, 'If I want him to remain until I come, what is that to you?'"

"Exactly, Cindy. These are the verses most people find obscure, if not a waste of precious space. But, as I wrote in verse 25, even the whole world could not contain all the books that could have been written concerning Yeshua's words to us."

"Why did Yochanan waste precious space then?" Yoseph asked, still somewhat skeptical.

"A saying went out among the believers that I would never die. I was trying to make clear that Yeshua did not say I would *never* die, but only that I would remain alive until He comes again."

"That's verse 23," interjected Cindy.

"You mean the apostle Yochanan is going to die when Yeshua comes again?" Yoseph asked, in a mixture of bewilderment and awe.

The room fell silent as the two elderly Jews glanced wistfully toward one another.

"Of course!" Eli belted out with great excitement. "The two witnesses are killed by the Antichrist at the end of the tribulation! Revelation says their dead bodies will lie here in the streets of—" Eli's voice trailed off, "the streets of Jerusalem. I'm sorry, I didn't mean to—"

"It's all right, brother Eli," Yochanan assured him.

Seated next to Eli on the couch, Sarah reached out and folded her arm in his. "We shall indeed die at the hands of the wicked one," Yochanan explained, "but not until we have told the world the good news about Yeshua, warned them of judgment, and seen our victorious Lord and His heavenly host beginning their descent to earth!"

"Amen," Stacy encouraged.

Freaks, Donna thought. *Total freaks.*

12

A Chosen Few

"Repent, for the kingdom of God is near!"

Eli, Moshe, Yoseph, and Zev stood near the edge of a surging crowd in the Western Wall plaza. "People are better behaved than two days ago," Eli observed. "They must have heard about the ring of fire."

The elderly Yochanan continued his proclamation in a powerful voice audible throughout the plaza. "Listen, that you may live! 'I am the resurrection and the life,' says the Lord. 'No one comes to the Father but by Me!'"

"That last Scripture will probably provoke a response." Yoseph nervously eyed the large crowd.

"Get out of here, you son of a harlot!" a young, black-bearded zealot shouted.

"Leave us alone!" cried a crinkled old woman wearing a blue scarf. "Take your false messiah somewhere else!"

As she spoke, a large rock whizzed past Yochanan's left ear and landed with a thud several feet behind him. Like

Elijah of old, the end-time prophet raised his right hand toward heaven. But this time the result was not a ring of flames. Instead, a bolt of fire flashed out of Yochanan's mouth, singeing the white stone plaza just inches away from the rock-thrower. The crowd gasped, and many screamed and ran for cover.

"What in the—I've never seen anything like—like that before!" stammered Yoseph.

"They obviously have supernatural power," added Moshe calmly.

"That's for sure!" Yoseph concurred, his remaining skepticism now melting in the heat of the flame.

"I'm convinced," asserted Moshe, shaking his head. "That does it for me."

"Me, too," averred Zev.

Despite the display of awesome authority, several hundred people stayed put in a circle around the apostles. Half were religious Jews and the others mostly secular Israelis or Palestinian Arabs. They were intrigued by the powerful presence of the two men.

Yochanan resumed his exhortations from the Word of God. After quoting Isaiah and Yeshua, he finished with a call for repentance and offered to pray for anyone wishing to receive the Lord into their lives. Seven Israelis and three Palestinians responded to the call.

As the two prophets ministered to the ten new believers, Yoseph, Eli, Moshe, and Zev lingered nearby. Eli felt an unexpected tap on his left shoulder. He swung around to greet Danny Katzman, a twenty-four-year-old Israeli he had met at a Messianic conference near Tel Aviv. The thin Ashkenazi had a keen wit, Eli remembered. He quickly introduced Danny to the others.

Yochanan eventually dismissed all but three of the ten new believers and smiled warmly at the eight brothers who remained standing before him. "Friends, it is no coincidence you are each here today. You have been carefully chosen by our Master, Yeshua, to minister with Natan-el and myself in the last hours of this age."

The three new believers, eighteen-year-old Eitan Ronen, thirty-nine-year-old Shimon Bickman, and twenty-four-year-old Abdul Wahab, gazed at each other in apparent bewilderment. The five veteran believers—excluding Eli—were only slightly less astonished.

"Yeshua wants each one of you to spend your time with us in the coming days," added Natan-el, standing beside his companion. "We have much to teach you."

Yoseph whipped up the courage to speak. "Sirs, I have a wife and congregation. I can't just walk away from my God-given responsibilities."

"Your wife will be fine, Yoseph," Yochanan assured him. "In fact, she will often minister with us in the coming days, along with several other women. Your congregation will do surprisingly well. Have faith and see."

And so each spring day around noon, except on the Sabbath, Yochanan and Natan-el spoke in the plaza below the ancient Temple Mount. The eight chosen brothers were usually there as well, helping to lead people to the Lord. Cindy, Sarah, Stacy, and other female believers often joined them.

Rabbinical circles in Jerusalem were in an uproar over the public preaching of the two old Jews, particularly after Israeli state television screened a feature report about them on the popular Friday evening news program, *Weekly Diary*. Chief Rabbi Yisrael Zotman issued a statement warning Orthodox Jews to stay clear of the two apostates. He was incensed that government officials seemed to be powerless in the face of their "provocative and insulting statements." The chief rabbi demanded that

Jerusalem Mayor Elran Merot banish the two troublemakers from the holy city.

Complaints began pouring into police headquarters charging that the witnesses were missionary agitators who were disturbing the peace. Police Chief Haim Dronen sent reinforcements to the area around the Western Wall to observe the two men and keep public order.

At the urgent request of Rabbi Amos Shimshon, an emergency cabinet session was held to discuss the situation near Judaism's holiest site.

"We must order the immediate arrest of these rabble-rousers!" maintained the Holy Torah party leader. "They are causing an enormous disturbance in our observant communities."

"We at least need to find out more about them," added Prime Minister Nimrod, uncertain what their course of action should be.

"Indeed we do," concurred Foreign Minister Sephres. "We must determine who, or what, is behind all of this."

Rabbi Shimshon grimaced. "If we don't do something soon, all hell could break loose in this city!"

The cabinet finally voted to instruct the police chief to arrest the two preachers. Dronen ordered a special contingent of Israeli Border Police—elite units known for their assertive approach toward security matters—to accompany his regular forces when the arrests were made.

More than a dozen army trucks were driven to the west side of the plaza opposite the Wall. Soon after Yochanan started speaking, Border Police units began to move out. Pointing their M–16 rifles in the air, the well-trained security force rapidly stationed themselves around the small crowd gathered to hear the apostles.

Wearing a green flack jacket and metal helmet, Chief Dronen walked toward the crowd and lifted a megaphone to his lips. "This is Jerusalem Police Chief Haim Dronen.

Everyone must evacuate the area immediately. No one will be harmed. The government has ordered us to take these two men into custody for questioning."

Eli and the other disciples stayed put. Eli whispered, "Aren't you going to do something, Yochanan?"

"No, my young friend," he replied calmly. "This action is the will of God. The Lord has made clear that we are to submit to the government at this time. Do not be afraid for us, Eli; Yeshua is with us. Move away now and keep us in prayer."

The Lord's ancient witnesses stretched out their arms to be handcuffed and were escorted to the waiting police van.

As the police convoy proceeded west along Jerusalem's main street, Jaffa Road, Yochanan reflected on his Master's arrest in the nearby Garden of Gethsemane. His sense of shame was renewed as he recalled how he had failed to stay awake as Yeshua agonized over His imminent crucifixion. Then he remembered that his mother had earlier gone before the Lord to ask for special positions for her sons in the kingdom of God.

"Are you able to drink the cup that I am about to drink?" Yeshua had asked the brothers in response.

"You said we would indeed drink that cup," Yochanan said under his breath as the convoy neared its destination.

The apostles were taken to a government office building near the Israeli parliament, the Knesset, and quickly escorted into a small concrete room with no windows. Minutes later, Israel's top officials marched in and encircled the two seated prophets.

"Who are you and where have you come from?" demanded an irritated Rabbi Shimshon.

"We are voices crying out in the wilderness of Jerusalem, 'Make ready the way of the Lord,'" replied Yochanan resolutely.

Staring at the sackcloth both were wearing, Rafi Hochman whispered to Shimshon, "These guys are real fruitcakes."

"How do you produce this fire, or whatever it is, from out of your mouths?" the defense minister bellowed as he loosened his tie.

"How did Elijah call fire from heaven onto Mount Carmel?" Yochanan remained tranquil in spite of the raging emotions around him.

"Uh, I'm not sure about that." Hochman backed down.

"You don't believe he even did it, sir," Natan-el stated with certainty. "You are not convinced yourself, Rabbi Shimshon."

Prime Minister Nimrod stepped forward. *What a strange, unique people we are,* he thought as he cleared his throat. "However you do it, these fire shows are causing disturbances and fear in our streets. We know you have a growing number of Jewish and Arab followers, but we will not release you until you promise to stop stirring up our people at the Western Wall!"

The two witnesses simply smiled at one another.

Michael felt elated. Jerusalem was his designated city, and he was finally receiving another assignment in it. His last one was during the Scud attacks of 1991 when he had warred high above the holy city.

Two angelic companions accompanied him to the underground pool hall bomb shelter. The archangel looked awesome in his mighty armor as he lightly touched the sleeping head of an Israeli security guard. The man would not awaken now. Then Michael and his cohorts floated down the hallway of the government shelter, gently brushing by the other guards as they went. Those half awake fell into a deep sleep, while those snoozing snored even louder.

The three angels halted in front of one of the bedroom doors, locked from the outside. The security guard suddenly felt the call of nature and went to a nearby restroom. Pointing his finger at the bathroom door, the archangel sealed it shut with the guard comfortably inside. Next he touched the locked bedroom door. Immediately it opened.

Yochanan and Natan-el were easily roused. Unlike their brother, Peter, they knew they were not seeing a vision. The Lord, through His Holy Spirit, had earlier made clear to them that a divine rescue would take place that night. It would be a sign to many people that the Lion of the tribe of Judah, the Root of Jesse, was Israel's true Messiah. It would also provide further encouragement that God was with His people.

13

The Emperor

On April 24, Prince Andre was crowned emperor of the European Union. The elaborate ceremony was broadcast live from Rome on worldwide television except where blacked out in China, Russia, and Iran. Presidents, prime ministers, kings and queens, diplomats, and industry leaders were in attendance. U.S. President Clifford Williams and his wife, Helen, sat in the second row. Yacov Nimrod and his wife, Esther, occupied the aisle seats in row three.

A one-hundred-twenty-member orchestra struck up the processional as four Swiss guards slowly opened the silver-plated doors leading into the ornate Roman hall. In marched the Queen of England and other European royalty, displaying their crowns and dressed in regal splendor. King Dan and Queen Dorothea appeared near the end of the procession wearing golden robes. Twelve young European girls attired in white satin dresses and carrying light turquoise baskets, followed close behind tossing pink and white rose petals onto the deep red carpet.

Ken Preston focused his World News Network camera on the opened silver doors. His heart skipped a beat as Crown Prince Andre appeared straddling a large white stallion. Trumpeters sounded triumphantly as horse and rider were led into the huge hall by two Swiss guards. Dressed in a white silk suit set off by a mauve robe with a gold trim, the youthful prince looked like a king already.

Preston slowly panned his camera up the carpeted central corridor. Andre soon arrived at the foot of a marble platform where he dismounted and slowly ascended the stairs.

"He looks like a million bucks," Ken commented into his television headset.

"He sure does!" agreed Roberta Byson in a nearby room coordinating the sixteen cameras placed strategically all over the gala hall. "Tighten up on his parents, camera three," she instructed him.

King Dan stepped forward. His eldest son knelt down on a soft purple pillow. Two lads dressed in golden pantaloons and blue velvet tops stepped forward holding a deep purple satin pillow with a sparkling jeweled crown resting majestically on it. Sounds of regal music filled every crevice of the large, ornate hall.

"Zoom in on the crown, six, and hold the shot."

The triple-tiered golden diadem glistened in the bright television lights.

A hush fell over the select audience as King Dan reached for the splendid crown. Andre bowed his head. "Andre, my son. In the name of the sovereign nations of the European Union, I crown you emperor of all United Europe!"

Amid ecstatic cries of "Long live the emperor," the new European monarch rose to his feet and embraced his beaming parents. As he exited the hall, he greeted European royals standing below the marble platform. He also shook hands with the American leader and made a point of grasping Nimrod's outstretched hand.

Billions remained glued to their television sets as the prestigious guests proceeded to a nearby banquet hall. Ken raced to man his position there.

"Camera five, zoom in on the silver goblet in front of the emperor," ordered Byson after the guests were seated.

"Will do," replied Ken.

"All cameras, our schedule says King Dan is about to propose a toast to his son. Then Andre will make a short speech. Camera two, tighten up on the king's face."

The suave and elegant king, born in Rome just before World War II, joyously held up his crystal goblet. "Ladies and gentlemen, honored guests, fellow citizens of planet Earth everywhere. I raise my glass to honor my son, Emperor Andre."

The new ruler stood up from his high-backed chair. "My dear friends, thank you," he began as the cheering died down. "I have had a tremendous honor and awesome responsibility bestowed upon me this day. But I do not bear it alone. It is primarily carried by the Great One, the exalted god of the earth, who chose me to be your supreme leader."

"Camera three, get a closer shot of the Queen of England," instructed Byson. "She looks so elegant today."

Andre continued. "Now it is time for you to meet the man who has been my spiritual mentor for many years. Venerable guests, I present to you the honorable Urbane Basillo."

The guests warmly applauded as a heavyset, olive-skinned man sitting four seats away from the emperor rose to his feet. With mock humility, the beady-eyed man in his early sixties bowed before the audience.

The young emperor went on. "Urbane is destined to play a very important role in our new world order. But for now, my treasured guests, enjoy the wonderful feast that has been carefully prepared for you!"

"I've read about Basillo," said Yoseph Steinberg as he switched off the television in his kitchen. He seems to be some kind of an occult guru that was brought into King Dan's court when Andre was about twelve. He was the prince's personal tutor during his teenage years. You know, many royals have their own private spiritual advisors."

"Yeah, even Nancy Reagan had somebody who did horoscopes for her," recalled Cindy as she cleared the supper dishes.

"They say this Basillo fellow is really close to Andre and well acquainted with most of the big wheels in Europe, including Catholic and Protestant church leaders. When Andre turned eighteen, Basillo left King Dan's employ and established a foundation in Rome to promote unity among all world religions. I think he may be the False Prophet spoken of in Revelation 13. He helps the Antichrist rule the world and performs miracles in his presence."

"Oh, my!" Cindy exclaimed as she ran water in the sink. "And what about the ceremony we just saw?"

Yoseph flipped open his well-marked Bible. "I think we may have witnessed the breaking of the first seal, described in Revelation chapter 6, verse 2. A man wearing a crown rides forth on a white horse to conquer the world."

"It's been a while since I read Revelation," said Cindy as she began washing dishes. "There are three more horses described. Correct?"

"That's right. The second horse signifies intense warfare. It says here the rider will take peace from the earth.

I suspect that will be Andre himself." Yoseph's brow was furrowed. "If so . . . nothing less than World War III is probably looming on the horizon."

"Good grief!" exclaimed Cindy.

"The third and fourth horses are famine and death, undoubtedly to follow the coming world war. After that, the fifth seal involves wide-scale martyrdom of those believers who remain faithful to Yeshua and resist the wicked Antichrist."

Cindy shuddered as she reached out for her husband's hand. "I am so glad I'm married to someone like you in these traumatic days, who knows and loves the Word of God."

Yoseph smiled and tenderly covered her hand with his. "Thanks, but you should be especially glad that we're both married to Yeshua. I suspect that only His mighty power will be able to hold us together as we enter the end of the age."

Ken Preston slowly opened the front door of his London apartment. "Betty, I'm back from Rome!" he announced as he dropped his black umbrella into the stand.

His wife soon appeared in the hallway. "Finally!" she exclaimed as she pulled her blond hair back with one hand and gave her husband a kiss on the cheek. "You look beat! Come in the kitchen and have some hot tea."

As Betty poured tea into Ken's cup, she revealed what was burning on her mind. "Honey, that Andre is not a good man! He is the prophesied Antichrist, spoken about in both the Old and New Testaments."

"You and your weird religion!" Ken spit out. "It's been twenty-five years since you were under the authority of your Southern Baptist daddy preacher. Don't you think it's time to lighten up and forget all that junk he taught you?"

"Ken, even you have to admit that something supernatural is going on, and what's going on fits in exactly with several prophecies about the end-time beast found in Daniel and Revelation."

"I thought I was the beast," he teased after swallowing some tea. "I suppose there must be some sort of Creative Force out there that's superior to us, as Andre thinks. I mean, I saw that knife protruding out of his bleeding head, and seconds later, he was as good as new! But whoever, or whatever, healed him, doesn't have anything to do with that fundamentalist trash you learned in your daddy's church."

"Well, dear, you think what you like," said Betty with her characteristic South Carolina drawl. "I'm going to continue studying my Bible."

"Fine. Just be quiet about it."

"Camera four, back up a little. We need a wider shot of the two men standing together," ordered Roberta Byson.

"Roger," responded Ken as he adjusted his lens.

"Camera one, you're getting too much sun reflection. Change your angle just a little, will you?"

The large courtyard in front of the European Union headquarters in Brussels was filled with international journalists and guests waiting to hear the emperor's first formal speech since his coronation. It was a sunny afternoon in May. Several billion people were expected to view the address live on television. Skilled linguists working at networks around the globe prepared to translate his speech, to be delivered in English.

The European sovereign emerged from the headquarters building wearing a light blue satin suit under a crimson cape. His jeweled crown was perched on his dark, wavy hair. He presented the outward picture of perfection. "My fellow citizens of Europe and the world, I am honored to be delivering my first address as supreme emperor of the European Union. My heart is humbled once more at the great task assigned to me by the Universal Force who has chosen me to give instruction and guidance to every person living on Earth, to save humanity from itself, to deliver us all from the dark powers attempting to destroy our planet."

"Camera four, get a shot of those people to the left of Andre who are already bowing low before him." Ken turned his camera to pan the worshipful crowd.

"I know that many of you have reservations about kneeling down before any man. Indeed, past decades have been marked by a series of brutal dictators who have enslaved many innocent people. However, more positively, they have also been marked by a turning away from the iron bars of religious superstition that imprisoned our ancestors.

"As the anointed channel of the benevolent Creative Force, I am worthy to be worshipped, just as he is."

Andre paused for several seconds and reflected on the orders he had just given to his top aides to begin drawing up secret military options against his Russian, Chinese, and Iranian enemies. "I have another wonderful announcement on this fine day. Citizens of the world, I want to present once again my tutor in all spiritual matters, Urbane Basillo."

The Milan-born man stood up and waved broadly to the cheering crowd.

"Come and stand next to me, dear friend." Andre motioned to his mentor.

"Ladies and gentlemen, Urbane has spent his entire lifetime listening to the voice of the great Universal Mind. He is prepared to lead all people everywhere into worship of the powerful Creative Force. On instructions from the Divine One, he will immediately begin to unify all existing religions into one new world order of worship. Citizens of planet Earth, pay very close attention to him. My brother, Urbane Basillo!"

The onlookers cheered wildly as the two men embraced and raised their entwined arms in triumph.

Yoseph Steinberg turned down the volume on the large color television set at Beit Yisrael. He had arranged a special congregational gathering so the believers could immediately go into prayer following the emperor's inaugural speech.

"I'm positive that Basillo is the false prophet spoken about by the apostle Yochanan in Revelation 13," he announced to the seventy believers gathered in the room.

"How can you be sure?" inquired Moshe from the middle of the room.

"Why don't you ask me?" said Yochanan, just entering the back door with Natan-el.

"Welcome, dear brothers!" Yoseph scurried toward the door to greet the unexpected guests and escort them to the front. A wave of excitement swept through the congregation as the two witnesses moved to the podium.

Yochanan spoke to the congregation in a deep, rich voice. "Basillo will exercise all of the authority of the first beast, who is Andre, as I wrote in Revelation 13, verse 12. He will cause people everywhere to worship the emperor, and he'll integrate all of the established world religions into this emperor worship. Statues of young Andre will be set up all over the globe. Anyone who doesn't worship him will be cut out of the new world economic system Basillo is about to build."

"People everywhere will be made to bow down to this human image of the beast. But God's true chosen ones will resist this false messiah. Many others will too, but not because they know the Lord.

"Basillo will perform great signs and deceive many. In fact he is about to do his first miracle right now."

Yochanan turned toward the television, prompting Yoseph to raise the volume. Andre was stepping back up to the battery of microphones.

"Citizens of the world, children of the one and only god. Many of you have assumed that spiritual matters are of little importance in our modern world. Others believe that their religion is the only true one. The Great Force knows these things. Therefore, he has granted an important sign on this special day. Just as I was raised from the dead to become the christ-force for the new age of universal peace, Urbane has been granted the power to perform miracles. And these miracles will confirm to you that I am the great, resurrected channel of the Universal Force.

"Urbane will now give you a small demonstration. It will be dramatic, but do not be afraid."

"Camera four, pull back to as wide a shot as possible," Byson directed through her headset to Ken.

"Will do, Roberta," he responded.

A cold and calculating look came over Basillo's robust face. He stepped back from the microphones. "In the name of the Universal Creative Force," he shouted with the voice of an army general, "I command fire to fall to earth from the highest heaven!"

Instantly, a stream of bright orange flames, about ten feet in diameter, cascaded to the ground, incinerating flowers and trees in a garden next to the courtyard.

"Return now!" he commanded. The blazing torch of fire rushed back into the sky.

"Oh no, another fire-caller!" exclaimed an exasperated Edna Satori as she sat with her colleagues in the premier's office. "Where are they all coming from?"

"Hard to tell," replied Rafi Hochman, sitting next to the set.

"There's a vast difference between Urbane Basillo and the two impostors operating near our Western Wall," Rabbi Shimshon maintained. "This guy is patronized by none other than the new emperor of the European Union. Our pair—despite their impressive escape from detention—are nobodies. The press isn't even paying very much attention to them anymore.

"But I'm not too sure about this emperor's theology," he added, thoughtfully stroking his bearded chin. "I don't really like the idea of this eclectic, one-world religion. Where will that leave Judaism?"

Sitting at his desk, the prime minister diplomatically nipped the budding theological debate. "It'll be interesting to meet the emperor's spiritual mentor, whatever his religious views. He is obviously a colorful character."

"Our people in Brussels tell me Basillo is eager to visit here in the coming months." Foreign minister Sephres crossed his legs and leaned back in the comfortable wing chair. *It will be good to get to know him,* he thought menacingly. *He might be of value against Nimrod.*

"He is eager to come," confirmed Nimrod, "and I expect each one of you to enthusiastically welcome him." He carefully eyed his senior ministers.

The leaders grew quiet and turned their attention back to the TV screen as Andre walked up to the podium and silenced the cheering crowd with a wave of his hand. "What a day of rejoicing for the world! We have seen with our own eyes a small taste of the awesome power of the great Universal Force! We will see his power manifested in many marvelous ways in the coming years!

"But I must warn you. Already there are some who have revealed themselves to be enemies of the exalted Creative Force! They are attempting to deceive the world and prevent the new age from taking hold. Their leaders are two old Jews who have recently appeared in Jerusalem, that city so central to the promulgation of the plans the Great Force has for us all."

The allusion to the two apostles caught the Israeli leaders and the Beit Yisrael believers by surprise.

Andre continued. "These two Jewish impostors are openly working for the dark force. They are the ones written about in the Christian Bible: the Antichrist and his false prophet! They deny the creative christ-force. They speak lies. They are for war, hatred, and division. Turn away from these wicked ones and follow the true god and his only savior, Andre!"

Dozens in the Brussels crowd began to prostrate themselves before the handsome emperor. The steely-eyed monarch showed no reaction. Although just a few years over the age of thirty, he had accomplished so much. He was destined to rule the world. The Universal Force was with him.

"Ken, get a close-up on that large group near the front bowing down toward Andre," Byson whispered. "Who would have thought. . . ."

Yoseph switched off the television set. "Please, brother Yochanan, speak to us!" The elderly apostle slowly stepped up to the podium in front of the silent congregants. "Little flock, do not fear. The God of Israel has long ago prevailed over this wickedness. The adversary will indeed take control of the earth during the coming days and will begin to persecute the saints of the Most High God."

Sarah grabbed Eli's hand as the prophet prepared to speak forth the powerful word of the Lord. Yochanan lifted his eyes and his hands. "But thus says the Lord: My little children, I will never leave you nor forsake you. I will be with you until the end. I will hide you in the shelter of My wings. I will guide you to the streams of life, for My name's sake. Just as the lightning comes from the east and flashes even to the west, so shall My coming be. Recognize this, I am near, even at the door. Work while it is still day, for the night of judgment is coming when no man can work."

Yochanan lowered his arms and closed his eyes. An atmosphere of holiness filled the room. Despite the fact that a black plague of darkness was descending on the tired old earth, the God of Israel, the God of the Universe, was in their midst.

14

The Face of God

Sarah was moving like a whirlwind. It was forty-nine days after Passover and the Jewish Feast of Shavout was about to begin. With last-minute preparations for the evening holiday meal awaiting her, she was hustling to get home. Still, she felt obliged to stop by and chat with her elderly friend.

"Here you go, Yitzhak. The last bite of chicken and rice."

"Thanks, Sarah. I hope I can recover enough one of these days to feed myself."

"Just take it one day at a time, dear friend. Have you been reading anything lately?"

"Only the paper. I don't have the strength for anything else."

"Well, at least you're keeping up with the news. I must be going now. I'll drop by after the holiday."

"I know you need to get home for your big meal, Sarah, but I need to ask you a question. What do you think about this new emperor and these two men who keep causing a stir at the Western Wall?"

"You rascal!" Sarah scolded with a gleam in her eye. "You know I love to talk about such things! But in just a few hours it will be sunset and the beginning of Shavuot. I will come by after the holiday to talk."

Sarah gently caressed her elderly friend's leathery hands. "For now, I'll tell you that my brothers and sisters in the Lord and I see the same spirit in Andre that was in Hitler. Both came as self-proclaimed saviors in a time of global upheaval. Both rose to power after economic depressions. Like Hitler, Andre appears to be a good man, a man who can restore order and get things moving again. But I believe he will end up persecuting us Jews, just as Hitler did."

"Oh, my! And what about the men who appear every day near the Wall?"

"Dear Yitzhak, I'm not sure you would believe me if I told you. Let's leave that one till next week. Get some rest now. Shalom!"

"Shalom," he replied as he put on his glasses so his eyes could follow the young Jewish widow out the door. *She sure reminds me of Rachel,* he thought.

When she arrived home, Sarah was pleasantly surprised to see Tali helping Stacy set the festive dining room table. *She is becoming a very mature young lady,* thought the proud mother. *These difficult times are turning us all into more responsible people.*

After donning her yellow cotton apron, Sarah checked to see that the table had the correct number of dinner plates for the holiday meal. She had invited the same people who were with her at Passover. Danny Katzman, the believer from Tel Aviv who had tapped Eli on the shoulder at the Wall, would be joining them. He had become roommates with Eli and Moshe. The two apostles had declined her dinner invitation; they needed to be in special prayer during Shavuot, the feast of Pentecost.

"Would you hurry up in there!" shouted Moshe as Eli checked himself once more in the mirror. "We're supposed to be at Sarah's in half an hour."

"Just a second," Eli called back.

"You'd think she was the fussiest woman on earth!" Moshe protested as he pushed open the bathroom door. "The way you make sure every hair is in place."

"I'm not doing it for Sarah, Moshe. I just like to look good on the Lord's feast days."

"Right," teased Moshe as he ran his rough hand over the back of Eli's head to mess up the carefully coiffured locks.

"Get away!" barked Eli, splashing warm water on Moshe's chest.

Danny stuck his head in the doorway. "You two studs better get moving if we're going to make it on time."

"Hey, you look great in my sweater!" Eli commented to his newly found friend. "The green really looks good with your red hair."

"I don't know, man," Moshe threw in with mock seriousness. "I think you look like a green forest on fire!"

"Yeah? Well, that hair on your chest makes you look like the Black Forest in Germany," quipped Danny.

After grooming themselves, the Israeli bachelors gathered together in their small living room for a word of prayer. The sun was just setting in the west, signaling the onset of Shavuot.

"Our Father in heaven," began Eli, "we commit this evening into Your hands. We rejoice that we can celebrate Your feast with our brethren. We rejoice at the outpouring of Your Spirit near the Western Wall, and that You have chosen us to be a part of the ingathering of the firstfruits in these last days. Help us to follow the Lamb of God more closely and to be men of God in all that we do and say. In Yeshua's name, Amen."

"Amen," affirmed Moshe and Danny.

The three Israeli men opened their eyes, only to feel a sudden strong pull by some strange unseen force. They quickly gazed at each other with puzzled expressions. In a flash they were gone.

Everyone arrived at Sarah's home on time—everyone, that is, except Eli, Moshe, and Danny.

"What could it be this time?" asked Stacy, chewing an olive.

"Well, Yochanan and Natan-el said they planned to be alone in prayer this evening, so the guys couldn't be with them," observed Sarah.

"Maybe I was right," Donna opined with a smattering of sarcasm. "The good fairy has finally arrived in town! The boys must have spotted her in the Old Hag City."

"You behave yourself, Aunt Donna!" scolded Tali, scurrying onto her aunt's lap.

Sarah ignored her uppity sister. "We'll just have to begin. The fish will be spoiled if we wait any longer."

Yoseph recited the traditional Hebrew blessing over the bread and wine. He then spoke about the outpouring of the Holy Spirit on the first Shavuot after the Lord's resurrection. "This Feast of Weeks, also known as the Feast of Firstfruits, reminds us of the great outpouring of God's gift to us, his Holy Spirit. It also reminds us of the large harvest of souls that occurred here in Jerusalem following that tremendous outpouring. I am certain we're going to see such power again in our day. The ministry of our two anointed brothers, present for that original outpouring, is a sure sign of that."

Sarah kept one eye open on Eli's empty chair, praying silently that he and his companions would soon show up.

"Could the guys still be over near the Wall?" asked Stacy after Yoseph had finished speaking.

"Not unless they went back for some reason," answered Cindy. "We left the plaza together about three hours ago."

"Glory to God in the highest! Glory to the Lamb!" The powerful male voices sang in perfect twelve-part harmony. Eli noticed he was no longer wearing the silk dress shirt and tan slacks he had put on for Sarah's special supper. A pure white robe, draped gently from his shoulders, clothed him now.

Moshe stood next to Eli. His face glistened as he joined in singing the new song to the Lamb. Danny, whose ancient ancestors were from the tribe of Benjamin, sang with a nearby group of twelve thousand men.

In all, 144,000 Jewish men now lined up in semicircle rows around half of a perfectly formed hill. Eli realized they were standing on the heavenly Mount Zion. Yeshua, the Lamb of God, stood at the top of the hill. His head and hair were radiant with light. His eyes sparkled like diamonds. Light emanated from His glorified body through His long flowing robe. A golden breastplate covered His chest, studded with twelve precious gems representing the twelve tribes of Israel. His burnished bare feet were as bright as the sun. His light was the only light in the midst of the assembly, and His brilliant luster lit up all the faces glistening below Him on the holy hill.

Eli's countenance reflected the unspeakable joy in his heart. He was finally beholding his beloved Lord, face-to-face! Tears of deep joy cascaded down his cheeks. The One who was sacrificed for his sins was alive and standing before him in resplendent glory!

The Israeli's watery eyes seemed to have a built-in magnifying lens. Somehow he could see Yeshua's awesome face as if He were standing just a few feet away.

After an indeterminable length of time, the male chorus ended its special song. The powerful voice of the Lamb rippled over the assembled crowd like the billowing waves of the sea. It was a deep, rich, commanding voice. It was a beautiful voice, like the voice of a groom calling his bride to the chamber of love.

The Lamb spoke tenderly to His chosen vessels in Hebrew. He spoke of things to come. He detailed the role they would play during the final days. The Jewish men listened intensely, savoring every precious word spoken by their beloved Lord.

After Yeshua had finished, the glorious song of worship began again. The magnificent male voices rang out in heaven until the dawn broke in Jerusalem. Then, just as quickly as they had come, Eli, Moshe and Danny were supernaturally transported back home.

Sarah was frantic with worry. It was not like Eli to miss an important festival. The young widow had slept very little through what seemed like an endless night. Despite the Shavuot holy day, she had been trying to reach Eli's apartment for hours. Finally, somebody answered.

"Oh, Moshe! Are you alright? I've been worried sick! Where in the world have you been?"

"Nowhere—in the world," answered Moshe. "Here, I'll let you speak with Eli."

"Shalom, Sarah."

"Eli! Where have you been? I've been calling all night. Yoseph went by your house after our meal, and nobody was home."

"We were home, sweet Sarah, if home is where the heart is. I can't explain to you over the telephone what happened.

I'm sorry we caused you anxiety and that we missed your meal. Read a couple of chapters in the Book of Revelation before we talk, chapters 7 and 14."

"Huh? Okay. Can you come over for lunch? We could talk then."

"That sounds great, Sarah. Shalom for now."

A sumptuous meal was waiting on the table when the three Israeli men appeared at the front door. Sarah and Stacy nearly fainted when they saw their male friends.

"What happened to you?" blurted Sarah as she flung open the door.

"What do you mean?" replied Eli. A broad smile splashed across his face.

"Well, you look so—different."

"Handsome, I'd say," Stacy murmured to herself.

Moshe's hearing was keener than ever. "What? You didn't think we were good-looking before?" His eyes twinkled at Stacy.

"Sure we did," responded Sarah. "But there is something different. Your skin is, well, it's glowing, and your eyes are radiant."

Their shoulders look broader, too, mused Stacy, before deciding that was ridiculous.

"We are different," Eli affirmed as Sarah's children rushed into the living room.

"Come here, tiger!" Eli scooped up Benny from the floor.

Sarah smiled. *Something may have changed, but not his great way with my kids.*

As Sarah placed grilled Saint Peter's fish and rice on her best holiday plates, Eli turned to Tali and Benny. "I want to share a true story with you both today, and with your mother and Stacy. But you have to promise me that you won't tell it to your friends, at least not yet. Do you promise?"

"Yes," they replied in unison.

Sarah interrupted. "Eli, I forgot to read the passages from Revelation. I fell asleep and didn't wake up until an hour ago."

"That's alright, you can check them out later."

Eli shared a few minutes of light banter with the children before revealing what was really on his heart. "Sarah, we weren't able to come to dinner last night because we were taken up to see Yeshua in heaven."

Stacy nearly choked on her mouthful of fish while Sarah fell back in her chair, her eyes wide as onions.

"Neat!" Benny responded as he ate a spoonful of rice.

"You were—what!?" gulped Sarah after catching her breath.

"We were ready to come. I had just finished saying a short prayer in our living room, and suddenly—bang! We weren't in our living room! In a flash, all three of us found ourselves standing on a mildly sloping hill, facing upwards. Thousands of men surrounded us. Everyone was clothed in pure white robes, and we all began to sing."

"What were you singing, Uncle Eli?" Benny gurgled through a full mouth.

"A special song of worship to our Lord, Benny. He was standing gloriously on the top of the hill, looking down at us. He was indescribably radiant and beautiful!"

Sarah felt a chill travel up her spine. Stacy's arms and legs were covered by significant goose bumps.

"Why were you taken up to heaven?" asked Tali matter-of-factly.

Eli gazed at Tali with eyes of fatherly love. "We are part of a large group of Jewish men, sweetheart, who've been chosen for a special task in these end days."

"The 144,000 single men from the twelve tribes of Israel!" proclaimed Stacy. "You are part of them? How absolutely awesome!"

"Awesome isn't even the word!" retorted Sarah.

"You really saw the Lord?" Tali inquired, twisting her long ponytail around her index finger as her excitement grew.

"We really did, sugar."

"Yeshua was as brilliant as the sun," added Moshe. "His eyes were like diamonds, and His voice like a powerful, yet gentle, sea."

Tears welled up in Sarah's eyes. Eli reached over and softly touched her shoulder. "We saw Him as He is, dear ones, just as Yonni also sees Him every day."

15

Who Can Resist Him?

The illustrious emperor had been having a bad morning. First, President Williams was not willing to let him take complete control of NATO. "I am the supreme authority in Europe!" he had shouted at his newly-appointed minister of foreign affairs, Burton Chiles, who delivered the unwelcome news. "The Americans are no longer needed on this continent. If they don't hand over control of NATO, I will take it by force!"

"You are certainly entitled to do so, your highness. Yet I would urge you to keep in mind that the United States is still a major world power," Chiles sheepishly admonished. "Despite their growing problems, their armed forces remain the most powerful in the world."

"Not for long!" barked Andre. "I will soon integrate all of Europe's armies, navies, and air forces into one body. Then we will see who controls NATO!"

Two hours later, the British-born Chiles informed the emperor that China was resisting his demand to link the Chinese currency—the yuan—to the newly renamed European currency, the Royal Euro. "What do you mean, they won't follow my orders? I won't have it!"

With a voracious appetite for power, the ruler made his carefully calculated decision. "Inform the media I will be delivering an important speech tomorrow afternoon," he ordered Chiles. "Set it up so it will be morning in the Americas and before midnight in the Far East. That way almost everyone on Earth should be awake to hear me speak."

"Forgive me, your worship," said Chiles as he bowed low before the much younger Andre. "What if Russia and China refuse to carry it?"

"If any nation refuses, tell them that European Union trade and aid will be cut off for good!"

"I will get on it right away, your majesty," responded Chiles, bowing low once again.

A surprised Ken Preston reported to the royal palace outside Paris early the next morning. Two days earlier he had received an angry call from network headquarters in Atlanta. His boss, WNN vice president Jim Dexton, had informed him that after one last assignment in Europe he would be moved to the network's Jerusalem bureau. His wife's statements about the emperor at a recent WNN staff dinner in London was given as the reason. Dexton had told Preston he would be out of a job if his wife did not keep her mouth shut.

An hour before that call, the fifty-four-year-old television cameraman had warned his spouse for the fifth time that her opinions should be kept to herself. "I don't care who you think he is, Betty. You must not talk about it in public."

But Betty Preston felt she had a duty to warn people who the emperor really was. "I can't keep quiet!" she had told her husband. "The force he speaks about is really Satan. We cannot bow down before this man! He is really a beast!"

"I don't care if he is a grasshopper in drag. Knock it off!"

The American cameraman spent several minutes studying the splendidly appointed room. Light from crystal wall chandeliers reflected softly off pearl-colored oak panels set in gold trim.

That gold-plated throne is a bit excessive, he thought. *I wonder what his five other palaces look like inside.* Preston growled to himself as resentment against his wife grew. "Sent to Jerusalem when the *real* action is here!"

Three cameramen were ready when Andre made his entrance.

"What a beautiful aqua-blue silk suit!" exclaimed Roberta Byson into their headsets. "He looks like a bull fighter! And what exquisite rings!"

Andre sat down on his throne and carefully adjusted his tight-fitting jacket, which followed the contours of his athletic build. His multi-tiered jeweled crown was fitted on his head as a last-minute touch of makeup was applied to his cheeks and forehead.

"What a knockout!" sighed Byson as she pressed buttons in the control room. "Okay, here we go. Ken, tighten up on his face. Three, two, one, take it."

"Citizens of the world, greetings. I am so pleased to be able to address you once again. I have been receiving excellent reports from the venerable Urbane Basillo about your growing devotion to me. He informs me that millions of you are burning incense and candles in front of pictures of me, as he instructed you to do."

"Camera two, get a tighter shot of Basillo."

Basillo, a broad smile crossing his face, stood to the left of Andre's throne. He was the picture of humility. The powerful man drew in the attention like a deep breath. It seemed to energize him.

"Urbane also tells me that people everywhere are already worshipping the creative Universal Force by bowing down before my magnificent statues. Others are worshipping my image on television. My master, and yours, is well pleased by such devotion!"

The emperor paused for a moment to frame his warning in the right words. "Friends, the creative Universal Force is slow to anger and full of compassion. But he wants everyone to understand that the time has come to worship him, and to honor and obey his anointed savior, Andre. Anyone who refuses to do so will receive the just penalty for his or her grave error."

Andre waited as Basillo stepped forward. With calm deliberation, the Italian raised his large hands and closed his eyes. "Hear this message from the Supreme Force: Leaders of the nations of my planet, you are to submit yourselves to me. The time for world unity and harmony has come. The age of peace has finally arrived.

"I will instruct my anointed vessel to use force to end all resistance to my rule. He will bring fire on any nation refusing to submit to me. People everywhere, give yourselves gladly to the beneficent reign of my beloved son, Andre!"

Basillo's words carried the power of an atomic bomb. He stepped back in the posture of a servant again, and the emperor spoke. "Friends, as you have just heard, the Universal Force has instructed me to govern beyond the borders of Europe. He has also revealed to me that I am to do so through the United Nations. It will be known from now on as the United World. United World headquarters will soon be moved back to the Old World where it belongs. The UN Secretary General, my good friend Batir Simdali, will host a special meeting soon in Geneva. All leaders *will* be there!"

Frantically Ken widened his shot as the emperor unexpectedly leapt to his feet, almost losing his crown in the process.

"My loyal subjects! Rejoice that your god is now with you! Join in celebrating the new age of peace that is dawning throughout the earth!"

"Why don't I feel like popping a champagne cork?" President Williams asked rhetorically as he motioned for the TV volume to be turned down. "We may be in deep trouble domestically, but we still have many more nuclear weapons than Europe."

"That is true, sir," affirmed Secretary of State Clayton. "But we clearly cannot stand in the emperor's way if he wants to move United Nations headquarters to Switzerland. He can easily muster the necessary UN votes, sir."

"But we are a sovereign nation. We're not used to bowing down to others, and we certainly won't to our European cousins. I simply cannot ignore the fact that millions of my citizens are not prepared to grovel before statues of this Andre, who most had not even heard of a few years ago."

Williams glanced at his notepad. "Maybe that preacher I watched on the Christian network last night is right. Maybe the emperor is some sort of false messiah."

Secretary of State Clayton sat down in the oversized chair. He wore a patronizing smile. "We must be realistic and acknowledge that the emperor now leads the world's greatest economic power, if not military power. He has forged peace in the Middle East. And the people adore him, including a majority in our own country. We must not let the religious right affect our agenda."

"Our agenda? And just exactly what *is* our agenda, Hugh?" Williams had grown impatient with Clayton's monologue.

"Our policies and world strategy, Mr. President. In your speech last month before the World Relations Council, you said that the United States must further integrate with Europe if we're to retain our superpower status. And you have wisely tied our faltering dollar in with the new Royal Euro."

"Which hasn't helped it very much," retorted Williams.

"True. Yet Andre remains the undisputed leader of the world's new economic giant, the European Union. He obviously has great supernatural powers. Basillo has united many religious groups in our country behind him. Cliff, the logical conclusion is to accede to Andre's demand for control of NATO and for the UN move from New York."

Williams loosened his silk tie. "I'm feeling hot, Hugh," he sighed. "Do you think that fire from heaven threat could be Europe's nuclear weapons?"

"We must assume so, sir."

"Well, find out details of this United World meeting in Geneva. I guess I have no choice but to attend."

Betty Preston thought the move to Jerusalem was the most wonderful development in a long time. Finally she would get to spend quality time visiting Israel's holy sites, and she would get to hear firsthand what the two prophets were proclaiming at the Western Wall.

To Ken Preston's chagrin, he quickly discovered that his main assignment was to cover these two wizened, weird Jews. Ken suspected that men in high places had ordered blanket coverage. It seemed that someone wanted to monitor their statements closely. The thought that the emperor himself might even be viewing his footage on a regular basis helped the disheartened cameraman carry on day after day with his boring assignment.

Although he had been filming the two men for almost a month, nothing dramatic had occurred. He had only filed one report for WNN, although all of his raw footage was being sent daily to London. Hundreds every week were professing faith in his wife's Baptist God, which did not impress him at all. The fact that many were being healed did not faze him either. To Preston, it was nothing more than phony emotion and faked miracles.

However, one warm, sunny afternoon the WNN cameraman sensed that he was finally going to see some real action. He smiled as two hundred black-clad Orthodox Jews headed determinedly toward the two witnesses. Preston quickly pointed his camera at the group and started recording.

"We come in the names of our revered rabbis!" shouted the leader of the group, who had moved within earshot of Yochanan and Natan-el. "We have a message for you. We agree with you that the new emperor of united Europe and his so-called spiritual advisor have not been sent by the God of Israel. And we appreciate your warnings to our people not to be taken in by their false claims. However, we cannot stand idly by while you steal sheep from our Jewish fold. Your Yeshua was long ago declared a liar and a false messiah by our sages. Stop preaching in this name, or we will be forced to take action! We are not afraid, because the true God of Israel is with us!"

Yochanan gently approached the spokesman. "My brothers, you are so loved by our Father in heaven. He sees your willing and obedient hearts toward His holy commands, and your love for this, His special city. But you have stumbled over the stumbling stone. How Yeshua longs to take you under His wings and comfort you, like a hen gathers her chicks."

An angry voice shot back from the group. "Deceivers! Get away from our holy Temple Mount wall!" The young zealot then turned and ran to join his friends on a nearby rooftop overlooking the expansive plaza.

The Orthodox spokesman looked with pleading eyes at the elderly Jew. "We wish you no harm. We are men of peace. But I must warn you: Some in our camp are not willing to tolerate your spiritual assaults on our people. We will not be able to prevent them from doing what they are convinced is necessary. For your own sakes please stop preaching in this name."

With that, the Orthodox group left the plaza. Aware that the disciples were shaken by the encounter, the two apostles decided to head home early as well. Before departing, they gathered their followers together for prayer.

Ken was disappointed that the encounter had ended peacefully. He had hoped to at least capture a good fist-fight on film. As he began to pack up his camera gear, the young zealot and his friends prepared to launch a shoulder-fired missile from the nearby rooftop.

16

Nearer to God

After the Orthodox Jews left the plaza, Betty Preston stationed herself between Sarah and Cindy. She was hoping to share some prayer time with them before her husband was ready to leave for home.

Over the past month, the soft-spoken southerner had become friends with the two Israeli women. She had met them at the Wall as they ministered to the growing crowds. Now she worked with them nearly every day.

Betty fit in well with her Israeli sisters. Although Gentile, she had been raised with a deep appreciation for the Jewish people. She vividly recalled the day-long celebration at her family's rural church when the state of Israel was proclaimed in May 1948. She wore a scarf over her hair in respect for the sanctity of the Jewish holy place and felt very much at home in Jerusalem.

The American pilgrim had been thrilled when Cindy informed her that a vibrant Messianic community had been growing in Jerusalem and all over Israel for several decades. She was moved when Cindy recounted how Yoseph had given up a well-paying job with a computer company in 1987 to start Beit Yisrael. The Israeli had felt that young Jewish believers were not being adequately discipled in the city's older congregations, she related. Betty was also pleasantly surprised when Sarah explained that many of the believers were from America and thus native English speakers.

The disciples formed a wide circle around the two apostles as Yochanan began reciting Psalm 20 from memory. "May the Lord answer you in the day of trouble! May the name of the God of Jacob set you securely on high! May He send you help from the sanctuary, and support you from Zion! May He remember all your meal offerings, and find your burnt offerings acceptable! May He grant you your heart's desire, and fulfill all your counsel! We will sing for joy over your victory, and in the name of our God we will set up our banners."

Betty Preston peeked through her eyelids to check on her husband, still busily packing up his video equipment. Sarah squeezed her friend's hand as Yochanan continued. "Now I know that the Lord saves His anointed; He will answer him from His holy heaven, with the saving strength of His right hand. Some boast in chariots, and some in horses; but we will boast in the name of the Lord, our God. They have bowed down and fallen; but we have risen and stood upright. Save, O Lord; May the King answer us in the day we call."

Suddenly Yochanan opened his eyes and shouted, "Quick! Move away! Now!"

Accustomed to bomb threats, Cindy and Sarah both turned and ran. The other Israelis instinctively hit the ground. But Betty was gripped by a paralyzing fear and froze like Lot's wife.

The shoulder-fired missile exploded seconds later on the stone pavement just four feet from the two witnesses. Hot shrapnel whizzed in every direction, but not a shred of metal touched the apostles. Some sort of invisible wall seemed to shield them.

Ken jerked his head around just in time to see shards of shrapnel bounce and fall harmlessly to the plaza floor. He saw large projectiles hit Moshe, Eli, Zev, and Danny. He was sure they were all dead.

"Oh, my God! Betty!" he screamed when he spotted his wife's body lying just behind Danny. As Ken rushed to her side he failed to notice the column of fire from Yochanan's mouth that landed squarely on a nearby rooftop.

The cameraman reached his wife just seconds before Cindy and Sarah. A thick pool of blood encompassed her head and chest and confirmed what he already feared—she was gone. He clutched her and began weeping. Sarah knelt down beside him.

After a few moments, a strong hand rested on Ken's left shoulder. He looked up to see Eli. "I'm so sorry, Ken," Eli began.

"You—you are still alive!" he exclaimed, both astonished and confused. "But I saw a piece of metal tear into your neck. How can that be?"

"No one on earth can harm us," Eli responded as he gently rubbed Ken's shoulder. "We have been sealed by God."

Ken frowned in bewilderment, trying to grasp Eli's incomprehensible words.

Eli attempted to comfort him. "Ken, I hardly know you, but I was getting to know your wife. We all really loved her. I want you to know that we are here for you in the coming days."

"That's right, Ken," affirmed Sarah as she pressed a handkerchief in his hand. "We are ready to help in any way we can."

The bereaved widower decided to bury his wife among the tall pine trees in the German Colony Cemetery, named after German Christians who had settled in the adjacent area south of the Old City in the late 1800s. Along with his daughter, one of their two sons, and Betty's seventy-six-year-old mother, approximately one hundred twenty people gathered on a cloudy afternoon in the dusty, walled cemetery.

Nearly a quarter of the mourners were media colleagues, who had come to pay their respects. Betty's death had received extensive press coverage around the world, and World News Network had decided to send vice president Jim Dexton to represent it. Ken was not overjoyed to see the man who had posted him to Jerusalem and avoided speaking with Dexton. The executive was just as eager to stay out of Ken's way.

Over seventy local Jewish and Arab believers showed up as well. To Ken's relief, the two apostles did not attend. In fact, he had asked several muscular friends to stand at the cemetery gate to prevent the rabble-rousers from entering if they showed up.

Appreciating Sarah's compassionate help in his time of need, and not knowing any other local ministers, Ken agreed to her suggestion that Yoseph Steinberg officiate at the interment.

Traffic bustled by on Emek Refaim, the busy street just beyond the cemetery gate, as Betty's metal casket was slowly lowered into the Jerusalem earth.

"I am the resurrection and the life," intoned Yoseph, quoting Yeshua's words from the Gospel of Yochanan. "He who believes in Me shall live, even if he dies."

Sarah squeezed Cindy's arm as he finished speaking. "I hope that Ken will soon be able to trust in the Lord's promises," she whispered as the husband threw a bouquet of flowers onto the casket. "I know that's what Betty's heart longed for."

Ken Preston returned to his job ten days later. But now he began to pay closer attention to the words of the two witnesses, and he found himself full of questions. *How can I continue to deny the fantastic things that are occurring here every day? Blind people are receiving sight; the crippled are getting up and walking. And what about that protection the men got from the missile blast? Could Betty have been right after all?*

Yet one thought kept preventing Ken from surrendering his life to Yeshua. Inside, he could not get away from the question of how a loving God could allow his wife to be killed in such an awful way.

"I've asked the Lord that question more than once about Jonathan," admitted Sarah one afternoon at the plaza. "And I always sense the same reply. God never promised us we wouldn't experience evil or suffering. Yeshua warned His followers to expect persecution during this age, but He promised that He would return and wipe away every tear from our eyes."

"Jesus may have accurately predicted that His followers would suffer, Sarah, but I want to know why He allows it."

"The Bible says that the entire earth is under a curse, resulting from sin committed long ago. The effects of that curse touch both the good and the bad, Ken, the redeemed and the unrepentant sinner. God promises to shield His faithful followers from some of those effects, but not all. Sometimes I think He wants us to experience the sorrow and suffering resulting from sin so we will remember throughout eternity what it was like."

"But Betty was really a good woman. She never harmed a flea."

"Neither did Jonathan. And right now they're reaping the rewards of their goodness, or more accurately, of their wise decision to trust in the Lord. Our spouses are savoring the eternal, beautiful presence of God. It is you and I who are suffering, Ken. We've been left in this world. But I know I'll join Jonathan one of these days. And I pray you'll give your life to Yeshua, so you can have that assurance as well."

The widower picked up his video camera. "Guess I'd better get back to work," he said as Sarah's words tumbled through his brain. "At least it gives me something to do besides miss her."

Moshe, Eli, Danny, and Zev spent most of their waking hours assisting the two witnesses in their extraordinary ministry. They had already quit their jobs after being caught up to the heavenly Mount Zion. The Jewish brothers were sustained by donations of food and money brought to them by the growing throng of Jerusalem believers.

Moshe was gifted in leading Palestinian Arabs to the Lord. His parents had immigrated to Israel from Morocco in 1951. Raised in an Arabic-speaking home, he held a special burden for his Arab cousins. The Sephardic Israeli frequently stood or sat on the ramp next to the Western Wall that leads up to the Islamic shrines on the Temple Mount. He encouraged the Muslims to come down with him and listen to Yochanan and Natan-el. As a result, dozens submitted their lives to the Lord. Some were even healed of their diseases and disabilities.

Eli discovered a delightful surprise one morning as he shared his faith with a visiting tourist. "Guess what, Moshe. I just shared the gospel with an Italian woman—

in perfect Italian!" he announced in awe. "I didn't even realize I was speaking her language until she told me she was from Naples! And I've never even been to Italy!"

"I spoke fluent Japanese only yesterday," replied Moshe with just a touch of pride.

"We seem to have received the gift of tongues in the same way the first believers did on Shavuot here in Jerusalem, and we didn't even know it!"

"The Lamb bestowed many gifts on us during our heavenly visit, Eli. He also gave us some heavy responsibilities. I feel a bit overwhelmed."

"So do I," admitted Eli, shading his eyes from the intense, midday sun.

The two buddies and their roommate, Danny, moved out of their north Jerusalem apartment into a three-story house on the Mount of Olives, donated to the believers by a wealthy Arab family who were relatives of Abdul Wahab, the Palestinian chosen to work closely with the apostles. Yochanan and Natan-el also moved into the large house, located on the western slope of the Mount facing the Old City. They were soon joined by the other single brothers — Zev, Eitan, and Shimon — along with Abdul.

The brethren usually gathered in the evenings to worship the Lord and hear a spiritual word from the two elders. Eli felt a growing love for Yochanan as he listened to his penetrating teachings. As the prophet spoke, Eli often found himself studying the cavernous creases in the man's well-worn face, with the evening light dancing softly around his cheeks. Eli deeply respected the powerful, yet humble, man of God.

One warm night in mid-July, Yochanan lingered in the living room after the others had gone to bed. Eli was puttering in the kitchen, pretending to do some chores but hoping to speak with the apostle alone.

"You wouldn't have a glass of water for an old man?" Yochanan inquired as he peeked his head around the half-closed kitchen door.

"Certainly, Yochanan," answered Eli, turning on the cold tap. "A glass of fresh Jerusalem water coming right up!"

"Why don't you get one for yourself as well, Eli, and follow me into the living room. I've been wanting to talk with you for some time."

Eli's heart nearly exploded. He had been wanting to talk privately for some time! The Israeli felt like a teenager invited out on his first date.

The humidity in Jerusalem that day had been high so Eli opened up another living room window to let in more of the night breeze. Then he plunked down into an old overstuffed chair.

"Son, you remind me so much of when I was your age," Yochanan said as he took a sip of cool water.

"I do?" replied Eli, feeling a little embarrassed yet complimented.

"Yes. You have a deep yearning for God inside of you, and this is, sadly, quite rare in human beings, even among the Lord's people. King David had a tender heart for God, too. I had it as well when I was your age. In fact, I still do."

"I know," replied Eli, clinging to every precious word.

"When Yeshua lived among us, He had a deep love for each of His disciples. But, for some reason He held a special love for me. He told me so one evening as the two of us sat alone around a campfire on the shores of the Sea of Galilee. I nearly melted when the Master looked into my eyes and told me. Can you imagine, Eli, the Lord of all creation saying something like that to you?"

The young Israeli brushed the perspiration from his brow. "It must have been exhilarating."

"It was. In fact," added Yochanan with a chuckle, "I still remember it quite vividly, even though it was a few years ago!"

"Yochanan, do you know why the Lord loved you so much?"

"He never exactly said, Eli. But Yeshua did tell me more than once that He perceived that my love for God was especially tender. He sees that in you as well, my young friend, and I see it too."

The aged apostle stood up and stretched out his arms. Eli eagerly rose from his seat to receive the warm embrace. A gently breeze blew back the cotton curtains.

"Thank you for sharing that with me," said Eli as he wiped away a tear. "We're so privileged to have you and Natan-el with us in these difficult times. I've heard that the body of Messiah around the world is beginning to understand who you are. To think that the Father would send Yeshua's closest associates to us in these critical last days. And especially you, who actually wrote down the prophecy in Revelation!"

"The Lord's book, Eli, and the Lord's revelation. I was only chosen to receive it and record it for posterity."

The two men looked out the large window toward the ancient stone walls of the Old City. They could hear the sounds of shopkeepers closing their metal shutters for the night along the narrow cobblestone streets.

"Speaking of Revelation, I would like to ask you a few questions."

Yochanan chuckled as his eyes took on a faraway look. "We were always bothering the Lord with questions, and he usually answered us. So please, son, go right ahead."

Eli blushed. "I was reading chapter 10, where an angel cries out with a loud voice, and seven peals of thunder speak. You were about to write down what the seven peals had to say but were told by another voice from heaven to seal up the things that were spoken. Yochanan, if the message wasn't to be revealed until later, why mention it at all? Was it that you knew you were coming back at the end of the age? And can you tell me what the seven peals of thunder uttered?"

"I bet you enjoyed mystery novels as a lad," smiled Yochanan, who sat back comfortably in the cushioned chair. "I cannot reveal those secrets now, Eli. They are for the very end of this age when the wrath of God is about to be poured out upon the earth. It's no coincidence that I am known as the Son of Thunder, because I myself will rattle the world with that final message. And yes, you are correct. When I wrote those words I already knew I would return to earth in the last days as one of the two witnesses.

"Do you remember when we talked about the Lord's obscure comments to Peter about my death?"

"Yes, at Sarah's house that first evening."

"Soon after Yeshua spoke to us on the beach, I privately asked Him to explain His puzzling words to me. He gave me an outline of my endtime role, although not all of the details. He said it would be better not to write these things down because people would claim to be me and would lead some astray."

Eli's eyes glistened as his mind pictured Yochanan talking with the Lord.

"Did you notice in Revelation what happened to me right after I was told to seal up those words?"

"I sure did," replied Eli, leaning forward to place his forearms on his trouser-covered thighs. "You were instructed to take a little book out of the angel's hand and to eat it—similar to what happened to the prophet Ezekiel at the beginning of his ministry."

"Exactly. I was told it would make my stomach bitter because it was a message of judgment. But the word in my mouth would be sweet as honey, because it was a message of deliverance for those who would hear and repent."

"The angel said that you must prophesy again concerning many peoples and nations and tongues and kings!" noted Eli, becoming more excited as he spoke. "And next the Scripture describes the two witnesses, who will prophesy to the nations in the last days."

"Another scriptural hint about my endtime, Elijah ministry, Eli, although few seem to have noticed it."

"But they're noticing now, Yochanan. In fact, I've even heard rumors that various church leaders from around the world are planning to come here to Jerusalem to hear you and Natan-el firsthand."

"They'd better come soon, Eli."

"What do you mean?"

"Emperor Andre, the Antichrist beast, has already received his crown. What follows the appearance of this false messiah?"

"The red and black horses, war, and famine," Eli answered.

"Correct. And after that, severe persecution of all believers in Yeshua."

"But we've always had false messiahs, wars, and famines. What will be different now?"

"The intensity, Eli. We're about to face wars and threats of wars like we have never seen before."

17

A Great Sword

When Andre's world summit opened on July 24, the leaders of China, North Korea, Iran, and Sudan were not in attendance. Chinese Premier Quay Chin, in office for more than a decade, ordered his foreign minister to turn down the invitation. The minister had faxed a stiff note from Chin to United World Secretary General, Batir Simdali: "We are an ancient and proud people, the largest nation on the face of the earth, with a highly developed culture far older than Europe's. We will not submit ourselves to any other nation or ruler."

Iranian President Ali Hajali agreed with his country's Islamic spiritual leaders that Andre was not the great, end-time prophet many Muslims expected to appear before the final judgment day. Attempts by Basillo to integrate Islam into a worldwide religious system, with Andre at its center, did not sit well with these fundamentalist leaders.

Russian President Vladimir Konstantine sat grimly in the new UW general assembly hall, mulling over an earlier telephone proposal from the Chinese premier. *Quay Chin is right. If Asia's two superpowers unite to resist Andre, we'll pose an unbeatable alliance. I know Williams won't voluntarily commit American troops to him. I'll see what happens today and then decide what to do.*

Clifford Williams entered the Geneva hall just before the first speech was set to begin. Cameras clicked as the distinguished American leader walked past reporters sitting at the back of the auditorium. Though smiling at his audience, he was angry. Andre's summit, he thought, marked the official end of America's reign as the world's leading superpower. The fact that the meeting was taking place at the new United World headquarters in Geneva, instead of New York, said it all. The United States was no longer the leader of the Western world.

The international dignitaries were welcomed by Batir Simdali. He told them a new day had dawned, a day of universal peace and justice. The United World would assist the new supreme leader in carrying out his task to unite all governments under his rule. Simdali acknowledged the pledges of support already received from most governments and from various peace movements, religious and business leaders, and many nongovernmental agencies around the globe.

The packed hall erupted in sustained applause as the emperor strutted down the center aisle toward the podium. He acknowledged the welcome with a wave. Then he ascended the stage and raised his right hand, signaling that he was ready to speak. The auditorium quickly fell into silence.

"Distinguished colleagues, honorable guests, and citizens of the world, greetings!"

The young ruler paused, and television cameras scanned the hall. Burton Chiles began to clap demonstrably, and the assembled leaders heeded the cue.

"Thank you. I bring you wonderful news this afternoon. The Universal Force has given me a new title to mark my ascension to world dominion: It is Son of the Dawn." Like a wound-up robot Chiles began clapping again, followed by the entire hall.

"What a load of garbage," muttered Russian leader Konstantine under his breath.

President Williams shook his head in dismay as his hands met to clap. He would have preferred to sit on them but he didn't dare.

"This is getting very old, very quickly," Yacov Nimrod whispered to his foreign minister.

"We have no choice but to play along, Yacov. At least he's brought peace."

"I'm starting to wonder," the rapidly aging leader replied. "I fear we are in for big trouble."

"Camera one, tighten up on Andre's face," ordered Roberta Byson as the clapping subsided.

The emperor's words hovered above the crowd like bald eagles searching for their prey. He continued. "My beloved subjects, with the help of the great Universal Force, I will govern our world and break down all barriers which have divided humanity for so many centuries. In time, I will restore the earth to the paradise of Eden."

Andre paused for effect. "However, I can only accomplish these divine goals with the cooperation of every one of you gathered today in this hall.

"If I do not succeed, then our planet will be plunged into the darkest age imaginable. War, poverty, and disease will wipe out billions of people. Pollution will continue to destroy our atmosphere.

"We stand this day at the crossroads. The exalted Universal Force is giving us one last chance. And so, I am now going to ask each of you in this distinguished assembly to pledge your full allegiance to me as the undisputed ruler of the world. In the coming days, meetings will be held here in Geneva to work out the details of world integration under my command. But right now, we must show our peoples that we are united for peace. Let us vote together to affirm my divinely appointed mission."

Williams frantically looked around. "I suggest a yes vote, Mr. President," Secretary of State Clayton advised. "Anything else will be political suicide."

"Andre is clever indeed! He has put us on the spot!" moaned an indignant Konstantine to an aide sitting to his left.

Yacov Nimrod pulled out his pocket handkerchief to wipe his brow. "I cannot surrender the sovereignty of our Jewish state to a Gentile," he said to Sephres while pulling on the arms of his shoulder-padded black wool suit.

"And how can we resist him and get away with it?" asked the foreign minister. "You have to vote yes."

"Have you found your voting buttons?" The emperor waited a few more moments. "Good. Now, give me your unanimous affirmative response!"

Each of the assembled leaders leaned forward. A large electronic tally board behind the podium began to flicker. Soon it glowed with the incandescence of the affirmative responses. Before long, all the lights except two had been illuminated.

The veins in the emperor's thick neck began to bulge. "I do not see a unanimous decision!" he screamed while pounding the podium. Burton Chiles bolted up on stage to calm his seething boss.

"Russia and the United States, I want an immediate explanation for these abstentions!" shouted Andre.

Williams shuddered as he dropped his pen and bent down to retrieve it. He glanced at his secretary of state and was surprised at how calm he looked. President Konstantine sat back defiantly in his chair, crossing his arms over his broad, medal-decorated chest. "The Chinese Republic has already made a grave error by not attending. I warn you to rethink your positions! You have exactly twenty-four hours!"

"So this is the great man of peace," quipped Craig Eagleman as television cameras followed the angry emperor stomping out of the hall like a spoiled child.

"Does his ranting and raving remind you of anyone?" Sarah asked the group gathered in her living room.

"Hitler," Stacy replied without hesitation. "When he gets angry, he moves just like Hitler did in those old newsreels."

"My thoughts exactly," said Sarah.

"And the evidence is mounting up that he'll end up acting just like Hitler," opined Yoseph. "It feels like we're back in the late '1930s when the world was heading toward a powerful and hellish explosion."

Sarah sighed. "And there seems to be nothing anyone can do to stop it."

Clifford Williams sipped some soda as his limousine drove down a sealed-off avenue toward the Geneva hotel where he and several other world leaders were staying. Canadian Prime Minister Renair, who had voted yes, rode in a limo just in front of him. The street was cleared except for a red sports car on the curb in front of a jewelry store.

The American leader was pondering his dilemma when the car phone rang.

"Cliff, this is Hugh. Burton Chiles has just informed me that Andre is demanding to see you early tomorrow. Shall I set up an appointment?"

"Do we have a choice?"

"I'll arrange it then."

What am I going to do? Williams, deep in thought, gazed out the window of his special armor-plated car.

Carefully and methodically, the small sports car pulled out behind the limo. A bearded head popped up in the back seat. "The big fish is being reeled in," he said into his cell phone.

The Canadian prime minister waited briefly for Williams to get out of his car so he could have a few private words with his American counterpart.

"Hello, John," Williams said, stepping on to the curb.

"Hello, Cliff," the Canadian replied, offering his right hand. "I'd like to speak with you for a moment. It's been a tough day for us all, hasn't it?"

Williams shook Renair's hand. "And it's going to be a tough night, I'm afraid."

The rifle bullet tore into the American president's neck, partially severing his spinal cord. As he fell into Renair's arms, blood covered the front of the horrified prime minister's gray suit jacket. The American president was dead.

18

The Dragon

Vladimir Konstantine flew out of Geneva soon after hearing that the American president had been assassinated. "They're not going to get me," he assured his frightened wife after ordering her to pack.

The emperor was livid over the Russian leader's midnight departure. It had not occurred to him that Konstantine would display such flagrant resistance to his royal will. Purposefully, he opened his desk drawer to store the delayed-reaction poison for another time.

After appearing briefly before reporters to say that a suspect had been captured by Swiss police and to offer condolences to the bereaved American people, Andre ordered UW Secretary General Simdali to begin assembling a large army, navy, and air force. It would be comprised of divisions and equipment from standing European armed forces and from friendly countries around the world. This United World "peacekeeping" force would be stationed initially in eastern Germany and Poland.

The new president, Vincent Rogel, was persuaded by Senate Majority Leader Frank Weston and Hugh Clayton to pledge firm United States allegiance to the European leader. Except for the fundamentalist Christians and some right-wing patriots, the move was strongly supported by the American people, especially by business leaders eager to receive Andre's European Union financial aide. This allegiance included turning over control of NATO to Andre as well.

However, the new president was not willing to integrate American forces stationed in Europe into the new UW force. "If we allow Andre to take charge of our troops, we could get pulled into a war not of our choosing," Rogel argued.

Clayton glanced knowingly at Weston as the new president scribbled a note. "If we withhold our troops, sir, Andre will be furious with us once more."

"Hugh, it seems clear that Andre intends to use his new force to threaten Russia and China. Both have already indicated to me that they'll not hesitate to hit us with nuclear warheads if we side with Andre."

Realizing that President Rogel would not change his mind, Clayton and Weston reluctantly acceded to his stand. However, they suggested that he compromise by publicly promising to use nuclear weapons in support of Andre if either Russia or China were to fire any atomic warheads at Europe. Rogel agreed that this was his best option under the circumstances.

Skilled craftsmen from around the world gathered in Jerusalem in early August. Construction of the temple was about to begin. It was to be a magnificent structure, overlaid with the finest Italian marble. Solid gold plating would frame the four corners of the rectangular building. Gold would also be used inside and out, along with other precious metals and jewels. The temple would rise over one hundred fifty feet, making it visible all over Jerusalem.

Under instructions from the emperor, newly appointed European Union Ambassador Julian Gambino scheduled the official cornerstone laying ceremony for August 13, the solemn fast day of Tisha b'Av. Long considered the blackest day of the Jewish calendar, the fast commemorates various disasters that had befallen the Jewish people, especially the destruction of the first and second temples.

As every year on Tisha b'Av, thousands of Orthodox Jews gathered at the Western Wall to pray. Gambino had requested that the area be closed off while the ceremony was taking place on the Mount above the Wall. But Israeli officials refused to go along, fearing a riot if they tried to keep religious Jews away from the sacred Wall on such an important fast day.

The emperor had arrived in Jerusalem on August 12. He was officially welcomed in an elaborate ceremony hosted by Prime Minister Nimrod, followed by a state banquet at the prestigious King David Hotel. Many world leaders were in attendance.

After spending the night there, Andre and his entourage were driven to nearby Jaffa Gate and then along the only auto-accessible road in the walled Old City. Soon he and his international guests, including Urbane Basillo, arrived at the entrance to the Western Wall plaza.

Over five hundred United World soldiers forged a human chain to keep Orthodox mourners away from the sealed area around the ramp leading up to the Temple Mount.

In the northwest corner of the plaza, Israeli policemen had secured a small area where Yochanan and Natan-el were preaching. Nimrod had reluctantly instructed Police

Chief Dronen to permit them into the plaza. He did not want a fire display today of all days.

When Yochanan and Natan-el saw the emperor step out of his black limousine, they began to tear their sackcloth clothes. They wailed, throwing handfuls of dust into the air. Hundreds of fasting Jewish men followed suit with a chant, reciting portions of Jeremiah's Lamentations against the Gentile emperor. Within seconds, nearly all of them had turned toward the hated ruler. Many angrily waved their fists in the air.

Andre had assumed that his two enemies would be banned from the plaza on his special day, along with all Orthodox Jews. He quickly decided that enough was enough. Like his Roman predecessors, he would have to teach these obnoxious Jews a lesson. Immediately, he ordered his illustrious seer to call down fire into the middle of the chanting throng.

The false prophet raised his arms and cried out. A tidal wave of red-hot flames descended from the sky, instantly engulfing several hundred of the chanting Jews. A stampede of frightened onlookers jammed the plaza's four exits. Within minutes, the area around the Wall was empty.

Yacov Nimrod and Foreign Minister Sephres had just arrived as the fiery torrent crashed onto the stone plaza floor. The livid premier ignored protocol and marched right up to Andre. "What in God's name are you doing? These are citizens of my country!"

If there was anything Andre hated it was uppity Jews, even if they were important government officials. "Nimrod, you will have to control your people better than this if you expect me to act with restraint," he replied without emotion. "Don't forget that I am the Anointed One. I will tolerate no such displays of disloyalty."

The premier begrudgingly stepped back from the emperor and bit his tongue. Andre then marched up the ramp to the Temple Mount. Swiss guards lining the ramp sounded silver trumpets as he passed by. Secretary General Simdali and other world leaders followed, including Frank Weston, who had just been appointed vice president by Vincent Rogel.

Sephres grabbed Nimrod's arm. "We must not make the emperor any angrier than he already is."

"But he murdered some of our people in cold blood on one of our holiest days!"

"Good grief, Yacov, these ultra-orthodox zealots had it coming to them. What makes them think they can provoke the ruler of this world and get away with it?"

The two men trudged up to the ancient Mount. The official procession passed through the gilded gate of the new stone wall, erected to divide the Muslim area from the northern third where Andre's temple was destined to stand.

Ken Preston had been assigned to cover the temple dedication ceremony. He focused his lens on Andre's mauve shirt and crimson velvet robe. He noticed again the emperor's muscular build, which was highlighted by the close-fitting shirt. Ken followed along as the emperor ascended his throne and donned his three-tiered jeweled crown.

Dressed in a satin suit, Urbane Basillo sat to Andre's right. Next to him were Batir Simdali and Frank Weston. Yacov Nimrod, still shaking, came next, followed by various rulers from all over the globe. Vladimir Konstantine and Quay Chin were not among them.

To the left of the throne sat religious leaders from all of the world's major faiths. Rabbi Amos Shimshon was positioned between a Japanese Shinto priest and the Muslim caliph of Mecca. The religious affairs minister was attending the ceremony with great reservations because he agreed with most Orthodox Jews that Andre's temple was an abomination to the God of Israel. He soon learned that the Saudi caliph viewed it as an affront to Allah.

"Camera two, tighten up on the podium," producer Mark Cranson instructed Preston. "Basillo should begin speaking from it at any moment."

Flashing a sparkling diamond on his right hand, the plump Italian slowly made his way to the gold-plated podium. The royal seal, prominently mounted on the front, pictured a red dragon with a gold crown on its head. Preston zoomed in for a close-up shot.

"Your exalted majesty, honored guests, citizens of planet Earth. We have gathered here in Jerusalem this day to initiate construction of the veritable house of God! It is a holy day, a day of great rejoicing! Let us begin by giving praise to the great Universal Force!"

Basillo lowered his tripled chin and humbly folded his hands on top of the podium. His black hair clung to his round head like wet seaweed on a piece of driftwood. The pious look on his face masked the evil lurking in his soul.

"O ruler of this world, prince of light! We come in your name to begin the most sacred task of raising up a temple to your glory. This temple will be a sign to all humanity of the new age of universal harmony. It will also be the place where your anointed servant will reveal his glory to the world! We praise you for this auspicious day."

"Camera two, get ready to follow Andre to the podium."

"I'm all set," replied Ken into his headset microphone.

Two blond boys dressed like altar boys elevated the train of his royal robe as the emperor descended from his throne to the golden podium. Hushed anticipation hung like a canopy over the assembled dignitaries.

"Distinguished and loyal rulers, my subjects around the globe, we are gathered today on holy ground to inaugurate a new temple—a temple that will not be anchored in the narrow concepts of the past or dedicated to some ancient tribal god, but a temple that will be universal, a house of prayer for all nations."

Rabbi Shimshon coughed nervously while his boss pulled at his tie.

"Camera three, get a shot of Nimrod," directed Cranson. "He really looks uncomfortable."

"For the first time in many centuries, this ancient city of Jerusalem is filled with love and peace. It is a peace that tears away the false divisions erected between the three old monotheistic faiths. Any doctrine that divides people from one another, or claims exclusive truth, must be destroyed."

Standing to the left of the assembled guests, Burton Chiles directed a round of applause.

"Every citizen of the world who acknowledges me as the supreme ruler will be welcome on this holy hill. Men and women, boys and girls from every nation and every race will come here in freedom to worship the Universal Force. Let the cornerstone now descend upon this holy ground!"

An enormous steel crane went into action. Slowly it lowered a three-ton cut stone onto the Temple Mount floor. A cheer arose from the throng.

"Camera two, swing back to Andre," instructed Cranson.

"What a glorious day for all humanity. The new age of universal love, peace, and restoration has begun!"

The emperor turned slightly to face the seated religious leaders. "Our eastern peoples have long venerated a symbol that accurately pictures the Creative Force. It is the noble dragon. This mythical creature holds great power and strength. It breathes fire from its nostrils and devours its enemies. Such is the exalted god of the universe. Yet he is also a friendly creature who bestows good fortune on those who revere him."

"Camera four, get a shot of the Japanese priest smiling at the Buddhist monk."

"This dragon, with its massive scales, symbolizes the atomic glue that holds the elements of the universe together. He is not concerned with petty rules created by misguided zealots. He is only concerned that we love and respect one another and honor him. We are all equal before him. Praise to our god!"

A nervous Chiles began to clap his hands together once again. The dignitaries followed suit. Andre acknowledged the applause and continued. "This temple we build will be the central place of worship to this enduring dragon, the Universal Force of love and peace. When it is finished, a golden dragon will be placed in its inner sanctuary, known in ancient days as the holy of holies. May the Eternal Force bless each and every one of you from this, his holy hill!"

The international leaders rose to their feet and cheered as Andre made his way to the cornerstone. Yudah Sephres clapped with apparent enthusiasm. However, the prime minister and Rabbi Shimshon did so with visible reluctance. Both were thinking about the anticipated Orthodox reaction to the Gentile temple, which they had discussed privately earlier that morning. Both were convinced that difficult days lay ahead.

19

"Operation Eagle"

"We're in big trouble," Yacov Nimrod sighed as he tapped his pencil on the desk.

The Israeli cabinet was meeting to discuss the escalating unrest following the temple dedication ceremony. Thousands of Orthodox Jews and Israeli nationalists had gathered in the Western Wall plaza the day after the event to protest the construction of the sacrilegious building. Several dozen zealots had attacked foreign construction workers as they attempted to walk up the ramp. Israeli police had intervened, arresting over fifty protesters and ordering everyone else out of the area.

The following morning, the police had attempted to prevent all Jews from entering the plaza, provoking widespread disturbances. The rioting spread to Mea Shearim, Jerusalem's Orthodox center located northwest of the Old City, as well as to other religious areas. Thousands of arrests were made. Muslim fundamentalists, unhappy with the building of a non-Islamic shrine on the Mount, also went on the rampage throughout eastern Jerusalem.

"We must stop this madness!" warned an agitated Edna Satori.

"It's not madness!" Rabbi Shimshon protested. "It's an understandable reaction to blasphemy! Such words have only been uttered once before on our holy Temple Mount—by the Greek pagan conqueror, Antiochus Epiphanes, and you know how our Maccabean ancestors dealt with him! I am warning you once again that my party will be forced to leave this coalition government if religious Jews are not immediately allowed to return to our sacred Western Wall!"

Nimrod twisted one of his solid gold cuff links as he gazed at his Orthodox colleague. "Amos, I don't want you to quit. I'm not exactly thrilled with Andre's temple project either, but Edna is right. The emperor has threatened to send in United World forces if we don't stop these disturbances. We have no choice but to continue blocking off the plaza."

But the rioting did not end. It intensified. Dozens were killed. The narrow, crowded streets of Mea Shearim resembled a war zone. Riot police chased angry, stone throwing zealots as fires raged unchecked in many buildings. The only calm spot was just outside the Old City's Dung Gate, where Yochanan and Natan-el continued to preach their message.

When it became apparent that Israeli forces could not quell the violence, the choleric emperor phoned Nimrod to inform him that six transport planes carrying United World forces were on their way to Ben Gurion International Airport near Tel Aviv. The prime minister protested that the action violated his country's sovereignty. But he admitted to his cabinet, with some self-loathing, that his protest was hollow. The Arab/Israeli peace treaty, which he had signed under Andre's tutelage, authorized the presence of such troops.

Only hours after touching down at Ben Gurion, United World troops were patrolling the streets of Jerusalem. They quickly brought the rioting to an end. One week later, several specialized units were given orders to carry out phase two of Andre's Jerusalem plan. They began arresting both Jewish and Arab believers and secretly confined them in a newly established UW camp just north of Jerusalem.

Somehow the Beit Yisrael congregants managed to hold their Wednesday evening weekly meetings. When the arrests of believers began near the Old City, Yoseph almost canceled the service. But after much prayer, he decided that the Lord's people must continue to meet, even with the increased danger.

The following Wednesday, two dozen UW soldiers burst into the congregation.

"We are troops of the United World," proclaimed the commander in English with a heavy Scandinavian accent. "You are to stand up and put your hands in the air. We are taking you in for questioning. Do not be afraid."

"Put your hands in the air, old woman!" shouted one of the soldiers at a Paris-born congregant in her late sixties. The Jewish woman trembled so hard her black shawl fell off. She instantly obeyed the command.

Craig Eagleman had been playing guitar on the platform with Yoseph. The blond worship leader, proficient in the art of karate, scowled.

"Don't resist them," Yoseph whispered.

"I suppose we are outnumbered," Craig responded softly. "And those don't look like toy guns."

"You two up there! Get those arms up!" barked the steely-eyed unit commander.

Yoseph cleared his throat. "Sir, most of us here are Israeli citizens. We have not been informed that we are suddenly under your authority. I must insist that we be allowed to contact our government immediately."

The commander was annoyed. "Our emperor is the supreme authority in Jerusalem, as in all the world. Your puny little government means nothing to him or to us. Now get moving!"

The forty believers were brusquely loaded into three waiting United World vans. Cool autumn air poured through the van windows. Moshe and Sarah sat quietly as the vehicle wove its way around burning tires in the road. The putrid smoke mingled with occasional rifle shots in the distance.

Moshe broke the silence. "Our city is still quite troubled," he whispered to Sarah, handcuffed next to him. "However, the Jerusalem above is free—she is our mother!"

"And my children are free. Thank God for that!" Tali and Benny were at home with Donna.

The bound believers soon arrived at the camp, where they were quickly processed and interrogated. One of the first people questioned was Craig Eagleman.

"I am an American citizen!" he proclaimed.

The balding interrogator pompously flicked ashes off his long cigarette. "Just answer our questions, Eagleman. Your United States is a full member of the United World, in case you did not know. And anyway, Washington is a long way from here."

Seated just outside the interrogation room, Sarah and Stacy waited calmly for their turn. Although full of trepidation when they were escorted into the waiting room, they had decided after prayer that remaining fearful would only make things worse. Sarah quietly hummed a worship tune. Stacy interrupted her.

"Sarah, what do you think Jonathan would do if he were here?"

Sarah thought a moment. "He might be reciting Psalm 23. We said it together on the last night I saw him, just before he left for the Golan Heights."

"The Lord is my shepherd," began Stacy, "I shall not want." The two friends recited the precious psalm together.

Since he was a university student from America and had no record of criminal activities against the emperor, Craig was released the next morning. He headed straight for the American consulate on Agron Street in west Jerusalem. "Lord, give me the right words," he prayed as he neared the complex. Seconds later he flashed his U.S. passport at two armed Marines and was escorted into the reception area.

"United World forces are rounding up American citizens, and for no legitimate reason!" he angrily told the receptionist after demanding to speak to the consul-general.

"I'll see what I can do," she replied.

After waiting for over an hour, Craig spoke with an official, who promised to pass on the information. He then raced up Agron Street to a nearby public telephone.

"Ken, this is Craig Eagleman," he puffed breathlessly.

"Hi, man, how are you? Long time since I last saw you."

Craig wasted no time. "Listen, UW forces broke into Beit Yisrael last evening and arrested everyone. They're being held at a camp north of town. I was let out a few hours ago."

"Really! Can you meet me at the studio in half an hour? I'd like to get this on video."

"I'm on my way. Thanks, Ken, and shalom."

When he entered the WNN office on Jaffa Road, Craig discovered Ken kneeling in prayer by his desk. "Hey, sorry to interrupt. I didn't know that you were a believer."

"I'm not sure that I am, Craig. But I've seen so many incredible things these past few months. I guess I've concluded there must be a God, and I can already tell that Andre is not him."

Craig knelt down beside his older friend. "If you will let me, I'll lead you in a prayer asking Yeshua into your life. He is the only way to the Father, Ken."

"I know you're smiling up there somewhere, Betty," Ken said as he bowed his head to pray.

The White House phone lines began to light up moments after Craig's interview was broadcast on WNN. Most callers were Christians strongly protesting UW detention of American citizens. The only caller who actually got through to the president was his wife, Betsy, who was in Wisconsin dedicating a new veteran's hospital.

"Hello, sweetheart. How's the weather in Madison?"

"Cold for mid-September," came the sharp reply. "Vince, I'm phoning about the WNN report on American Jewish Christians being rounded up in Jerusalem. Andre has gone too far this time."

"I agree, Betsy."

"Well, what are you going to do about it?"

"Hugh Clayton and I have a conference call scheduled with Burton Chiles in ten minutes. I'll let you know later tonight."

Rogel's conversation with his wife was much more pleasant than his talk with Andre's minister of foreign affairs. "These people are citizens of my country. I have every right to demand they be released!"

"Mr. President, let me remind you that they are also citizens of Israel, and their arrests are being carried out by direct orders of our esteemed emperor. These Jews are not nearly so innocent as you suggest. For one thing, they have clearly stated to our interrogators that they will never agree to bow down and pay homage to Andre. Any

American citizen, whether at home or abroad, will face difficult days if he or she refuses to give glory to the emperor."

"Rogel swallowed hard. "Mr. Chiles, we will not allow U.S. citizens, wherever they are, to be arrested because of their religious opinions or practices."

"We shall see about that. At any rate, they'll be freed shortly. And, for your own good, I won't report your response to his highness. Good day, Mr. Rogel."

"Well done!" commended Andre as his faithful servant carefully placed the receiver down on the speaker phone. A smile flickered through the minister's subservient eyes. "We'll not have any more trouble from him. And soon we shall lock up those Jewish rebels for good!"

"They plan to use one of the air force bases in the Negev Desert—the one that they helped build in the early '80s," the prime minister reported to his security cabinet on September 21.

"This is an extremely risky enterprise," Edna Satori protested when Nimrod finished his presentation.

"It is bound to get us into deep trouble," sighed Yudah Sephres. The power he had hoped for was now beyond his grasp. Israel was just a pawn on Andre's international chessboard.

The ten ministers were meeting in the prime minister's Jerusalem office to discuss President Rogel's request to send several dozen giant U.S. transport planes to Israel to evacuate those American passport holders who wished to leave the country. Rogel had dubbed the evacuation "Operation Eagle."

"But European radar is sure to spot them flying into our airspace," Rafi Hochman warned.

Nimrod rubbed his unshaven chin. "So, do we refuse this humanitarian request from Israel's most faithful supporter or should we risk offending Andre?"

Rabbi Shimshon quietly studied the faces of his cabinet colleagues. His bushy eyebrows hung over his dark brown eyes, almost shielding them from the fluorescent lights.

"Yes, Amos, go ahead," instructed Nimrod, who sensed that he had something to say.

"All of us in this room are Jews, even though you are not religious as I am. In the last century, one-third of our people were slaughtered in Nazi death camps. Now we are living in our sovereign Jewish state. Fellow Jews are being rounded up in our own country, right under our noses.

"We may not be strong enough to prevent it, but the United States is still powerful enough to rescue those Jews born in America. We must support this. We have no choice."

Most of the shamed ministers looked down at the floor as Shimshon finished his admonition. The cabinet voted unanimously to let "Operation Eagle" proceed five days later in the Negev Desert.

Sarah and her children cautiously entered the five-story building, located on a quiet street in southwest Jerusalem, and climbed the back stairs to Miri Doron's third floor apartment. Those already inside had staggered their arrivals so as not to arouse the neighbors' suspicions. Yoseph had instructed them to make sure absolutely no one was following them. Altogether,twenty-five believers had gathered in Miri's living room.

Benny skipped over to Eli while his mother greeted everyone. She was glad to see Yochanan and Natan-el seated next to the Steinbergs. *They'll know what we should do,* she thought.

Yoseph called the special meeting to order. "Brothers and sisters, this is an important, yet sad day for all of us. Still, I am glad that we are together again so soon after our brief detention. As all of you know, we have been offered an escape from the clutches of the Antichrist. Yochanan and Natan-el have already warned us that intense persecution will soon break out here in the Lord's land as well as other parts of the world. It will reach the United States, but it won't be as severe. Each of us must choose whether to stay in our beloved Jewish homeland or seek temporary refuge in America."

Yoseph paused so Yochanan could speak. The apostle realized the struggle that most were going through. With concern on his face, he leaned forward on the couch so he could see each believer in the crowded living room.

"Little flock, some of you are being called to remain, others to leave. Each of you must hear from the Lord for yourself because you will have to bear the consequences of your decision.

"Danny and Zev, who have ministered so faithfully with us, will accompany those who decide to fly to the States. As recorded in Revelation 12:6, the specially sealed celibate males who were caught up to the heavenly Mount Zion will help to nourish the chosen woman, Israel, during the coming years of worldwide tribulation. Sealed Jews in America will join them in this spiritual and physical nourishment."

"Excuse me, Yochanan," interrupted Danny, running his fingers through his short red hair. "Are you saying that the male child in Revelation, who is caught up to the throne of God before ruling the world with a rod of iron, is not Yeshua but the sealed 144,000?"

"Yeshua will rule the earth with a strong hand during the soon-coming millennium, Danny. But the traditional interpretation of this verse is wrong even though Messiah is a son of the woman Israel."

Danny frowned, so Yochanan went on. "Our Savior was never caught up to heaven as a child in the way described in Revelation 12. He ascended as a fully-grown adult from the Mount of Olives. Natan-el and I witnessed this ourselves with great joy and astonishment.

"I wrote in verse 6 that the woman who gives birth to this child is immediately given sanctuary from Satan, the dragon, manifested in the Antichrist. They will nourish her for 1,260 days. The 'they' in this verse refers to the male offspring of the woman Israel—the supernaturally sealed Jewish males of Revelation 7 and 14. These males are the sons of Israel who were caught up to heaven."

The believers began to stir at this revelation. Eli winked at Moshe as Yochanan continued. "The Scriptures reveal that Yeshua will not rule the nations alone during the coming age. All believers who are faithful until the end will be given authority with Messiah over the nations, ruling with a rod of iron. That is recorded at the end of Revelation 2. But the Jewish males who have been caught up to heaven will rule with even greater authority during the millennium, as hinted at in Revelation 12."

Yochanan surveyed his small Israeli flock. Tears welled up in the beloved apostle's ancient eyes. "Those of you who choose to stay in Israel will witness continued revival and blessing in the land. But you will also see and experience tremendous persecution from the beast. The blessings will be great but so will the trials. May the Holy Spirit guide you as you seek His perfect will!"

There wasn't a dry eye in the place. The believers would soon be divided. Softly, Eli led them in a familiar song of hope—a song about the promised return of the great Shepherd of the sheep. The song brought joy back to their hearts. Whatever else lay ahead, their Savior would return.

20

Carried Away

Sarah was having trouble hearing from the Lord about the evacuation. Not only did she have herself to consider, but also her two young children.

"Jonathan, I miss you so much," she sighed, all alone on her king-sized bed. "You always seemed to know just what to do."

Suddenly, Sarah sat up against her pillows. A soothing warmth pulsed through her body. Then, almost as suddenly, Sarah's mind caught the clear, sweet promise from Yeshua, "I will never leave you, nor forsake you."

"Lord, thank you!" she exclaimed as assurance filled her soul.

The next morning the Israeli widow set off for her last hospital visit. *What will I tell dear Yitzhak?* she wondered while riding the crowded bus toward Hadassah Hospital.

After entering the main lobby, Sarah headed for the cafeteria to pick up a tray of food before going to Yitzhak's room on the fourth floor.

"Good afternoon, Yitzhak," she greeted him while trying to balance a tray in one hand and a Bible in the other.

"Hello, Sarah. It's great to see you again. What goodies do you have for me today?"

"Well, the best thing is the Bible you requested the last time I visited. And let's see, we have some caviar, roast duck in orange sauce, creamed onions and peas, cherry supreme for dessert, and the finest of French wines!"

Yitzhak chuckled as he rolled up the sleeves of his cotton pajamas. "I see they've lowered the standard again!"

"Here we go. Open wide for some duck!"

"Funny how it looks like chicken." The elderly man revealed his yellowed teeth as he obeyed Sarah's command.

"They just do that to fool your sensitive stomach."

As he finished his custard dessert, Yitzhak noticed the look of heaviness on Sarah's face. He gently reached out to touch her arm. "You look worried today, my dear. Is everything alright?"

"To be honest, Yitzhak, no. The emperor's United World forces are rounding up many of the protesting Jews and Arabs. They even briefly detained me and some of my friends last week."

"They did what?!" Yitzhak could see the pain in Sarah's eyes. A flood of World War II memories stormed through his head.

Sarah recoiled at the sudden look of terror on her elderly friend's face. "Dear Yitzhak, it's alright. They didn't harm us. But they did warn us that we're in for further trouble if we keep associating with the two witnesses near the Western Wall.

"But something else is troubling me right now. The United States government is offering to fly American citizens out of Israel in a one-time emergency evacuation. It's scheduled for three days from now. I have to decide what to do."

"You mean, you might not ever be coming back?" Yitzhak slumped down on his pillows. "I will miss you so."

Sarah sat on the side of the bed and stroked the old man's thin white hair.

"Sarah, I want to tell you a story," he said quietly after a few minutes had elapsed. "I want you to know this about me before you leave.

"After my parents were arrested by Nazi forces in our German hometown, my thirteen-year-old sister and I were hidden in the attic of an elderly Gentile couple. I was only ten, and I couldn't stand being confined like that. So one day when they were out I persuaded my sister, Rachel, to slip down to the kitchen with me to find some cookies.

"As we were waltzing down the stairs, a Nazi SS guard spotted us through the front window. He knew that no children were supposed to be living there. He banged on the heavy wooden door. I turned tail and ran back upstairs, but Rachel froze in fear. The soldier forced open the locked entrance with his bayonet and boot and grabbed her. For some reason he didn't come after me.

"I watched in horror from the attic window as my terrified sister was dragged away. I knew I would never see her again. Two days later, several Nazi guards arrived at the house and forced Mr. Presinger to take them to the secret hiding place. I was cowering under a wool blanket when they banged in the door. They called me a 'dirty-Jew-boy' as they tied me up with a rope. Then another guard shot Mr. Presinger dead in front of me as I was being carried down the stairs."

Tears streamed down the holocaust survivor's time-worn face. "You remind me so much of my Rachel, Sarah. I lost her, now I'm going to lose you."

The widow hugged her elderly friend and realized that her dilemma had been resolved.

Craig entered the Goldmans' front door with grim determination on his face. "I've decided to stay," he declared.

"But Craig, you're not even Jewish," retorted Stacy. They headed toward the dining room table to sit down. "Why remain in Israel and risk getting caught in Andre's evil web? You could return to the States and finish your studies there."

"God called me to study and work for his kingdom right here. I've been in Israel for over a decade, Stacy. It's my home, not America. The Lord hasn't annulled that call, so I'm staying put."

"I wish I had your courage, Craig. I don't know what to do. Sarah is leaning toward staying. The Steinbergs are for sure. Eitan and Shimon phoned an hour ago and said God wants them to go with the believers."

"What about Eli and Moshe?"

"Sarah talked with them this morning. The apostles want them to remain here for now and minister with them. But they'll be going to America fairly soon."

"Stacy, do you think Sarah has romantic feelings for Eli? I mean, he is a marked man, as it were, and not available for marriage."

Stacy poured Craig a cup of hot coffee. "She realizes there won't ever be anything between them, but she cares for him just the same. Women can't just turn feelings off like a lightbulb, like some of you men."

"But that isn't why she wants to stay in Jerusalem, is it?"

"I don't think so." Stacy poured herself some coffee. "She murmured something strange as she was running out the door this morning. She said, 'I can't leave Israel. I'm Yitzhak's Rachel.' Whatever that means."

"What about Donna?" Craig stirred some sugar into his cup.

Stacy smiled. "Afraid to lose a secret admirer, Craig?"

"She's not so secret. I've had to tell her to cool it. I'm not interested in a nonbeliever."

"Well, Donna says she has no reason to fear Andre or his forces since she isn't a practicing Jew and doesn't believe in Yeshua."

The phone rang in the living room. Stacy excused herself to answer it.

As Stacy was finishing her ten-minute telephone call, Sarah walked through the kitchen door. "Who was that on the phone?"

"My dad in the States."

"That's the fourth time he's called in the past two days, isn't it?"

"He's really worried. He's been so lonely since Mom died, and the thought of losing me—it's just too much for him. I told him I would decide what to do by tomorrow."

"That reminds me, I need to phone my parents, and Jonathan's as well."

Stacy took the bag of groceries from Sarah. "Did you decide on their offer?"

"What offer?" Craig asked as he poured a second cup.

"My in-laws offered to keep Tali and Benny if I decide to stay. In fact, they fairly begged to take them. You wouldn't know, Craig, but Benny is named after Jonathan's grandfather, Benjamin Goldman, who perished at Auschwitz. Dad just can't bear the thought—" Sarah's words disappeared in emotion.

Stacy picked up where Sarah left off. "He can't bear the thought that he might lose his grandson to some Jew-hating tyrant, just like he lost his father and son."

A short while later, Sarah dutifully carried two cheese sandwiches to the basement. Her heart was heavy with anticipation. "Oh good! I'm starved!" exclaimed Benny as the youngsters ran to greet their mother.

"Hello, my babies." Sarah sat down in an old rocking chair and lifted her offspring into her lap. "Before you begin eating, we have to talk one more time about the airplanes. Your grandpa will be calling soon, and I promised him a final answer today."

The wistful mother stroked the hair of her little ones. "Children, I've decided to stay here in Jerusalem for now. I just don't feel right about leaving, and I think God wants me to stay. But it's a dangerous time. It's best if you go to be with Grandpa and Grandma Goldman. You can also visit Grandpa and Grandma Hazan in California."

"I want to stay here with you," protested eight-year-old Tali.

"Me too," piped in Benny.

"I'm sorry, Benny. Mommy has decided that you're going to Grandpa Goldman's house, and that's final."

Sarah cuddled her son in her arms.

"Tali, you know what I said this morning. I agree that you are old enough to make up your own mind. I will let the final decision be yours, but I still think it's best if you go."

"But I'd miss you too much." The youngster buried her head in her mother's blouse.

"We'll be together again, honey."

"I've prayed a lot about it, Mom. I want to stay here, no matter what happens." Sarah embraced her daughter, then kissed her son's little forehead. Even though she knew it was risky, she was relieved that at least one of her children would remain in her care. "It'll be alright, Benny. We'll all be together again soon. I'm sure of that."

Two tourist buses were leased by the American consulate to pick up the evacuees at four different Jerusalem locations, all well off main streets. The pickup would take place before dawn. If stopped at UW checkpoints, the drivers would show their U.S. embassy papers and say they were transferring American citizens to the Negev town of Beersheba in order to escape the continuing violence in Jerusalem.

A small group of believers gathered at the south Jerusalem rendezvous point. Sarah cuddled Benny in her arms, glad that her five-year-old was too drowsy to realize what was going on. Tali stood quietly next to her mother.

Ken Preston showed up with his television camera. The bus driver momentarily panicked until several believers assured him they knew Ken, who quickly promised not to send any shots to network headquarters in Atlanta until the rescue operation had been completed.

The cameraman spotted Craig on the other side of the bus and walked over to greet him. "Hey, the man who lost me my job!"

"What? Lost you your job?"

"This will be my last shoot for WNN. A very important person in Europe ordered them to can me after my piece featuring you ran on the network. I think it was that British guy, Chiles, who always seems to be two steps behind the emperor. He apparently didn't like what you had to say, or that I had filmed you saying it!"

"I'm really sorry, Ken. I didn't mean to get you in trouble."

"Don't fret for me, Craig. I was already on the emperor's hit list because of Betty. Fret for your homeland. All of the media there have fallen under Andre's control, except for that Christian network."

"That's one of the reasons I'm staying put here in Israel," said Craig as Ken turned on his camera and started filming people boarding the bus.

An early morning mist created a slight chill in the early Autumn air. Sarah was glad she had insisted Benny wear his sweater.

"The bus departs in five minutes," announced a consulate official. "Anyone with luggage not yet on board, bring it now."

"I better get on," said Stacy, who had decided to leave and had promised to take care of Benny on the journey to America.

"Give me one more minute, Stace."

Benny rubbed his eyes as Sarah roused him. "Is it time to go, Mom?"

"It's time, son. I want you to promise Mommy that you will be good for your grandparents."

"I promise. When will I see you again?"

Sarah's last moments with Jonathan flashed through her mind. "I hope very soon, honey."

"Do you think Yeshua will come to Jerusalem before I get back?"

"I don't know, Benny, but I do know He's coming soon. Dear heart, don't ever forget that He loves you so much, and so do I."

"I love you too, Mommy."

Sarah brushed the tears from her cheeks as she carried her only son over to her best friend near the front door of the bus.

"Here's my big boy! Take good care of him."

After final farewells had been exchanged, the driver shut the door. Sarah silently prayed as Benny, Stacy, Danny, Zev, and Miri waved from the rear window of the accelerating bus.

O, Lord, do come quickly!

21

On the Wings of an Eagle

"There must be some way to stop this!"

"Your majesty, I suggest we see what Urbane Basillo can come up with," Burton Chiles responded diplomatically.

The emperor had just learned about the planned U.S. evacuation. Senior government sources in Washington and an aide to Foreign Minister Sephres had alerted him. "Get Basillo in here at once!"

Chiles scurried down the corridor to summon the man on whom Andre always relied. The minister did not like Basillo. He terrified the emperor's staff and treated Chiles as if he were an idiot.

"What is it now?" the deep voice barked...

"Sir, his majesty want to see you again," Chiles said gingerly. "He says it's important, Mr. Basillo. He's in his private chamber."

The emperor was pacing the floor impatiently when his supporting-role duo arrived. He rapidly sketched the situation for Basillo. "You must find a way to halt this American insubordination!" he raged with a clenched fist.

"I will consult the dragon," the rotund man solemnly replied. He then closed his eyes and shrieked in a hideous voice, "Lu-ci-fer, god of this world! Shine on me and show me your will!"

Instantly, Basillo's voice dropped several octaves. "I am with you, my child. I will guide you. When I command, call out to the sky over Palestine. Call for my minions to pour forth water like a flood! We will destroy!"

More than fourteen thousand people assembled at the sprawling air base surrounded by barren rolling hills. Two-thirds were Orthodox Jews and the rest either Messianic believers or Gentile Americans. Hundreds of non-U.S. citizens were numbered with the American throng as well, having been granted special permission to join the urgent exodus from Israel.

The giant C-5 Galaxy transport jets glistened in the midmorning sun. The final group of twelve planes had landed just before the last set of buses drove in from all across Israel. There was almost not enough room for the jets on the sprawling base runways, built with American assistance following the 1979 Egypt-Israel peace agreement.

Each Galaxy could carry three hundred fifty people. Holding clipboards with the names of the assembled evacuees, American officials boarded passengers on the planes, checking off names one by one. As the desert sun intensified, Israeli soldiers circulated through the crowds with water and fruit juice.

"What was that, Stacy?" Benny asked as they waited in line.

"I suppose it's thunder, honey. Looks like lightning over there, although it's a bit early in the season for that."

But the thunder quickly intensified and became deafening. And then they saw it: A wall of water fifty feet high was heading straight for the Israeli air base! The billowing tidal wave reached the nearby canyon's mouth, just a quarter mile from the base. It sounded like a roaring sea.

"O God, help us!" Stacy pressed Benny's face to her shoulder.

People fell over each other as they tried desperately to run in the opposite direction. Stacy grabbed Benny's hand and yanked him into a mad dash. The youngster's Chicago Bulls cap flew off his head and landed on the pavement. But it all seemed in vain. The rushing water was traveling at the rate of fifty miles an hour. They could not run fast enough.

A sharp jolt knocked them onto the asphalt runway. It was an act of Israel's God. The earth had split in two, creating an eight-foot-wide trench. The surging flood poured into the deep abyss. Those still standing turned around and stared in awe as the earth swallowed up every last drop of the Antichrist's raging tide.

When news of the successful U.S. rescue operation reached the young emperor, he flew into a rage.

"Our master is humiliated by this!" he screamed at Basillo, whose catlike eyes did not move. "But he will get his revenge."

Basillo nodded coldly. "It is time for the final phase of our program to begin. The system is almost completely in place, your majesty. We can begin to arrest those who refuse to bow down to you."

"See that it is done, and quickly!" Andre commanded as he turned to admire his trim and muscled image in a nearby mirror.

Sarah switched on the radio. "The weather bureau reports that an unusual late September thunderstorm occurred around noon in the Negev Desert, causing localized flash flooding. No damage was reported."

She was not entirely surprised by the news, having just read chapter 12 of Revelation. Trusting that Benny was safely on his way to the States, she decided to join the two witnesses just outside of the walled Old City.

"Hello, sister!" Eli was glad to see her. "Any word about Stacy and Benny?"

"Not yet. However, I did hear a radio report about a freak thunderstorm in the Negev around noon. They said it caused flash flooding, but no damage."

"That was Satan trying to disrupt the American evacuation, Sarah. The apostles warned me several days ago that it would occur and that Satan would fail. I didn't say anything because I didn't want to worry you. Anyway, it'll be the last thunderstorm anyone will see for awhile."

"What do you mean?"

"Yochanan just proclaimed that no rain will fall in Israel until the people repent and turn to God. Listen, he is still talking about it."

"Turn and be saved, says the Lord! I will grant authority to my two servants to shut up the skies so that no rain will fall! Turn to me and be saved, says your God!"

"Wow, that's powerful!" exclaimed Sarah.

Eli's expression turned serious. "Sarah, you must remain close to us for the next few weeks. Go get Tali and bring some clothes with you. You can stay with us at our Mount of Olives home."

"What's going on, Eli?"

"The Lord has shown us that Andre will react swiftly to the American rescue operation. Many will be arrested and persecuted. We can protect you if you stay close."

Sarah returned home and hurriedly packed bags for

herself and Tali. Within two hours, they joined the believers near the Old City. They arrived just as United World troops approached the disciples.

Ken Preston ran to pick up his camera. He was now working for the Virginia-based Evangelical Broadcasting Network.

The tall and trembling commanding officer pointed his rifle at Natan-el. "Where is your companion?" he inquired.

"He's over there," the apostle replied, pointing to a nearby public rest room.

"We are here to arrest a number of your followers who are charged with disturbing the peace. Do not try to resist us."

Sarah pulled Tali to her side as UW soldiers surrounded the throng of believers. "It will be okay, sweetheart. God will protect us."

As she spoke, a bolt of molten fire struck the officer. Yochanan had emerged from the rest room. The remaining soldiers quickly scattered as Ken filmed the smoking remains of their slain commander.

Sarah was happy enough to be helping with the daily ministry next to the Old City's Dung Gate, despite several more attempted arrests. Her sister Donna was looking after her south Jerusalem home. Jonathan's compassionate widow desperately wanted to visit Yitzhak at Hadassah Hospital, but she knew that would be dangerous.

One morning in November, however, she decided to slip away. She intended to stop by her home before visiting Yitzhak.

A half hour after the others left the Mount of Olives house, Sarah exited through the back door. In order to escape notice, she wore a black Arab shawl to cover her hair and face. While riding on the city bus toward Beitar

Street, she prayed that God would protect her. With UW forces finally off of the streets, everything seemed back to normal. People were driving their cars. Mothers were taking their children to school. Shopkeepers were conducting business as usual.

""Just a second!" Donna shouted when she heard the knock on Sarah's front door.

"It's me, Sis. Undo the bolt and open up."

The sisters hugged each other. Sarah entered her home for the first time in almost two months.

"So, when did you become an Arab?" Donna's smile was cold, but Sarah shrugged it off as stress.

"It's just for today. It's almost nine and you're still in your nightgown!" Sarah laughed as she took off the shawl and threw it on the coffee table.

"I'm taking it easy this morning."

"The place looks good, Donna. Thanks for watching things for me."

The new immigrant turned serious. "Sarah, United World soldiers have come here three times looking for you. It isn't safe. Why didn't you call before coming over?" Donna's voice seemed unusually loud for the small living room.

"I didn't want to give away my plans in case someone was tapping the phone. I'm actually on my way to see Yitzhak. How are you doing?"

"Fine. I'm just fine." Donna spoke tersely as she smoothed the wrinkles in her gown. "Jonathan's father called again. I told him you are well and so is Tali. But that's not the truth, is it?"

"Things aren't bad."

"Except that you'd be dead if it weren't for those flame throwers!"

"They're not flame throwers; they are very godly men — something you wouldn't understand."

"Oh, I know a lot about men, although I still don't quite know why our handsome friend Moshe wouldn't slip into the sack with me."

Sarah was irritated. Her shapely sibling was always bragging about the men she had captured. She thought it was Donna's way of getting back at her for being the star pupil in the Hazan household, a fact frequently mentioned by their well-educated father.

"Cut it out, Donna. We've talked about this already, and I've said all I care to. How are my plants doing?"

"Your kitchen plants are greener than ever! Come in and take a look!" Donna raised her voice almost to a yell.

"Don't you ever wash the dishes?" asked Sarah as she ran some hot water over several crusty pots in the sink.

"I was just about to when you knocked on the door," Donna replied coolly as she tossed an empty wine bottle in the garbage.

When Sarah decided to leave the kitchen and head toward her bedroom, Donna bolted in front of her. "Don't go in there yet!" she directed harshly. "Let me straighten up a little."

Sarah waited uneasily in the hall for a few minutes. "Can I come in now?"

"Yeah, although it's still a bit of a mess."

The widow glanced around.

"Sorry your bed is so disheveled," apologized the house sitter. "I've been staying here most of the time. You know, your house is so much nicer than my tiny apartment."

After placing some clothes in a shopping bag, Sarah headed for her daughter's room. Donna followed. "Why is Tali's bed unmade?" Sarah asked as she straightened up the sheet and blankets.

"Oh, I had a friend over the other night. Sorry, I forgot about it. I haven't been in here since then."

Donna wished her sister good luck as Sarah headed out the front door. She bolted the lock as she watched her sister cross the street. "It's all right, love you can come up now."

A tall, muscular UW soldier, holding his wadded up uniform and wearing a towel around his trim waist, bounced up the basement stairs and into Donna's welcoming arms.

Yitzhak felt overwhelming joy when his young female friend appeared in his hospital doorway. "Sarah! Thank God you are alright!"

"Dear Yitzhak, I am fine, by the grace of God. I haven't been able to come until today. How have you been?"

"Worried to death over you! I thought you must have left for the States—without even saying good-bye."

"I would never have done that, sweet Yitzhak. UW soldiers have been rounding up believers again. Only this time, they aren't letting anyone back out. I've had to stay off the streets."

The two chatted about the serious situation in Jerusalem until Yitzhak changed the subject. "Sarah, I've been reading the Bible you gave me the last time you were here. I looked at Isaiah 53." The old man propped himself up on his pillows and straightened the bed sheets around his legs before he continued. "Sarah, my dear, I think you might be right. Yeshua was definitely a Jewish Israeli, and he may be our promised Messiah."

"Oh, Yitzhak, I'm so thrilled to hear you say that! It makes it all worthwhile."

"Makes what worthwhile?"

"Oh, nothing. Are you ready to invite the Lord into your life? I know He's ready."

"Can you show me how?"

Sarah placed her left hand with her wedding band on Yitzhak's pale arm and led him in prayer. Yitzhak repeated each sentence after Sarah.

"Father in heaven, I believe that You exist, and that You sent Your anointed Messiah, Yeshua, to be the Savior of Israel, and of the entire world. I acknowledge that I am a sinner, in need of salvation. I ask you to wash me clean in the blood of the sacrificial Lamb of God, Yeshua the Messiah, and to grant me the eternal life that You have promised to give to all who believe in His atoning death in Jerusalem two thousand years ago. Thank you Lord for dying for me, for forgiving my sins and for granting me everlasting life in Yeshua! Amen."

Yitzhak wiped a small tear from the corner of his right eye. "I guess you really are my sister now," he chuckled.

"I certainly am! And you are my brother in the Lord forever!"

Sarah's heart was singing like a robin on a spring morning. She wanted to stay forever but knew she had to get back. "I'd better be going now, sweet Yitzhak. I'll try to come again soon. Pray for me, will you?"

"I don't even remember how to pray."

"God will guide you, and He'll listen to whatever you say. Shalom, dear friend!"

The elderly patient waved a leathery hand at her and then let out a small shout of joy.

Sarah rushed down the hospital corridor with the shawl wrapped around her head. Suddenly two UW soldiers emerged from a side doorway. The stocky one grabbed her wrist.

"Sarah Goldman, you are under arrest."

22

World War III

By late December, a massive United World force was ready to move out from its staging ground in eastern Germany and Poland. Its first target was Moscow. The powerful force, commanded by General Jules Fontaine, would be bolstered by troops from the Ukraine, whose leader had pledged his support to Andre.

The order to advance in the direction of Russia was given on January 1. The decision to set out in the dead of winter was made mainly for strategic reasons. A winter campaign against the poorly equipped Russian army would be a military nightmare for them. The European-dominated UW force was adequately prepared and ready to fight.

Vladimir Konstantine privately feared that the emperor's attack would parallel the American-dominated UN force's crushing defeat of Saddam Hussein. Andre's awesome military machine would undoubtedly outperform

Russia's army and air force, substantial as they were. Although the fifty-nine-year-old Russian leader's potent naval fleet outnumbered the combined European and Ukrainian forces, he knew the war would be decided on the ground.

Any use of nuclear weapons—Konstantine's only serious hope of defense—was sure to bring a swift nuclear response from Europe and possibly from the United States. On top of this, the fascist Russian dictator could not be sure of the loyalty of his own troops. Although officially banned, emperor worship was openly occurring in many places, especially among younger Russians—the very group most represented in the armed forces.

Konstantine's only real hope of victory lay in his alliance with China and Iran. He was particularly counting on military support from Chinese ground and air forces since Chinese leader Quay Chin realized his nation would come under attack if Russia fell.

The well-armed United World juggernaut reached Minsk, the capital of the Republic of Byelorussia in just eight hours. Ukrainian brigades, marching northward along the west bank of the Dnepr River, met up with General Fontaine's military machine in eastern Byelorussia. Armed Russian resistance began as the UW force proceeded north of the nearly frozen waterway.

With Russian forces on the defense, the emperor's skillful army rapidly captured the city of Smolensk, situated on the Dnepr just inside the Russian border two hundred miles from the western suburbs of Moscow. Two days later, long-range artillery pounded the Russian capital as UW strategic bombers pummeled military and civilian targets, including the Kremlin.

Konstantine's forces were doing much better on the open seas. His warships engaged European vessels in several locations, including the Indian and North Pacific

Oceans and in the Baltic and Mediterranean Seas. Casualties were equal on both sides with hundreds of ships destroyed and thousands of sailors killed.

Warplanes based on Russian aircraft carriers in the Mediterranean launched numerous successful air attacks on military targets near several southern European coastal cities, including Barcelona, Marseilles, Naples, and Athens. Cruise missiles were used in three of the attacks, which destroyed dozens of NATO jets and two large weapon factories. However, the Russian pilots were thwarted in attempts to bomb targets near Rome.

Vladimir Konstantine pleaded with Quay Chin to send ground reinforcements to western Russia, now rapidly falling under United World control. But the Chinese leader decided to reserve all of his troops for the expected UW attack against his own country.

With his ground and air forces crumbling, Konstantine realized that he had no choice but to surrender. Russia was lost, but the dejected leader promised his weary government comrades that the humiliating defeat was not the end of the story. He would get his revenge on the upstart European despot in time.

Though drunk with victory, Andre was willing to let the Russian strongman remain in office, as long as complete control of Konstantine's military forces and nuclear weapons passed to United World commanders. More importantly, Russian troops would be forced to join Andre's upcoming campaign against China.

The UW assault left Moscow decimated and the countryside in ruins. Besides the hundreds of thousands of soldiers and civilians killed in fighting, over ten thousand Russians starved or froze to death in January alone. With medicines in short supply, tuberculosis and influenza spread at epidemic rates. By April more than one million people had perished.

After quickly consolidating his hold on Russia, General Fontaine ordered his men to head southeast. Their new destination was the Shiite Muslim fundamentalist stronghold of Iran. United World troops passed through the Muslim republic of Azerbaijan the first week of February. Officials in Baku, the capital, decided to offer no resistance, despite pleas of help from Iran.

On February 12, Fontaine ordered his soldiers to cross into northwest Iran, where they swiftly overcame Shiite Iranian revolutionary guards and Mujahedeen fighters as well as thousands of volunteers from Afghanistan and Iraq. As soon as the victorious UW forces entered Tehran, Urbane Basillo flew to the Iranian capital to integrate the Shiite Muslim establishment into his growing worldwide network of emperor worship.

The emperor was so satisfied with Fontaine's brilliant campaigns that he ordered the general to meet him in Rome for a celebration. His royal band greeted the Lyon-born military leader as soon as he stepped off his jet at Leonardo da Vinci airport. Hundreds of Romans behind police barricades waved the new United Europe flag picturing Andre's golden crown surrounded by stars in a light blue background. Fontaine was then whisked away to the Venezia Palace.

Built during the 1400s and once the headquarters of Mussolini, the palace had housed an art museum until the emperor took it over. He usually stayed at either his Rome or Madrid palace during the winter but preferred one of his northern European mansions when the weather turned hot.

Dressed in a crisp army uniform, General Fontaine slowly walked through the front corridor and into the dining room where dinner was set for two. Large portraits of Charlemagne, Charles V, Napoleon, and Alexander the Great adorned the walls. He then heard a servant announcing the arrival of Emperor Andre. A four-man chamber orchestra in one corner of the large dining room began playing softly as two gilded doors opened. The emperor, wearing a white tuxedo with matching gloves, greeted Fontaine with a warm handshake.

"I am extremely pleased with your operation," Andre announced between bites of caviar. "In fact, I believe we're at least one month ahead of schedule."

The sturdily built general swelled with pride. "The Russians crumbled much faster than we anticipated, your majesty, and the Iranians hardly put up a fight. But the Chinese, I fear, will be quite another matter."

Andre sipped his Chablis. "The Chinese are an obstinate people, but they will not prevail. I am certain Quay will see the light when our forces arrive along his border."

"If he doesn't, your majesty, my men are prepared to make him see it."

"I'll drink to that!" The emperor victoriously raised his crystal glass in the air.

Fontaine soon returned to Asia. In mid-March his forces set out from northeastern Iran. By April 1, his military machine had reached China's northwestern border. Several Russian divisions, now under his command, poured into Mongolia from the north. Troops also massed along the Argum River next to China's northeastern border. Officials in New Delhi soon joined Andre's alliance, sending Indian soldiers to the border between India and Chinese-occupied Tibet. Burmese troops were poised to move into the southern Chinese Yunnan Province. During the second week of May, Fontaine informed the emperor that the United World tiger was ready to pounce on the world's most populous nation.

As Fontaine positioned his forces, Andre ordered his finance minister, Hans Brecht, to begin integrating Russia into the Brussels-based economic system that would eventually link all of the world's economies. The intricate network—dubbed "Black Dragon" by Andre's top aides—was essentially Brecht's brainchild. Millionaires, corporate executives, and international bankers provided expertise and capital. The system's centerpiece was the assignment of computerized identity numbers to everyone on earth, beginning in industrialized nations and ending in the Third World. The system had begun operating in Europe and Japan before Christmas and was beginning to function in parts of North and South America, South Africa, Australia, and New Zealand.

Finance Minister Brecht had a well-deserved reputation for being hard-nosed and ruthless. The former bank president from Bonn had been instrumental in helping European Community leaders forge close economic ties in the sixties and seventies. He eagerly began carrying out Basillo's order to tag every human being with an implanted computer chip containing an ID number and other personal information such as age and religious affiliation. These minuscule chips, readable by electronic scanners, would be implanted either on a person's hand or forehead. No one could buy or sell without this number.

Sarah Goldman was confined all winter in a tiny prison cell with three other women in the United World detention compound north of Jerusalem. The guards allowed only one small kerosene heater to be lit a few hours each evening, but this barely reduced the chill and dampness that permeated the dark cell.

Food was scarce. Two pieces of bread and cold soup broth were all they had to eat. Every other day a few small pieces of chicken were thrown into the soup for protein. Exercise took place in the prison courtyard twice a week.

One of Sarah's cell mates was Naomi Blum, an Israeli-born mother of four and a Jewish believer from Tiberias. The two women often prayed quietly together in Hebrew.

Naomi had been arrested while grocery shopping. She had no idea whether her husband had also been nabbed from their apartment that overlooked the Sea of Galilee. Male prisoners were kept well away from the females in a separate section of the UW camp. She was certain her youngsters were alright under the care of some relatives in Tiberias.

Sarah also prayed each day in English with Yasmin Nakouri, an Arab believer who shared the cell with them. The Bethlehem-born woman of twenty-three, who had only come to faith the previous summer, understood some Hebrew, but not enough to pray with the two Israelis.

After several weeks of imprisonment, Sarah felt like she needed to do something to keep her mind sharp, so she decided to pass the time teaching more English to Yasmin. Sarah in turn improved her Hebrew with Naomi's help and picked up some Arabic from Yasmin.

The fourth cell mate was an Orthodox woman named Zipporah Epstein, whose husband, a Jerusalem baker, had been arrested three days before her. The thirty-eight-year-old mother cried constantly during her first few days in prison. She feared that she would never see her seven children again. Zipporah listened with rapt attention to the Hebrew prayers of her fellow Israelis. She quickly became interested in this Messiah they spoke about.

One Monday in March, the female inmates were taken to a newly constructed auditorium on the outskirts of camp. For the first time, they were able to see the male inmates over a three-foot-high partition running down the middle of the auditorium.

As the prisoners made their way to their seats, they frantically searched for familiar faces on the other side of the divide. Sarah spotted Reuven Sassler, a young single member of Beit Yisrael, and she waved conspicuously until he saw her.

Naomi grabbed Sarah's hand. "There's my Avi!" she exclaimed as she began to blow a cornucopia of kisses his way.

Before too long, a large female guard abruptly stopped her visible display of affection. "Sit down and keep quiet! You Jews act like a pack of animals!" she growled as she pushed the woman to her seat.

Yasmin spotted several believers that she knew, including her cousin, Yusef. But Zipporah could not locate her husband. She leaned on Sarah's arm as her eyes desperately raced up and down the other side. Then she spied a familiar face. It was her second oldest son, Boaz. She tried to raise her arm to get his attention, but the stone-faced guard gripped her hand and pulled it down. The program was about to begin.

"Good morning, detainees." The United World camp commander greeted the inmates in a deep monotone English, which was immediately translated into Hebrew, and then Arabic. "You are being housed in Camp Shining Dawn, run by the United World. Your incarceration is not meant to bring you harm. We want to educate you and enlighten you.

"To achieve this goal, we will be meeting here in this wonderful new hall every day from now on. Those of you who successfully complete the education process will be able to leave Shining Dawn. Those who do not—and we hope that no one will fit into this category—may find that conditions rapidly deteriorate as the camp is transformed into a high-security prison. We have your best interests at heart. Simply cooperate and you will go free. Your education should be completed in just a few months."

Sarah and Zipporah grabbed each other's trembling hands.

"Each of you has demonstrated that you do not yet understand the truth about our exalted emperor, Andre." The commander paused to turn and acknowledge a life-size picture of the European monarch hanging to the left of the stage. "He is the manifestation of the Universal Force. He is the true reflection of god in human form."

"Blasphemy!" The word hurled through the air like a stone from King David's slingshot.

"Ah, good." The surly commander's teeth shone through a glazed smile. "We have an early opportunity to demonstrate to you today what will happen to anyone who disrupts these meetings. Guards, bring the rebel here!"

Two blue-uniformed guards with clubs hanging from their belts yanked an Orthodox Jewish man in his late twenties from his seat and dragged him to the front of the auditorium. A heavy-set man appeared out of nowhere. He wore a surgical gown and carried a black metal box with wires. The guards tied the heckler's hands and attached a tiny electrode to the back of his neck.

"Are you ready?" asked the commander.

"Yes, sir," came the guttural reply.

The man turned a knob on the device, and the prisoner let out a blood-curdling scream before writhing in agony to the floor.

"Is that enough?" the commander calmly inquired as he towered over the jerking victim.

"Y . . . e . . . s," the prisoner moaned.

"Turn it off."

A dropping pin would have made a crashing sound in the stunned auditorium. Sarah and Naomi did not even realize they had joined hands. Zipporah had grabbed Sarah's arm so tightly that her fingernails were cutting into it. Naomi's hand was dripping with sweat.

"I am sorry you had to witness this," the commander lamely apologized as the limp victim was carried off the platform. "We hope we do not have to repeat it. But let this serve as a warning to each of you. Cooperate and all will be well."

The stern commander gripped the sides of his metal dais. "Your lessons begin tomorrow. You will soon be joining the ranks of billions around the globe who are already displaying their devotion to our emperor. At the end of your course, you will be integrated into the new world economic system and given the necessary credentials to buy and sell. An exciting time lies ahead, ladies and gentlemen! Class is dismissed."

"But how can Sarah go with us when she's locked up in that dreadful camp?" Eli asked when Yochanan informed him the Lord would soon be transporting them to other parts of the world.

"Surely you must know by now that with God all things are possible. Walk in faith, my young friend."

That April night, Yochanan asked Eli to drive him north to the UW camp. The midnight April air blowing in through the open car windows was perfumed with the scent of wild flowers. The bewildered Israeli soon parked his Renault a quarter mile from the main entrance and quietly accompanied the apostle. UW soldiers carrying machine guns manned two high towers on both sides of the eight-foot chain-link gate.

Yochanan nonchalantly raised his arms into the air. "Now we can go in, Eli," he announced as he lowered his arms.

"But the guards will see us! And besides, the gate is locked."

"Didn't I tell you this morning that all things are possible with God?"

Yochanan boldly walked up to the steel-reinforced gate while his younger companion followed behind like a frightened puppy. Four German shepherds began to bark, prompting nearby soldiers to raise their semiautomatics in the air. Floodlights scanned the area. Eli froze in fear. Yochanan pulled him past the guards and directly through the closed gate.

"Michael taught me that one," quipped Yochanan as they emerged on the other side.

Yochanan then led an astounded Eli past several more guard posts and through a locked door. Soon they were approaching Sarah's dank cell. When the apostle touched the handle, the lock instantly sprang open.

Eli leaned down and gently shook Sarah awake while holding his hand over her mouth. She instantly recognized him and gave him an excited hug. Then she jumped up and embraced the beloved apostle as well.

"Wake up the others, Sarah, but do it carefully," Yochanan directed in a soft voice.

"What about Zipporah?" Sarah asked with a worried look across her face.

"She would not understand and create a scene." Yochanan reached into a small bag he was carrying. "Here is a pen and paper. Write her a quick note explaining that Yeshua has set you free."

Sarah woke Naomi and Yasmin. The apostle told them not to fear, but to follow him quietly and quickly out of the prison camp.

"The Mighty One will cover us with His wings," he assured them.

As they passed through the closed gate, the three Israeli women marveled at what had just occurred. Truly Yochanan was right. Nothing is impossible with God.

23

Precious Mothers

Tali switched on her bedside light. The clock read 1:15 A.M. It had been more than five months since the eight-year-old had seen her imprisoned mother.

Tali missed Sarah terribly. Her distant grandparents begged her to join them in the United States, but she refused their pleas. She told them she had to wait in Jerusalem for her mother to come home.

Every day Tali prayed for Sarah's safety. "God, I lost my abba, and Benny is gone," she repeated amid tears. "Please don't leave me an orphan. Please let me see my mom again!"

Eli informed Sarah on the way home from the UW prison that Tali knew nothing about the planned rescue. He had not said anything to her just in case something went wrong. In turn, Sarah revealed that Yitzhak had become a believer during her visit to Hadassah Hospital just before she was arrested. Eli decided to wait awhile before telling her his news concerning the elderly Holocaust survivor.

He knew she would have mixed emotions when she learned that Yitzhak had gone to be with the Lord during her incarceration.

The widow trembled in anticipation as she darted up the tiled stairs of the communal home to her daughter's tiny bedroom. Tali was sobbing when Sarah entered the room. She had just awakened from another vivid dream. In this one, an angel, dressed in a white robe and carrying a silver menorah, was leading her mother out of prison.

"Tali, sweetheart, I'm here!" whispered Sarah gently as she approached the bed.

"Mommy!" The young girl shot up from under her covers. "Oh, Mommy! You're alive! Thank you, God!"

Eli stood in the doorway. "Bless you, Lord," he prayed under his breath.

"The cold was the worst part for me," lamented Naomi over eggs and toast the next morning.

"That's for sure," confirmed Sarah. "But it didn't get really bad until they started indoctrinating us in emperor worship. They unveiled a ten-foot statue of Andre and told us we would have to bow down and worship it before the end of April—or else! They claimed his image would actually speak when we worshipped before it. Just the thought is revolting!"

Yasmin nodded. "And the statue was completely, how do you say—"

"Completely nude, like Michelangelo's David," Sarah finished.

"Yes, nude. To even look at such a thing is completely foreign to our Arab culture."

"This emperor-worship thing has ungodly sexual overtones," Eli observed as he finished his last bite of toast.

"Indeed it does," confirmed Natan-el. "Sex is the honey Satan often uses to lure people into his trap."

Sarah reached over to touch Yochanan's hand. "We are so thankful to you for rescuing us from that nightmare."

The apostle smiled through his beard and winked at her.

"I hope my Avi will be alright," said Naomi. "I realize you couldn't rescue every believer last night."

Yochanan put down his butter knife. "We can't say for sure what will happen to him, Naomi. The Lord has shown us that the time is at hand when many believers will be called upon to lay down their earthly lives for Him." He paused. "Millions of Yeshua's followers will accept death rather than bow down before Andre's idolatrous image."

Natan-el covered Naomi's hand with his. "Don't worry. The Lord will protect you as you return to your children in Tiberias. But you must remember that those who die in the Lord from now on will receive a very great reward."

After breakfast, Naomi and Yasmin accompanied the others to the Western Wall plaza, now reopened to limited numbers of Jewish worshippers. Both women had heard many reports about the two anointed prophets and wanted to hear them speak.

Sarah was thrilled to be back. She chatted amicably with Cindy as they walked toward the plaza, catching up on the local news.

"Cindy, have you seen my sister?"

"No, but I did talk with her by phone a couple of times. She didn't seem very surprised when I told her you'd disappeared. I asked if she'd seen you the day you were arrested, and she told me no."

"That's a lie, Cindy. I went by the house before going to the hospital. Something fishy was going on."

"Sarah, do you think it's possible that Donna turned you in?"

"I'm afraid so. She was acting so strange, almost shouting at times. I think someone may have been down in the basement. I had a lot of time to think about it in the camp. It's so sad," Sarah's voice trailed off.

"Imagine! Your own sister turning you in! Why?"

"Well, I know this sounds incredible, but I think it's at least partly because she wants to hold on to my house. She was used to luxurious living in California and hates her small apartment."

Cindy was dumbfounded. "That is so wicked!"

"The Lord warned us people would grow more selfish and evil at the close of the age and would even betray their own family members."

"Yeah, but it's still shocking when it actually happens."

"True, yet not so surprising when it comes to Donna. You know how she's resisted the Lord. And she's always been a bit man crazy. I never told you this, Cindy, but she tried to seduce Jonathan one time soon after we were married. I'm afraid my sister is under Satan's spell. But I pray that will change one day. Oh, praise God! There's the Wall! I've dreamed about this day for many months."

A crowd of nearly four hundred people, over half of them believers, were already waiting in the plaza for the apostles. Harassment of believers had eased because the internment camps could not hold the number of people who were becoming followers of the Lord. The emperor himself had ordered a temporary halt to arrests in response to intensifying complaints from Prime Minister Nimrod, who bristled at the fact that an outside Gentile ruler was rounding up his citizens, and he could do little about it. Andre gave in to his protests after deciding that getting rid of Nimrod might only spark more trouble on the streets of Jerusalem.

It was the Friday before Easter and Passover. However, for the first time in decades, no Christians would be marching down the Old City's narrow Via Dolorosa carrying wooden crosses and singing hymns. No public services would be held at the Garden Tomb, located just north of the Old City below a hill that many believe to be Calvary. No public prayers would be recited in the Garden of Gethsemane at the foot of the Mount of Olives. Open worship of Yeshua had been banned.

Yet even Satan himself could not stop the Lord's two appointed witnesses. After praying with some of the brothers, Yochanan began prophesying in his usual, powerful voice. "The kingdom of God is at hand! Repent, and draw near to God, and He will draw near to you. His kingdom is not of this world. The Messiah, Yeshua, came into the world to bear witness of the truth. Everyone who is of the truth hears His voice. Obey His voice and live forever!"

The Lord's beloved friend raised his ancient hands and reverently closed his eyes. "Repent of your wicked ways, house of Israel, descendants of Abraham. Return to the Lord and be healed. The wrath of God is about to fall on all the earth! Every mountain and island will be moved out of their places. The sun and moon will grow dark. The stars will fall from the sky, which will be rolled up like a scroll."

Sarah shuddered as the Son of Thunder uttered his warning. "The hour of God's judgment has come! Worship Him who made the heavens and the earth. Do not worship Andre or his image. He is not god, but a son of Satan. Do not receive his mark, or you will drink of the wine of the wrath of God!

"Fallen, fallen is Babylon the great—the economic, political, and religious system that worships itself instead of God. 'Come out of her, My people, and do not partake of her sins any longer. My plagues are about to destroy her! For in one day, My wrath will come, and she will be burned up with fire.' If anyone has an ear to hear, let them hear what God's Holy Spirit is saying to His people."

After Yochanan finished thundering, Natan-el and the disciples joined him in ministering to the crowd of people. Some were healed of diseases while others were freed from demonic oppression. Many surrendered their lives to the Lord.

As the crowd dispersed, Yochanan called together the one hundred believers who lingered behind. "Brethren, it is now one year since Natan-el and I began ministering here in Jerusalem. Thousands have repented of their sins and returned to the living God of Israel, through his Son. Many more around the world have heard our message through modern communication methods and have surrendered their lives to God.

"We have much more to say to Israel, but the Lord is calling us to other parts of the world—to warn people directly of the judgment to come and to proclaim the good news of salvation freely available in Yeshua. This will be our last day of ministry for awhile here at the Western Wall."

The local believers had mixed emotions about Yochanan's announcement. They were happy that other nations would get the chance to hear the two witnesses firsthand but sad that the apostle's words of life would no longer be their daily portion.

When Yochanan finished, Sarah spotted Ken Preston filming the dispersing crowd. She walked over and warmly greeted him.

"Shalom, Ken, how are you?"

"Sarah Goldman! How good to see you! I heard you were arrested. How did you get out?" Ken immediately hoisted his video camera back onto his shoulder. "Here, wait a minute, let me record this."

"Ken, I don't think your news network would be interested in my story."

"You're mistaken, Sarah. I'm now working for EBN, sending back daily footage of the two witnesses. I'm told that my reports are being widely copied, and underground videos are being sent to believers all over the world."

"I'm so pleased! But haven't you been harassed by the UW?"

"A few times, but I think they realize it would create trouble to arrest a prominent American journalist. You see, I'm not only filming for EBN, I'm also the on-site correspondent. And I'm told that many thousands have given their lives to the Lord as a result of my pieces!"

"Ken, that's great! But doesn't EBN get in trouble for airing them?"

"They've been harassed by some folks in Washington, but freedom of the press is still somewhat operational in America. However, the pressure against born-again Christians is definitely growing. I've even heard of wide-scale arrests of those resisting Andre's mark."

Sarah's thoughts wandered off to Benny in Illinois.

"Sarah?" Ken could tell she was suddenly miles away.

"Sorry, I was just thinking about my son near Chicago. I haven't spoken to him in months." She forced her mind back to Israel. "Betty would be so proud of you, Ken!"

As the Good Friday sun set over the holy city, the two witnesses and their brethren journeyed back toward their Mount of Olives home. They passed several dozen empty tourist shops along the Via Dolorosa. Arab children played marbles where crowds of pilgrims used to march. Venders pressed fresh bread under their noses in hopes of making a sale.

The believers exited the walled Old City through Lion's Gate, also known as Saint Stephen's Gate, the place where Israeli forces had breached Jordanian defenses when capturing the Old City in 1967. Then they dipped down past the Garden of Gethsemane, situated in the narrow Kidron Valley between the Old City and the Mount of Olives.

A small, unsanctioned Good Friday service was in progress inside the garden's ancient church. Sarah prayed silently as a sacred hymn floated past the aged, twisted olive trees in the venerated garden. *Lord, I was truly willing to drink the cup of death that you drank from,* she prayed. *Please help me always feel that way.*

Yochanan walked in silence behind her, his thoughts in another century. Mary's sorrowful eyes kept appearing in his mind. He remembered holding her hand as the nails were being driven through Yeshua's wrists and feet. Together, they had watched the Roman soldiers raise the wooden cross off the ground. Yochanan did not know how to comfort her as her dying Son hung naked for everyone to see. He was not able to bear her sorrow and his own at the same time.

Then, somehow, the Lord lifted his blood-drenched head and looked directly at His weeping mother. "Woman, behold your son." Yochanan melted into tears as the Lord turned His gaze on him and said, "Behold your mother." The words of the hymn made the Lord's beloved friend remember how he had leaned over and embraced Mary. Yeshua's cherished Jewish mother would remain in his care until her death.

That evening, the disciples fixed a festive Friday evening meal of roasted chicken and mashed potatoes. It would be their last Sabbath together in the holy city for some time.

Yochanan broke the Sabbath "challa" bread. "Baruch Ata Adonai, Eloheinu, Melech ha Olam," he prayed, blessing the God of Israel for the Sabbath bread in the traditional Jewish manner. *O, Lord, how I long for Your feet to return to this Olivet Mount!* he prayed silently as he handed the bread around the large table.

Natan-el blessed the Lord for the wine and said a special grace. "Our Father in heaven, You have blessed us with this wonderful meal, provided by Your generous servants here in Jerusalem. We are grateful. And Lord, we ask You to bless this city, now in chains but ordained to become the seat of Your glorious throne."

He paused as if listening to someone. "Yeshua, how Your heart yearns for this city! On this very hill You cried out over it, 'Jerusalem, Jerusalem, if you had only known the things which make for peace!' Then You said our enemies would surround us and hem us in until we say 'Blessed is he who comes in the name of the Lord.' Come, Yeshua, and deliver Your holy city."

After the Sabbath meal had ended, Yochanan explained how they—the fourteen adults and Tali—would soon be transported to their overseas destinations. "Do you remember what happened to our brother Philip after he shared the gospel with the Ethiopian on the road to Gaza?"

"Yes. He was snatched away by the Lord, just like that!" Tali snapped her fingers as she recalled the event recorded in the Book of Acts.

"He suddenly found himself in Ashdod, the town located north of the Gaza Strip on our Mediterranean coast," added Cindy.

"Correct. In just the same way, the Lord is going to snatch us away and take us to our destination. You will be coming too, Ken, in order to keep encouraging reports going out to believers around the world."

"But what about clothes?" asked Sarah, as down-to-earth as ever. "We'll need some clothes."

"Women!" Eli let out an exaggerated sigh.

Yochanan smiled. "After the Sabbath, everyone should pack one bag of essentials. We will take off early Tuesday morning. Our first stop will be Rome."

Shortly after the Sabbath, Sarah decided to phone Donna.

"Shalom, sister."

"Sarah! How . . . ah . . . great to hear your voice! When did you get out of jail? Cindy told me you'd been arrested."

"Late Thursday. I didn't get a chance to phone before the Sabbath. Are you alright?"

"Fine. Are you?"

"Yes. Listen, Donna, will you be able to look after the house for awhile longer?"

"Sure. Why? You need to stay around those two old flame throwers some more?"

"I guess you could put it that way. Say, what's that noise in the background?"

"I'm just having a few friends over."

Sarah paused as she mustered up courage to ask her next question. "Donna, I need to ask you something. I was arrested right after you saw me. Did you turn me in?"

"Don't be ridiculous! Despite your fanatic religious views, you're still my sister. I would never have you arrested."

"Is it possible somebody close to you, like maybe a United World soldier, knew that I was on my way to the hospital?"

"Uh, no, I don't think so."

"Do you have someone staying with you?"

"Of course not," Donna said, smiling at her handsome lover.

"Well, please try to behave yourself. Tali and I will be out of town for a few months. I'll phone when I can."

"Out of town?"

"I'll explain later."

"Glad you're safe, Sis. Take care."

"You too. Shalom, Donna." Sarah hung up the phone feeling that her sister was slipping ever closer toward the abyss.

Two days later, the believers were packed and ready to be transported to foreign harvest fields. After a hearty breakfast, they gathered together in the living room to sing songs of praise to their God. Then, in the twinkling of an eye, they were gone.

24

The Image of the Beast

Trumpets sounded as four tanned, muscular Italians carried the triumphant sovereign into the banquet hall of the Venezia Palace in Rome. It was the first anniversary of Andre's ascent to the European throne. Royal relatives from across the continent paraded with dignity behind his elevated chair. Leaders from around the world watched in person, along with millions of others on live television.

The emperor's gilded throne was carefully lowered at the head of a long banquet table as the invited guests were shown to their appointed places. Everyone then listened to a ballad sung by Venice opera great Ambrose Scarcelli, extolling the emperor. When the lengthy song ended, Andre rose during the applause to address his auspicious guests.

"Camera one, keep Andre in full view. He gets more gorgeous each time I see him!" The voice of WNN producer Roberta Byson carried into the cameraman's headset.

"My loyal friends and relatives, to our father, the dragon, who reigns supreme!" Andre lifted his jewel-studded silver chalice.

"Camera four, get a shot of President Rogel and his wife. They don't look too excited."

"My distinguished guests, we have come together on this glorious evening to celebrate the new age, an age where humanity is free to be itself, no longer enslaved to the false concepts of the past. It is an age that does not look back to yesterday's saviors but to the new messiah, Andre!"

The guests applauded.

"Thank you, loyal subjects. Because a few nations have tried to stand in the way of our new world order, I want us to pause for a moment to honor the many brave soldiers who are showing such valiant courage in the struggle for world harmony."

Andre motioned for General Fontaine to stand up. The dignitaries applauded again.

"With the help of the great Universal Force and General Fontaine and his men, the world is now rendering the worship that is due me—that is, except for one nation, the People's Republic of China. I urge Quay Chin to join in the universal age of harmony and love. Set your people free!"

The guests exploded in rapturous applause. Byson ordered various shots of the assembled leaders, including Vladimir Konstantine, who was clapping politely at the far end of the table.

"Now, my friends, I have an exciting announcement. I have already informed you that the Creative Force will reveal cures for all diseases when the world is completely united under my rule. I am delighted to tell you that my highly esteemed scientists, working night and day under the inspiration of the great dragon, have discovered a cure for the virus that has plagued humanity for well over two decades. We now have a cure for AIDS!"

Andre's guests leaped to their feet, many of them cheering. A few fell to their knees and bowed in the direction of the emperor, who basked in the adulation as he motioned for silence.

"No longer will this horrible scourge devour precious lives. A simple immunization shot is all that will be needed. The vaccine will soon be available to everyone who is registered in the proper manner."

The emperor's dark eyes panned the audience. *The world is mine!* The thrilling thought lingered in his mind like the sweet fragrance of an expensive perfume.

"Our AIDS cure and the upcoming venereal vaccines will allow humanity to throw off the heavy chain of puritanical sexual restrictions, inherited from our misguided forefathers. Men and women will now be completely free to express their sexuality as they see fit, unhindered by false human chains.

"Men may marry other men, if they so wish. The same for women. This freedom will help us solve the growing problem of over-population. Abortions will be available without cost. The elderly and terminally ill who desire to end their lives with dignity will be assisted in doing so."

The monarch then looked tenderly at his mother and father, seated on either side of him. "Dear friends, from now on April 24 will be known as Coronation Day, a glorious annual holiday for the world. It will be celebrated with great joy. We will dispense with such other festivals as Christmas, Easter, Passover, Mohammed's birthday, and Buddha's birthday. We will no longer look backward to history but forward to the future!"

Andre leaned over and kissed Queen Dorothea on the cheek. The charmed guests warmly applauded. Then he straightened up to speak one more time.

"Under the expert guidance of Urbane Basillo, we are now integrating everyone into the new economic order. In time this will bring prosperity to all corners of the globe. Unrestricted trade will shortly begin between all nations as local currencies are replaced by our new Royal Euro. Do not despair. Rejoice!"

Andre triumphantly raised his long, muscular arms high in the air to acknowledge the acclaim of his esteemed guests.

"And now for my final announcement. I have spoken with many of our European royal cousins who are here in Rome for this glorious celebration. Together, we have decided to give the world a marvelous anniversary gift: the nectar of the gods from the finest wineries of Europe. We have decided to remove all import duties on wine and slash prices to virtually nothing. Everyone will be able to enjoy the fruit of the best vineyards in the world!"

Roberta Byson ordered a shot of the entire banquet hall, including the sparkling crystal chandeliers and marble columns, as the guests roared their thunderous approval. "And now, let the festivities begin!"

Eli turned down the sound on the old black and white television set. "Half the world is starving, and our leaders are feasting on the finest delicacies. And now Andre is going to make the world drunk with illicit sex and wine!"

The believers were watching the televised festivities on the patio of a large house in the southern section of Rome, not far from the catacombs. Their Italian hosts, a Christian family, had already been forced to hide in one of the catacombs when UW troops attempted to arrest them. With Eli sat Sarah, Tali, Moshe, Yoseph, Cindy, and the two apostles.

Moshe shook his head. "As if we didn't already have

enough sin in the world!"

"I'm surprised Andre didn't mention you," said Yoseph, tilting his head toward the apostles.

"He didn't want to spoil his party with talk about the 'antichrist and false prophet.' He knows that we're here." Yochanan adjusted his position on the wrought iron chair.

"The Italian people have certainly noticed your presence, especially after you were forced to defend us with fire last week," added Eli, who was leaning over the banister and looking at the city. "I'd say several thousand have heeded your words and turned to the God of Israel."

"That's correct," said Natan-el. "However, it is about time to move on. We have nearly reached the limit of our potential harvest here in Rome."

"What did he mean about doing away with Christmas and other religious holidays?" asked Sarah as she turned her gaze away from the beautiful city.

Natan-el reached for his Bible. "Daniel chapter 7, verse 25, tells us the Antichrist will reign for three and a half years. During that time, he will persecute the saints of God and make alterations in times and laws."

"And, as we heard, he condones sexual abominations," Yochanan added. "He is giving the fallen world what it wants—a religion that glorifies humanity instead of the transcendent God."

Tali looked particularly glum. "I don't like Andre!"

"Cheer up, little one," said Natan-el as he lovingly patted her head. "It says here in verse 26 that his dominion will be taken away, annihilated, and destroyed forever. It won't be long before we reach the very end of this age and the beginning of the true age of peace under our Lord, Yeshua."

Cindy pulled her hair back behind her head. "It seems to me that Andre is returning the world to the pre-Christian religions of Greece and Rome. All those bronzed nude figures of him everywhere. They've even placed one in Saint Peter's church!"

"Yes, Andre embodies a return to the pagan religions of ancient Babylon, Greece, and Rome." Natan-el's mustache moved in rhythm with his beard when he talked. "His empire comes out of those earlier ones, as God revealed to Daniel."

Eli turned up the volume when he noticed that Andre was preparing to speak once again.

"My esteemed guests, we hope that every one of you has thoroughly enjoyed this marvelous feast. Now, my friend and confidant, Urbane Basillo, has an even more wonderful surprise for you."

The secretive master of religious seduction stood on the far side of the banquet hall in front of a scarlet velvet curtain. "Ladies and gentlemen, it is my extreme pleasure to unveil before you tonight this magnificent statue."

Basillo reached over and ceremoniously tugged on a gold cord. The assembled guests gasped. Many fell on their faces. In the Greek tradition, a forty-foot, nude, white marble statue of Andre towered before them.

Pride oozed out of Basillo like blood from a pricked finger. This was a moment of triumph. "Friends, it is right for you to worship before this exquisite image. Now, you must listen—for the statue will speak!"

"What did he say?" Byson asked quickly. "Camera two, zoom in on the statue's face."

"I am the mighty dragon, your savior and god!" The statue's lips moved as the ear-splitting voice echoed across the hall. "You will worship me!"

Chairs fell over as the assembled dignitaries pitched themselves onto the floor. Everyone except President and Mrs. Rogel prostrated themselves before the huge human idol. Fear gripped every soul. Smiling triumphantly, Andre stood up and lifted his hands toward his image.

"Please, turn it off," pleaded Sarah.

"This is only the beginning," warned Yochanan.

Eli frowned. "What do you mean?"

"I recorded this in Revelation 13. The False Prophet will give life to Andre's images around the world and make people everywhere worship before them. The statues being erected all over the globe will be imbued with this satanic force. All who refuse to bow before the beast's image will be put to death."

25

Dragons Collide

The day after his coronation anniversary, Emperor Andre summoned President Rogel to a private, late-night meeting. He was extremely unhappy with reports that the American leader was continuing to resist his authority.

"Vincent, how are things going with preparations for my upcoming visit to your country?" Burton Chiles poured the men some Courvoisseur as they talked.

"Very smoothly, your majesty," Rogel said with slight hesitation. "Your summer tour will be most splendid, I'm sure. My nation is looking forward to your arrival. You can expect huge crowds in every city you visit."

"I should hope so. Vincent, I want to talk straight. I am quite disturbed over reports that my programs are not being taken seriously by many of your people. Urbane tells me resistance is openly tolerated in many parts of America. He also informs me that his economic integration program is several months behind schedule in your country."

Rogel sipped the soothing liqueur and nervously cleared his throat. "Your highness, we are doing the best we can to get everyone plugged into your world system. However, as you know, we've had so many disasters recently. The Midwest drought, combined with the locusts and our bank failures, have left our farms in deep trouble. Our wheat crop has been massively reduced, and the price of flour has skyrocketed."

"I understand your troubles, Vincent. But we cannot effectively help you until our programs are fully in place. Do you understand?"

"I understand, your majesty. However, it is hard to promote emperor worship in the United States. Americans have a strong tradition of religious freedom and a belief in the separation of church and state. We cannot change their habits overnight. We are doing all we can to encourage your programs."

Andre tried to smile through clenched teeth. He did not like this answer. "I am encouraging you, Rogel, to do much better. If you do not, I will be forced to take care of the problem myself!"

The American leader bit his lower lip. He did not like threats.

"Basillo tells me you have not really attempted to make all of your citizens sign up for our worldwide economic network. I also understand that those people you snatched from Palestine—without even informing us—have not yet been registered at all. I want these things taken care of—immediately!"

Rogel winced as Andre's voice reached the shouting stage. "I also want that insulting Christian television network shut down, right away!"

"Your highness, I am doing everything within my power to please you, but do try to understand. We are a proud and independent nation, not used to taking orders. Most of my citizens own private arms, and many will use them to defend their self-perceived rights, which, by the way, do coincide with our written constitution."

"Change your stupid constitution!" The emperor was now sweating profusely. Chiles handed him a handkerchief and tried to get him to sit down. "Let me put it to you straight, Rogel. I no longer need your nuclear shield; the Russian nuclear arsenal is now under my direct control. If you don't straighten up, you could be next in line after China!"

"Your worship, may I get you some water or something?" Chiles was trembling. He did not like to see his sovereign get into this emotional state. No telling what might happen.

Andre took the cue and fell back into his lounge chair. "That's all I have to say to you, Rogel. Think very carefully about your future action."

The European emperor, wearing his tennis outfit, glared at Rogel with the eyes of a cobra. The president knew this snake meant business. He left the room without even saying good-bye.

"Is there anything else, your eminence?"

"Yes!" Andre snapped. "Get Quay on the phone for me and send up Charles."

The foreign secretary returned ten minutes later. As he entered the suite, he pushed his glasses up on his nose and spotted twenty-two-year-old Charles Monet, wearing a beige silk robe, in the emperor's private chamber.

""Your highness, are you in there?" Chiles called weakly from the living room.

"Yes. What is it?"

"The Chinese premier will not speak to you."

"What?!"

Chiles moved closer to the open bedroom door. "He says he will not speak to a gangster who is maliciously threatening his country, and that he is not going to give up his sovereignty nor allow his citizens to bow down before any naked statues."

Andre pounded his fist on the mahogany bedstead. "The decision is final! We attack China in two days!"

The insolent emperor flew secretly to Tokyo to personally oversee the coordinated assault. Operation China Storm would be launched simultaneously on three fronts: in the north, from the Gobi Desert in Mongolia and southeastern Russia; in the west, from Kazakhstan and northern India; and in the south, from Burma and the South China Sea. Air support would come from bases in Russia, Burma, Thailand, South Korea, and Taiwan, as well as from aircraft carriers stationed off China's eastern and southern coasts.

Andre ordered the attack just before dawn on May 12, almost two years to the day after Israel uncorked the nuclear genie over Damascus. News that the last phase of the emperor's war of world conquest had begun sent food prices soaring around the globe. Panic buying was especially pronounced in southeast Asia and Africa.

By the end of the first week of fighting, General Fontaine's forces had penetrated one hundred miles into the southern uplands of the Gobi Desert. Russian troops, supported by UW air cover and artillery, were nearing the northeast city of Harbin. Air force bombers, flying out of South Korea and from aircraft carriers in the Yellow Sea, were striking military and economic targets around the capital of Beijing. Sea-borne jets and long-range bombers stationed on the island of Taiwan pounded the coastal city of Shanghai and surrounding districts. In the south, UW marines were nearing the city of Canton after fighting their way on shore not far from Hong Kong. Warplanes flying from UW carriers in the South China Sea were assisting the advancing marines.

On the eleventh day of China Storm, Fontaine ordered UW marines ashore in Tientsin Province, southeast of Beijing. They would march northwest toward the heavily defended Chinese capital while ground forces from Mongolia moved south around the Great Wall.

With his capital city under threat of imminent invasion, Quay Chin phoned Andre in Tokyo. They spoke in French.

"I will not hesitate to use my ultimate weapons to defend my nation!" Chin warned.

"You do not frighten me, old man. Your time is past. The new world order is here, and China will be a part of it. Surrender now or risk total devastation!"

"I will never surrender to the likes of you! We are still a powerful people. And I have friends overseas who are ready to assist us, if necessary."

"If you're speaking of the Americans, Quay, forget it. Rogel won't lift a finger to help you."

Because of the frightful Asian war, Yochanan and Natan-el found the people of London to be especially open to the gospel message. Thousands came to the Lord as they preached each day near Speaker's Corner in Hyde Park. British police tried once to arrest the two witnesses, but fiery blasts rebuffed them.

One afternoon, the apostles received word that the Queen herself wished to meet with them. She invited the two men to Buckingham Palace. Swiss guards at the gate initially blocked their entrance but gave way when the Queen's personal secretary intervened.

"We're very honored you asked us to speak to you privately." Yochanan bowed his head in respect.

"Thank you for coming here to the palace this evening," she graciously replied. "I have heard many things about your messages in Jerusalem and Rome. I must admit that I have grown quite disenchanted with Andre. Please speak what is on your hearts."

The apostles took turns talking to the British monarch. They spoke about the emperor's true identity and how he would meet his inglorious end. Finally, they answered her questions about the Lord's return.

"I am most impressed," she revealed after Natan-el had finished speaking. "I do believe that Jesus is the way to God and that Andre is a false messiah. However, I cannot say such things openly at this time—and I am the official head of the Church of England."

"If you confess with your mouth that Yeshua is Lord, madam Queen, and believe in your heart that God raised Him from the dead, you shall be saved."

"I do believe. Will you both pray for me?"

Yochanan held one of the Queen's hands while Natan-el grasped the other. England's sovereign wept as the two prophets prayed for her.

Three floors below in the basement, a silent tape player recorded every word. "Wait till Andre hears this!" exclaimed a balding man with stubble on his chin.

"Yeah, the old gal will be history," quipped his secret service companion.

Chinese forces had a difficult time slowing the military juggernaut advancing toward Beijing. Although outnumbered, Andre's troops were better armed, commanded, and trained. Many young Chinese soldiers were secretly sympathetic with the one-world goal and were fighting halfheartedly. They saw an opportunity to throw off the yoke of the elderly Communist clique that had kept China in its backward state for decades. They wanted the progressive lifestyle and, in particular, the free love offered by the powerful European demigod.

Nearing collapse, Quay Chin decided on day thirteen to fire his ultimate weapon. He was confident Andre would want to preserve his troops and would not respond in kind. He was wrong.

Quay's first round of ballistic missiles was launched at 10:14 A.M. on May 25. European satellites immediately detected the firings. Taipei was hit, along with the Indian cities of Bombay, Madras, and Bangalore. The Burmese capital, Rangoon, was leveled, as were the Russian cities of Novosibirsk, Gorki, Vladivostok, and Perm. Military targets were also attacked in various parts of Asia.

Within two minutes, Andre ordered Russian and Ukrainian missiles airborne, aimed at the major Chinese military bases and the cities of Beijing, Wu-han, and Chung Ching.

Fearing a preemptive atomic strike on American targets, Rogel quickly ordered nuclear-tipped cruise missiles to be shot toward several of the emperor's ships in the Pacific and Indian oceans. The president was making a show of force in the face of Andre's threats to destroy American cities if he so much as lifted a finger to help China. Although realizing he was taking a deadly gamble by targeting the ships, he wanted Andre to understand that he was prepared to immediately launch nuclear missiles toward Europe if there was any sign of a preemptive strike on America. U.S. firepower wiped out over a half dozen UW vessels, including a French aircraft carrier. Ten minutes later Andre responded in kind. United World missiles annihilated fourteen U.S. ships, including two giant aircraft carriers. Dozens of Chinese vessels were also destroyed. The oceanic nuclear explosions killed thousands of sailors, along with millions of fish, leaving bright red pools of blood and radiation in their wake.

The news of atomic exchanges propelled the world into a state of mass shock. Panic-stricken people throughout

Japan and the Koreas retreated to underground bomb shelters to avoid the fallout. President Rogel ordered Americans into their shelters, as did the leaders of Canada and Mexico. The emperor ordered precautionary measures in Europe.

Seething with anger over Rogel's naval strike, Andre toyed with the idea of obliterating several American cities, but his top advisors convinced him the president would probably destroy Europe if he did. Attempting to hide his fierce disdain, he telephoned Rogel and asked for a truce, vowing he would not launch any further missiles against U.S. ships or North American targets. Rogel curtly agreed to a cease-fire.

Sheltered in a deep underground bunker outside Beijing, Premier Quay decided that another nuclear strike would be pointless, since a substantial portion of his nation had already been decimated. He placed an immediate satellite telephone call to Andre offering China's unconditional surrender. World War III, which began near Moscow in January, officially ended with the destruction of Beijing in May.

The intense Asian war unleashed unprecedented destruction on a third of the world. In less than two weeks, sixty million civilians and soldiers had been wiped off the face of planet earth—a greater number than in all of World War II. Several of the earth's largest cities lay in utter ruin. Radiation poisoned rivers and lakes throughout Asia. Fires ravaged forests everywhere. Clouds of smoke and radioactive dust rose into the earth's atmosphere, ultimately reducing the sun and moonlight in the northern hemisphere by a third for several months and making it impossible to see all but the brightest stars.

The nuclear blasts over Vladivostok and Taipei triggered a powerful earthquake near Tokyo. The rolling seismic disturbance shook the city only two hours after Beijing was leveled by the bomb. Buildings swayed and collapsed into rubble during the quake that measured 8.2 on the Richter scale. Highways buckled and apartment buildings crumbled. Over one million people were killed in the devastating earthquake while millions more were seriously injured.

Although knocked to the floor in his heavily reinforced underground government shelter, the virile emperor was not injured. Three hours after the quake and five hours after the disastrous nuclear exchange, his image was transmitted by satellite to every part of the globe.

"Citizens of our common planet Earth, it is an extremely sad day for us all. Millions of innocent civilians have been killed throughout Asia due to the madness of a rebellious Chinese leader. He has now surrendered to our United World forces.

"However, despite this tragedy, there is a new dawn on the immediate horizon. The rebel nation, China, was the last great obstacle on the road to world unity. We now expect North Korea to surrender peacefully. Like Alexander the Great, your exalted emperor has brought order out of chaos. We shall now begin to rebuild our bleeding planet and put war aside forever. Citizens of the world, the new age has now begun!"

26

In God We Trust

As a result of the devastating Asian war, Yochanan and Natan-el received new travel instructions. The apostles had already appeared in Rome, London, Paris, and Madrid; now the Holy Spirit was directing them to China, where a large spiritual harvest was expected.

With the ability to speak local dialects, Yochanan and Natan-el spent two months preachingin those areas not totally destroyed by the war. Several million people surrendered their lives to Israel's Messiah. The word of life, accompanied by testifying signs, brought a bright beam of hope to the death-soaked land, where millions were already showing symptoms of radiation poisoning or dying from starvation and disease.

After traveling through most of China, the two witnesses decided to visit the three cities destroyed by nuclear blasts. Only Eli, Moshe, and several other sealed Israeli males were permitted to accompany them. Sarah, Tali, the

Steinbergs, and the others stayed behind in a safe, remote section in western China with a large Christian community and no UW forces.

In an instant, the Jewish evangelists were transported by the Lord to a dirt road on the outskirts of Beijing. They proceeded by foot toward the center of the decimated Chinese capital, sharing the gospel with each person they met.

The disciples' hearts grew heavy as they proceeded through the hellish inferno. The results of the nuclear catastrophe were beyond imagination. Only Yochanan was not completely numb. He had seen nuclear devastation before, in his endtime vision on Patmos. Vultures circled overhead, waiting to enjoy the feast of human carcasses that littered the streets. Piles of gray stone and rubble covered the charred ground. Glassy-eyed Chinese survivors milled around in a daze, haunted by the ghosts of a life that would never again be. Naked children huddled together for protection against the weather.

After five days of sharing the gospel and healing many sick and dying, the disciples were transported south to the outskirts of Chung Ching, another city annihilated by Andre's nuclear warheads. Then they proceeded to Wuhan, laying hands on thousands and healing them of radiation poisoning. They also provided food for the hungry, much like the loaves and fishes of old.

When the evangelists reunited with the brethren, they described the total devastation they had witnessed. They also related the thousands of conversions. Then Yochanan announced it was time to move on.

"But the needs are still so great here!" Sarah protested, her heart speaking while her mind was telling her to keep quiet. "Forgive me, Yochanan. I know our steps are completely guided by the Lord."

"Don't apologize. The wounds here are deep and the potential harvest great. But rest assured, more Chinese will come to saving faith through the testimony of their countrymen. Healings will also continue."

Yochanan rubbed the back of his hand over one eye, wiping away a small tear. "It won't be long before the False Prophet sets up Andre's images all over this vast nation. Some of these dear ones will fall away, but most will enter the Lord's eternal peace, having washed their robes in the blood of the Lamb."

The believers sat in silence for several seconds before Tali asked, "Where are we going next?"

"In a few months, little one, we will visit India. But before that, we are heading to the Americas."

"Mom, did you hear that? We'll get to see Benny!"

"Yes, sweetheart, by the grace of God."

"Thanks for the juice, Sam. It really hits the spot. This July is a scorcher."

"My pleasure, Mr. President."

"I guess I'm still a bit jet-lagged."

The Secret Service chief faked a look of concern. "You do look slightly under the weather, sir."

"That's what Patricia said this morning. She isn't feeling well herself. The Queen's funeral was an emotional drain for us both. Her death was so unexpected."

The president took a big swig of juice before changing the subject. "Sam, I've checked over the report you sent me, and it looks good.

"I don't want any disturbances while the emperor's here. People are already complaining about the announced curfews. How many dissidents have you rounded up?" Rogel wiped his brow with a handkerchief. *My, it's hot in here.*

"Tens of thousands, sir," Sam Peal answered with pride. "I think we can expect the crowds to be well behaved. The National Guard will help. We've also contacted local Android gang leaders, and they've pledged to cooperate with our men."

Rogel took another sip of juice. Andre's first scheduled stop was Washington. Rogel wished he were not coming.

The following day, the emperor's two mortal enemies appeared on the Capitol Mall.

"Repent, for the kingdom of God is at hand!" the powerful voice cried. "Every valley will be lifted up and every hill made low. The day of the Lord is near; it will come as judgment from the Almighty!"

"Oh, my God!" Sam Peal had been summoned to the Mall by his top aide. He quickly darted to his official car. "Get me to the White House—fast!"

After entering the president's official residence, Peal learned that Rogel was not in his office.

"The president is feeling ill this afternoon. He is resting upstairs," Rogel's personal secretary informed him. "He thinks it might be something he ate for lunch."

Sooner than I expected, Peal thought as he replied, "It is extremely important that I speak with him. Can I go up?"

"I suppose so, seeing that it's you. I'll let him know you're coming."

Peal straightened his narrow tie while walking upstairs to Rogel's private quarters. Once again, he had to play the part of a devoted colleague.

"Yes, come in. Hello, Sam."

"Thank you, Mr. President. I'm sorry you're not feeling well this afternoon."

"I'll be alright," sighed the American leader, sweating

noticeably in his tailored pajamas. "Must be the lasagna I had for lunch. I just hope it's not the flu."

The flu of fools, thought Peal. "Sir, I have some bad news. Those two troublemakers and their motley crew from Jerusalem have somehow sneaked into the United States. They're speaking right now in front of the Capitol."

"At the Mall? I thought you had their pictures posted at all the entrance points?"

"We did, sir. I can't explain it. Do you want me to have them arrested?"

"No, I don't think so. It might cause problems."

"What else can we do? We can't let them continue, not with the emperor arriving in just five days!"

"I have another idea. See if you can get them to come to talk with me. They met once with Yacov Nimrod in Jerusalem, while under arrest. I hope we can avoid that. Maybe I can persuade them to leave the city. I'll get dressed and wait for them in my office." The president winced in pain as he pulled back the bed covers.

He has less time than I thought. "I'll have my men get on it right away, Mr. President."

The day was a scorcher, but the emperor did not notice from his air-conditioned box at the bullfighting arena near Barcelona, Spain.

"Your grace, Burton Chiles is calling from Rome."

"Pardon me for disturbing you, sir, but WNN has just reported that those two slimy Jews from Jerusalem and their followers are in Washington."

"What?!" Andre clutched the phone as if it was his prisoner. "We have everything perfectly timed. I cannot delay my arrival. Phone Peal and see to it that he gets rid of them—today!"

"Your majesty," Chiles timidly ventured his next sentence, "disposing of them will not be so easy. We may have to alter your travel arrangements."

Andre bolted up from his cushioned seat, causing his loyal subjects throughout the arena to scramble to their feet in observance of proper protocol. "I will not be humiliated! Make sure Peal moves them out, or he will face my wrath!"

"Yes, your eminence, I shall see to it immediately."

The forty-nine-year-old president could not stand up to greet his guests in the Oval Office.

"Welcome, gentlemen. Please sit down."

"Thank you, Mr. President." Yochanan placed his Bible on a table next to the leather chair.

"Would you like something to drink?"

"No, thank you," responded Natan-el.

"Gentlemen, let me be candid. We were surprised to learn that you had entered our country. How did you get past our customs agents?"

"We flew directly to your lovely Capitol Mall," quipped Yochanan almost in a tease.

"You did what?"

Natan-el shifted forward in his chair. "Do you remember the story of Philip the evangelist in the Book of Acts, Mr. President? He was transferred supernaturally after sharing the gospel with the Ethiopian eunuch."

"Yes. You mean to say that you came here the same way?"

Yochanan took over. "Indeed. That's also how we got to China so quickly from Madrid."

"Ah, I heard them talk about that on EBN. In fact, I've seen quite a few reports about you from that Ken Pres—" Rogel's deep cough filled the last syllable. He reached for a glass of water on his desk. "Excuse me, that Ken Preston fellow."

"If you have seen his reports, then you must know what our message is."

"I believe I do." Rogel's cough was becoming relentless. Why wasn't the medicine working?

Yochanan stood up and walked over to the president's desk. "Sir, you are a very sick man. In fact, you are dying. Without God's intervention, you will be dead within twenty-four hours."

Rogel's bloodshot eyes darted back and forth between the two witnesses.

"You've been deliberately infected with a man-made virus that kills within seventy-two hours. It was concocted by scientists working for Andre."

Rogel blew his nose. "How do you know that?"

"The Lord revealed it to us. The same poison was used to murder the Queen of England."

"Murder?" Rogel collapsed in his chair. Could this be true? "You mean she did not die of a heart attack following pneumonia?"

"She did, sir. But her illness and heart attack were caused by the poison. You were given the same virus by the man who told you about us, the head of your Secret Service. It was concealed in tomato juice."

"Oh, no! My God, what can I do?"

"You are addressing the right one, Mr. President—God. Only He can save you. And in His mercy, and in answer to many, many prayers for you, He will do so now."

Yochanan followed the perimeter of the large desk and placed his hands on Rogel's burning forehead. "In the name of Yeshua of Nazareth, the Lord of all creation, I cancel the effects of this virus. You are healed."

Immediately the president's body was free of fever and muscular pains. He felt completely normal.

"I don't know what to—how did you do that?"

"I didn't. It was the Lord."

"How can I thank you?"

"All thanks and praise belong to the God of Israel. We are simply His servants. But He would love to receive your thanks and in return bestow on you eternal life."

"I'm ready. What should I do?"

"Just pray with us, and God will do the rest."

"God knows your heart, Mr. President," responded Natan-el after they had prayed. "He will guide you. The birth pangs of the Lord's kingdom are coming closer together, as the day of His return draws near. Whatever occurs, He will never leave you or forsake you."

Yochanan placed his weathered hands on Rogel's shoulders. "You have many enemies, sir. But you now have the best friend anyone could ever have. Do not fear. Simply trust, and Yeshua will see you through."

Vice President Weston leaned back in his leather chair as he practiced his speech. "My fellow Americans, it is an extremely sad day for us all."

"No, Frank, that's not good enough. You've got to try and *sound* sad." Sam Peal stared out the plate glass window behind Weston's chair into the White House garden. Yellow roses and mid-summer tulips lined the red brick path.

"My fellow Americans, it is an extreme—" Weston's phone abruptly interrupted his second attempt.

"How can I rehearse? I thought Cathy understood that I didn't want to be disturbed!"

"Maybe it's the call we've been waiting for." Peal's face registered unfeeling malevolence.

"Perhaps it is. Yes, Cathy? The president?" The Secret Service chief's expression ripened into merciless glee.

"—is dead!" whispered Peal with delight.

"Of course I'll take it."

Peal let out a nervous laugh. "I bet Rogel wants to read you his will while he still has breath!"

"Good afternoon, Vince. Are you feeling better?"

"Yes. Much better, Frank, thank you."

"Really? Your doctor informed me that you were quite ill." The vice president could feel the lump in his throat as he switched on the speaker phone so Peal could hear the whole conversation.

"I was, Frank. But I feel like a million bucks now, maybe I should say a hundred million, with the sharp drop in the value of our currency." Rogel leaned back and propped his feet up on his desk. He was enjoying himself.

"Great! What a relief!"

"I understand Sam Peal is there with you?"

The Secret Service chief, shocked that Rogel was still alive, stiffened at the mention of his name.

"He is, Vince. Do you want to speak with him?"

"No. Just tell him I've found a solution regarding the two elderly gentlemen from Jerusalem."

"Yes. Sam told me that they'd gotten through our border nets. May I ask what the solution is?"

"I met with them here in my office and convinced them to leave Washington. They've promised to stay away from Andre during his upcoming tour. I think everything will work out fine now."

"But Vince, they're a menace. The emperor is sure to be angry if we let them remain anywhere in our country during his visit."

"He'll have to be angry. I'm still the elected leader of

the United States, not him."

"Elected only as vice president, remember."

"The same as you, Frank. At least I was voted in by the people, not just the Congress. And I intend to remain the president. Pass that information on to Sam, will you?"

"Uh, I will, Vince. Glad to hear you're better." Weston's face soured as the words turned bitter in his mouth.

The conspirators stared at each other in numbed silence. Finally, Peal spoke. "He should have been dead by now. Do you think he somehow knows about our plot?"

"How could he unless one of us told him? Sam, something has obviously gone wrong. Andre is going to be furious!"

The emperor's reaction to the botched assassination frightened even Chiles. His foreign minister reassured him it would only be a matter of time before Rogel was six feet under.

On August 8, Andre's royal jet landed at Washington's National Airport. As the plane touched down, the demigod was pleased to spot a long green tarp covering the Washington Monument. The unveiling of his surprise would be sheer scurrilous pleasure.

President Rogel and Vice President Weston officially greeted Andre and his entourage at the airport, with the latter falling to his knees before him. Then the leaders made their way to the White House.

Rogel politely opened his Oval Office door for the emperor. "Please be seated, your majesty."

"In a regular chair?" The incensed world monarch bristled at the thought.

The president caught the hint. "Please be seated in my chair, your highness," he offered, bowing his head in respect.

Andre's face beamed with delight as he sat down. *I am now truly the supreme ruler of planet Earth! No one can resist my will. At last, I have reached my destiny.*

Andre got right to his point. "I hope I have been misinformed, Vincent, that you have allowed those two old Jews to stay in your country during my visit."

"I really had no choice, your majesty. These men have some sort of supernatural power." The president looked at Urbane Basillo as he spoke. "Haven't you had problems yourselves restraining them?"

The fat pockets in the Italian's jaw became rigid with anger, but he kept silent.

"Anyway, your majesty, they've promised to stay well out of your way."

"They'd better!" Andre snapped back, incensed once again that the deadly virus had somehow failed. "I suppose I will just have to deal with them myself!"

27

Tour America

It was over ninety degrees when Yochanan and Natanel began to prophesy in Manhattan's Central Park. A crowd of nearly ten thousand people had gathered to listen. Several hundred sealed Jewish males from the New York area were there as well. Reporters from the major American television and radio networks, along with print journalists, recorded every word.

"Do you see those great, tall buildings behind me?" Yochanan thundered. "Not one stone shall be left upon another which will not be torn down. Repent, for the day of the Lord is at hand! Though your sins are as scarlet, they will be white as snow! 'I, even I, am the one who wipes out your transgressions for My own sake,' says the Lord, 'and I will remember your sins no more!' If we say that we have no sin, we are deceiving ourselves, and the truth is not in us. If we confess our sins, He is faithful and just to forgive us our sins and to cleanse us from all unrighteousness. 'I am the way, the truth, and the life; no one comes to the Father but by Me.' "

Sweating television cameramen strained to get better shots of the two apostles as Natan-el took up the discourse. "Fear God, and give Him glory, because the hour of His judgment has come. Who is the liar but the one who denies that Jesus is the Messiah? This is the Antichrist, the one who denies the Father and the Son. Do not worship the beast or his image, or take his mark on your hand or forehead. Fallen, fallen is Babylon the great!"

After the witnesses had finished, the believers led many to the Lord, but most in the dispersing crowd seemed indifferent or even hostile toward the apostle's message.

Reporters nudged their way up to the two witnesses and began firing questions. Ken Preston decided to stand back and let his secular colleagues have their day.

"Bob Wortan from the *New York Times*. What is all this business about impending judgment and doom? It seems that with the fall of communism in China, an era of world peace is beginning, as Andre claims."

Yochanan moved closer to the jostling journalists. "It may seem that way to you, but it is not the truth. Andre is the last in a series of satanic demagogues who claim to bring peace by means of war and oppression. He will fail, as have those before him. The source of his power is not God, but Satan, the father of lies."

Wortan laughed. "So the world is going to the devil?"

"No, young man. The earth is the Lord's. The devil is going to the pit, while the world will be made new by the true Savior of humanity, Yeshua the Messiah."

"So, then, we should run and hide?" Denise Penell of ABC News wore an exaggerated smirk on her face.

"The entire world will soon be judged. Only those who know the Lord, and are known to Him, will live in the coming kingdom of God. All others will be cast out of His presence forever."

Penell shook her head in disdain. Natan-el took up the response. "The God of Israel is mindful of the good deeds that have come out of the United States over the years, especially support for the spread of the gospel and the concern for His ancient Jewish people. In judgment, He will take these things into account. But God also sees the moral filth and rampant materialism in this nation. He will bring an end to those who destroy the earth."

"Duncan Bond from the *Chicago Tribune.* Can one of you explain these spectacular fire stunts we've seen on television?"

Yochanan replied, "We've been empowered by God to warn the world that Andre is Satan's son. We have also come to deliver a message of hope and salvation in Yeshua the Messiah. God has entrusted us with this supernatural fire to demonstrate His power. It is also a means of protection as we deliver His word."

"Why should we believe your message over Basillo's? He can do the same thing!"

"We speak the truth. He speaks lies."

"That's pretty subjective, isn't it?" Penell asked.

"Our message is verified by God's holy Word, recorded for many centuries in the Bible."

"Sir, Carol Mason from NBC. What about the reports that you are actually John the apostle, or maybe John the Baptist, and your companion an ancient disciple of Jesus named Nathaniel? Doesn't that make you both a little old?" Chuckles rippled through the crowd.

"It is not so important who we are, but what we say. If our words are those of the God of Israel, then woe to any who fail to heed them. Blessed is the nation whose God is the Lord!"

Suddenly, Denise Penell directed her cameraman to swing around. "Here come the Androids!"

A large group of young males were marching up a wide tree-lined path carrying nude statuettes of the emperor and toting banners reading "Death to the Rebels," "Kill the Jewish Pigs," and "Sex, Love, Power." The gang members began chanting, "Kill—the—rebels" when they spotted Yochanan and Natan-el.

One of the leaders, wearing tight leather pants and a red tank top with Andre's picture emblazoned on the front, stepped forward. "You swine, get your Jewish carcasses out of our city. This is our territory, not yours!"

Hundreds in the nearby crowd roared their approval, but others remained silent, especially Jews. Several dozen sealed believers, including Moshe and Eli, moved closer to the apostles, along with the disciples from Jerusalem.

The reporters quickly moved away as gang members began to encircle the Lord's people. Some brandished long metal chains. Soon, the nearly two hundred Androids had surrounded Yochanan and his companions.

Apparently on cue, six muscular fascist thugs pulled homemade firebombs from brown paper bags and hurled them toward the believers. Simultaneously ten hand grenades were tossed at the corralled group.

Tali clutched her mother's waist and screamed as the bombs detonated. The explosions reverberated throughout the park. Flaming metal shards flew everywhere, but nothing touched the believers. It was as if an invisible shield had been erected around them.

Both Yochanan and Natan-el extended their arms toward the hazy New York sky. The surrounding believers instantly dropped to the grass as bellows of fire blazed toward the screeching thugs, incinerating most of them. Those who were left shrieked as they fled into the protection of the park's shrubs.

Yochanan's mighty voice thundered a prophecy found in Isaiah 24. "Behold, the Lord lays the earth waste, devastates it, distorts its surface, and scatters its inhabitants. The earth is also polluted by its inhabitants, for they transgressed laws, violated statutes, broke the everlasting covenant. Therefore, a curse devours the earth, and those who live in it are held guilty. Therefore, the inhabitants of the earth are burned, and few men are left.

"Fallen, fallen is Babylon the great—"

"Hello, your exalted majesty. This is Samuel Peal."

"Yes, Peal. Is everything ready for tonight?"

"Yes, your majesty. Three of my best marksmen will be waiting in strategic locations. Rogel doesn't have a chance."

"Splendid." Andre clenched his fist and admired his bulging biceps. "Remember, the shooting must commence after I exit the platform. I don't want anything to detract from my performance."

"We will obey your instructions to the letter, your highness." The chief pursed his lips before relaying the next bit of information. "I'm afraid that I have some bad news, your kingship. The attempt our agents made to kill those two Jews and their associates in New York has failed." Peal's body tensed as he waited for the explosion.

"Yes, I know. I was watching WNN," the emperor said calmly.

Peal was taken aback. "Your majesty, if you will permit me to speak frankly, I have an observation."

"I am listening."

"Well, your eminence, I'm no theological expert, but I've risen to the highest rank in my secret order." Peal's voice trembled but he held on. "Forgive me for saying so, but isn't it written in the Christian Bible that these two Jews will remain alive for three and a half years and then be killed by you in Jerusalem? If so, why bother to try and get rid of them now?"

Andre snarled like a rabid dog. "What is written in that dreadful book is not irreversible! I rule the world! I will prevail over those Jewish swine and their crucified master! I will prevail!"

Peal trembled down to his toes. "Yes, of course, your majesty. I'm sorry, I didn't mean to—"

"Do what you are told, Peal, and don't insult me again!"

Sarah stared blankly at her melting ice cream. She was weighed down with worry. She knew Stacy was in serious trouble. Why else would she fail to show up for their dinner reunion?

Cindy squeezed Sarah's arm. "Are you alright?"

"No, not really. I'm sure something dreadful has happened to Stace, just like I felt the night Jonathan was killed. I just know it."

"New York is a big city," submitted Craig, "and we picked this restaurant deliberately because it's small and out of the way. Maybe she just got lost?"

"Craig, she knows Manhattan like the back of her hand," Sarah pushed the ice cream away, "just like you do, Yoseph. When I spoke to her on the phone today she knew exactly how to get here. I've called twice already, and nobody is answering, not even her father. Something is terribly wrong."

Cindy knew intuitively that Sarah was right. "Stacy told me that she doesn't go out much these days. She doesn't have Andre's mark, and she said the police are cracking down on anyone not registered in the system."

"We have you to protect us," Sarah looked appreciatively at Eli and Moshe, "but Stace is all alone."

Craig pulled out his pocket Bible and opened it. "Didn't Yochanan say that some of the 144,000 sealed

Jews will protect and minister to the Jewish woman mentioned in Revelation 12, who fled into the wilderness? Stacy was part of that evacuation."

"But Stacy chose to live here in New York with her father, not in rural communities like most of the evacuated believers," Eli responded.

Sarah sighed. "Can we stay here a little longer? It'd be too dangerous to try to go to her apartment. Maybe she'll still make it."

"Sure," replied Yoseph. "We'll stay. Anyway it's still early, and this is the first restaurant meal most of us have had in over two years. Let's order coffee."

Sarah did not sleep very well in the stuffy church basement where she and the other Jerusalem disciples were spending the night. Just before dawn, she noticed a light coming from the small classroom where Yochanan was sleeping. She gently knocked. The apostle, kneeling beside his cot in prayer, told her to come in.

"I'm sorry to disturb you, Yochanan. I couldn't sleep, and I noticed your light on. I thought I might ask you—"

"About your friend Stacy," interrupted Yochanan. "In fact, I've just been shown something about her in a vision."

"Is it good news?"

"Blessed Sarah," he said tenderly while reaching out for her warm hands. "It's good news for our sister but difficult news for us. I saw her dressed in a pure white garment, standing humbly before the throne of God. She will serve the Lord there day and night from now on."

Tears rolled down both of the Israelis' cheeks. The apostle wiped away Sarah's tears with his thumbs. "I saw something else, dear one. Her earthly father is with her before the heavenly Father's throne."

"Praise the Lord!" Sarah blew her nose. "Did the Lord show you how it all happened?"

"Yes. Some Androids—that group who attacked us in the park—went to her apartment last night. They forced Stacy and her father to a local church, now a center of Andre worship. There, they ordered the two of them to bow down before the Antichrist's image or be killed."

Yochanan paused. "Your friend was ordered to bow down first. She refused, saying that she trusted Yeshua as her Lord, not Andre. At that moment her face shone like the face of an angel, and she cried out, 'Lord Yeshua, receive my spirit!' Instantly, fire bolted from the idol's mouth and killed her. Her father was likewise murdered. Sweet Sarah, they are both now in Yeshua's presence forever."

The apostle sat back on his cot and leaned against the concrete wall. "When you knocked on my door, I was thinking about my brother's death. Yacov was the first apostle to be martyred for his faith—by King Herod Agrippa. The Roman soldiers rammed a sword through his stomach. An eyewitness later told me that he cried out the same words Yeshua did when He was crucified, 'Father, forgive them, for they do not know what they are doing.'"

"It must have been very difficult for you."

"Death is never easy, even when we know that our loved ones have gone to be with the Lord. These are difficult days for us all, but we will get through them. As the prophet Isaiah wrote, the Lord is exalted, and He shall be the stability of our times."

President and Mrs. Rogel arrived on Capitol Hill as the U.S. Army Band struck up "Hail to the Chief." Over one hundred thousand Americans packed the area west of the Capitol stretching out along the Mall well past the Washington Monument. Warm August breezes blew over the Mall as the sun set in the west.

The celebration to welcome the emperor began with a colorful fireworks display over the Mall. At 9:00 P.M. sharp, the president introduced Andre. The pompous European dictator stepped up to the podium and basked in the rapturous cheers of the surging crowd.

"May the exalted Creative Force, the dragon, bless you!" his voice echoed as the cheering began to subside.

"Citizens of America, I am honored to be in your great country, so long a beacon of freedom in the world. Working in partnership with me, the United States will continue to be a great nation. Soon, American soldiers will begin serving with our United World forces. Together, we shall spread the light of western civilization to every corner of the globe. We shall remake Russia and China into free, enlightened nations, enjoying the fruits of economic prosperity and peace. We shall liberate countries dominated by outdated religious codes. With your support, we shall accomplish our goals."

The audience erupted in enthusiastic applause. The emperor knew he had the crowd exactly where he wanted them. This was going to be easier than he had expected.

"My precious American children, I have a present for you on this glorious evening.

"Rejoice with your exalted emperor!

"Gentlemen, the lights!"

Suddenly, a mass of floodlights lit up the green tarp that had been concealing the giant Washington Monument for more than half a year. At Andre's command, the covering dropped to reveal a five-hundred-sixty-foot nude statue of the emperor. The bronze image had been constructed over the stone monument behind a solid wall of scaffolding, and it faced east toward Capitol Hill.

Andre smiled defiantly at Rogel. His naked profile would now be the tallest structure in Washington and would be visible from the White House Oval Office.

"And now, citizens of the world, it is time for my image to speak!"

Urbane Basillo strutted up to the podium and bowed low before his master. He leaned into the microphone. "Mighty dragon, manifest yourself through our emperor's powerful image," he bellowed.

A deep, reverberating sound rolled out of the statue's moving lips. "I am the god of all creation! Bow down and worship before me!"

Like well-trained Hitlerian youth, everyone fell prostrate to the ground. "Worship the dragon through me!" the emperor shouted through the microphone as he watched the crowd grovel before the blasphemous idol.

Only the president and his wife Patricia remained in their chairs. "Rogel will not spoil this moment!" he spit at Basillo. The spirit of death clung to each word.

Sam Peal was waiting near the northwest corner of the Capitol building. "Everything is set," he reported when Basillo approached him. "It'll be easier than killing Kennedy."

"I'll be in my limo. Don't screw this up!"

As they spoke, three highly trained marksmen aimed their high-powered rifles from their hidden positions. The president would not have a chance. However, before they could shoot, Rogel suddenly collapsed in his chair.

The first lady grabbed him. "Vince! What's wrong?"

"I feel like I'm going to throw up. Help me get off the platform, right now!"

Assisted by Patricia, a pale and doubled-over Rogel weakly struggled to reach the stairs leading down from the platform. A murmur passed through the front of the crowd. Peal gasped in horror as the sick man hobbled down the platform steps. He then ran to his nearby Cadillac, pulled a revolver out of the glove box, and shot himself squarely in the mouth.

28

Fiery Trials

A recovered Vincent Rogel turned up the volume on his Oval Office television set by remote control. He was in a meeting with Secretary of State Clayton when informed that a potentially damaging report about him would soon air on the WNN evening news.

"In other developments, the two Israeli rebels who have caused unrest in various parts of the globe showed up in Chicago today after spending two days in New York. The leading rebel, who goes by the name of Yochanan, brutally murdered a government agent outside City Hall. The incident occurred soon after the elderly Jew used his apparent magical powers to turn the Chicago River into blood, which also polluted a portion of Lake Michigan. The Israeli claimed his action was a warning of impending judgment on America. City officials said that liquid samples taken from the river showed that it had indeed been turned into blood."

The WNN anchorman paused as a video of angry Chicago residents standing near the river, shouting and shaking their fists at the apostles, was screened.

"Minutes later, government agent Patrick O'Brian was murdered when federal agents ordered the two Israelis and their accomplices to leave the area. When the forty-four-year-old agent pointed his pistol at the rebels, fire proceeded out of Yochanan's mouth, instantly killing O'Brian. The other agents then retreated to the nearby federal building.

"Mayor Rodney Blake condemned the brutal murder and the earlier pollution of the local river, as did state and federal officials and several church leaders. Vice President Frank Weston pledged that attempts will be made to arrest the two Israelis, despite their apparent ability to use deadly supernatural power to defend themselves."

Rogel sighed as the anchorman continued: "In other news, White House doctors report that President Rogel has made a full recovery from the illness that struck him during welcoming ceremonies for the emperor near the Capitol building two nights ago. He is now fully fit to work.

"Meanwhile, senior administration sources have told WNN that President Rogel is secretly working to harm the interests of his majesty, Emperor Andre. We have this exclusive, live report from John Thorton at the White House. John?"

"Thad, high ranking sources close to President Rogel have told WNN that the president is secretly working to slow down the completion of the emperor's 'Black Dragon' national registration program, in which all Americans are being assigned a number to prepare for the introduction here of the Royal Euro currency. According to current government plans, U.S. citizens should begin to trade in their dollars for Royal Euros next month. However, our sources say the worldwide program may be delayed in the United States due to unwarranted meddling by the president."

"John, these are pretty serious charges against the president. Can you tell us exactly who in the administration is making them?"

"My sources wish to remain anonymous at this time, but they are very senior officials. On top of this, Thad, they maintain that President Rogel is blocking emperor worship in America. They say the president, along with the first lady, may actually be secret fundamentalist Christians. Emperor Andre may very well return to Washington at the end of his tour to confront Rogel with these accusations."

A disgruntled Clayton walked over to the set and turned down the volume. "That report certainly won't do you any good, Vince."

"Who do you think Thorton's senior sources are?"

"I don't know," the secretary of state replied as he sat back down in front of Rogel's desk.

"It wouldn't be Weston, would it? He and Peal were in cahoots, and now Peal is dead. You're close to him these days. What do you think?"

"Mr. President, I've known Frank for over twenty-two years, and I don't believe he would leak such allegations to WNN against your best interests."

"I suppose you're right." Rogel did not believe a word of it. He knew Weston and Clayton were the leaky faucets.

"Vince, have you become one of those born-again, fundamentalist Christians?" Even Clayton was hoping this had not happened.

"I don't exactly know how to label myself, Hugh. I do have a personal faith in Jesus, and I do have grave doubts about Andre.

"Let's face it, he is demanding we surrender our sovereignty and let him rule America! I've been sworn to uphold the Constitution, not to step aside in favor of a foreign ruler."

"But he's extremely popular here, Vince. The latest poll shows that 84 percent already view him as the supreme ruler of the world, and that includes America."

"But I've been told by the FBI that resistance remains strong, especially in rural areas of the South, Midwest, and Rocky Mountain states. We'd have to put to death millions of our citizens if we actually carried out his correction program. I will not do that!"

The secretary of state nervously fingered his pen, wondering how long it would be until Rogel found out that many thousands had already been killed secretly in the twelve government detention centers since the emperor landed in America. Clayton carried on with his charade. "Vince, don't forget what happened to Cliff in Geneva. You can't resist him; he's too powerful."

"I must stand firm in my beliefs and uphold the integrity of this office. I couldn't live with myself if I did anything less."

Then, sucker, you won't live at all, Clayton thought as he snuffed out his cigarette and stood up to leave.

Sarah's anticipation grew as the van turned onto Chicago's Edens Expressway. She and Tali would soon be at the Goldman family home in Skokie, just north of the city limits. Eli was driving the borrowed van. Craig was sitting in the front passenger seat.

"Turn off the freeway at the next exit. It's just two blocks from there," instructed Sarah as she leaned forward from the backseat. "How do I look; is my hair okay?"

"As beautiful as ever," replied Eli, glancing in the rearview mirror.

The passengers traveled in silence until Tali spotted her grandparents' house. "Uncle Eli, there it is!"

"You remembered, pumpkin," exclaimed her surprised mother. "You were only here once before, and that was four years ago."

Sarah had not phoned to say they were coming, fearing that the line might be tapped. She figured that her in-laws had probably seen the news reports about the two witnesses in downtown Chicago and realized that she and Tali were in the area.

Tali straightened up her summer dress as her mother rang the front doorbell. Abe Goldman answered.

"Shalom, Dad!"

"Hi, Grandpa!"

Abe Goldman let out a whistle. "Sarah! Tali! Oh God, thank you. You've made an old man glad!"

Six-year-old Benny raced to the door just as his mother and sister were entering. "Mom! Tali!" he cried as he jumped into Sarah's open arms, nearly tearing them from their sockets.

Eli and Craig, who stood at the door, greeted Abe Goldman, who they both knew from his previous visits with his wife to Jerusalem. Benny darted over to them as Sarah warmly embraced her mother-in-law.

"You've grown so much, Benny." Tali's heart was filled with joy. "Grandma has really been feeding you."

"He isn't hard to please," Rebecca Goldman added with a chuckle, wiping one hand on her blue cotton apron. "My, Tali, you have grown so!"

"We sort of expected you might show up." Abe motioned everyone into the living room. "We spotted you on the local news, so we knew you were in Chicago. The report was not very positive about your group."

"That's an understatement," Rebecca added. "They made you sound like murderers!"

Eli smiled broadly. "We're not very popular these days, but we're not murderers, Mrs. Goldman. The message that Yochanan and Natan-el bring is one of everlasting life and peace. That fire is only directed against those who threaten our lives."

Grandpa Goldman pulled Tali onto his lap and squeezed her. "You really do have your father's eyes, young lady." Then he turned to face his daughter-in law. "How long can you folks resist the emperor and get away with it?"

"We have to speak the truth, Dad, whatever the cost. The Lord will take care of us."

Sarah and the children followed Rebecca into the kitchen to help with supper while Abe and the men talked.

"Eli, do you know that Andre's forces have even begun arresting Jews here in Skokie? They're rounding up the evangelical Christians, too. They say we're resisting worshipping the emperor. Well, I sure the heck am! I won't bow down before some nude statue. Rebecca and I have managed to avoid getting those stupid microchips implanted in our hands. My father had a number tattooed on his right arm in Auschwitz. It'll be a cold day in hell before I'll let them do that to me in America! Who would have believed that such things could happen here?"

The phone rang next to Abe's chair. The two believers knew something terrible had happened when they saw the stricken look on the elderly man's face.

"What's wrong?" Eli asked.

"That was Henry Berg calling from down the street. The authorities are arresting members of our synagogue in the neighborhood—those without Andre's mark. Henry says they're heading in this direction. We'd better move fast!"

Abe bolted out of his easy chair toward the kitchen and rushed the visitors downstairs.

"You stay down here," he ordered as he opened the heavy steel door of a large coal bin. We'll all be captured if Rebecca and I stay with you, and I won't risk the lives of my grandchildren. The authorities will break in and search the whole house if we don't answer the door." The aging Jew took his daughter-in-law's hand. "Here I was worrying about you in Jerusalem, and now some Nazis are coming to get us right here in Skokie!"

Sarah and the children hugged the elderly couple. "Dad, Mom, please know that Yeshua does love you, as we do. Trust in Him as your Messiah, as the Messiah of Israel. We love you both!"

"We love you too." Rebecca blew a kiss as she hurried back up the stairs behind Abe.

Moments later, a loud pounding began on the front door. Abe grabbed his newspaper and undid the lock just as the authorities began kicking in the door. "Good gracious, men," he exclaimed. "What in the world is this all about?" Rebecca stood in the kitchen doorway, a spatula in her hand.

"Abraham Goldman?" A rough-looking officer followed by three men with clubs burst into the entrance hall. "You and your wife are under arrest for failing to register for your economic identification numbers."

The three agents immediately left to search the house while the officer remained with the Goldmans.

"What are all these toys?" one shouted gruffly from a bedroom door.

"Our grandson was over this morning," Rebecca replied.

The suspicious officer glanced down at a clipboard he was holding. Some of your grandchildren live in Jerusalem? Is that correct?"

Abe shuddered before responding. "Yes, two of them."

"Our grandson Todd was here today," Rebecca quickly added. "He stays here often, so we even keep some clothes for him. His folks live in Franklin Park, not far from the airport."

"Yes, I see you have a daughter in Franklin Park, with two boys and a girl. They are properly registered. Hank, take a look downstairs."

Two burly agents stomped down the basement stairs, making the house almost shake. One of the men spotted the coal bin. "Want me to look in here?"

"Sure, Jack. Check it out."

Sarah held her hand over Benny's mouth as everyone prayed furiously.

"This stupid thing must be rusted over. It won't open!" The man yanked on the long, metal handle, but it would not budge.

"Don't worry about it. It doesn't look like it's been used in years."

Holding down the matching handle inside the bin, Eli and Craig said silent prayers of thanksgiving for their apparent deliverance. When they emerged from the dark coal bin a half hour later, they discovered that the house was empty. Sarah knew her children would never see their grandparents alive again.

After visiting twelve major cities, the emperor finished his triumphant American tour and returned to Washington. Sensing that his enemy, the God of Israel, was somehow protecting the president, he arranged to drive with Rogel from National Airport to the Washington Monument, now renamed the Tower of Andre.

After crossing the Potomac River, the driver continued up 14th Street to stop directly in front of Andre's grandiose likeness, glowing in the afternoon sun. The two leaders got out of the car.

"It is marvelous, isn't it, Vincent? It looks so radiant in the sunlight!"

"Stunning, your majesty. Tens of thousands pay homage to you every day here." Rogel had to force the words out of his mouth.

"And you, have you done so, Vincent?"

"No, not quite, but I see your image every day from my office window."

I've got him now! he thought as he gazed into nearby television cameras recording the scene.

"It's one thing to see it, Mr. President, and quite another to worship before it. We would be most honored if you would do so now, in our presence. Bow down before my image or pay the price!"

Rogel's heart began to race like a horse in the Kentucky Derby. He looked directly at the devil incarnate and announced loudly, "You are not God! I will not bow down to you!"

The emperor stepped back a few paces and motioned to Basillo, who raised his hand toward the statue. A column of glowing, red-hot flames arced down from the Tower of Andre and instantly reduced the president to a heap of smoking ashes.

The Man of Sin was well pleased by his latest triumph. He did not anticipate that Vincent Rogel's televised martyrdom would help inspire millions around the globe to choose a similar path toward eternal life and glory.

29

Tribulation

Emperor Andre was present when Frank Weston was sworn in on the White House lawn. After taking the oath of office, the new president pledged his undying loyalty to the emperor. He told senators, supreme court judges, and the other officials gathered for the ceremony that Rogel's death, while regrettable, showed that the era of independent nation-states had come to an end.

When he finished speaking, Weston turned and bowed in the direction of the Antichrist, seated pompously on a nearby throne. The assembled dignitaries warmly applauded.

Following a ceremony at Andrews Air Force Base, the emperor flew back to Europe to spend time consolidating his united world empire.

After Rogel's death the campaign to imprison Americans who refused to worship the beast and take his mark was stepped up. By Christmas over one million people had been incarcerated, and that was just the beginning.

To Andre's great dismay, large numbers of Christians followed Rogel's courageous example and chose suffering and death over the emperor's lies. This incensed the sadistic despot. In the end, most were beheaded—a method of slaughter especially pleasing to Andre.

Most of the Israelis evacuated in "Operation Eagle" escaped harm. They were sheltered in rural parts of America. The sealed Jewish males who ministered to them played a large role in their protection and even produced food through miracles when supplies ran out.

Among those benefiting from such blessings was Miri Doron. She had been directed to a rural refuge set up by Gentile Christians near Fort Collins, Colorado. Danny Katzman accompanied her, along with 170 other Israelis.

United World agents tried several times to arrest the Israelis. Each time they did so, Danny or one of the other sealed males prayed aloud, and the agents went temporarily blind.

When local believers could no longer supply food to the camp, Miri approached Danny for solace. "It's so cold, Danny, and I haven't had a bite to eat in two days," she complained while plopping down next to her redheaded friend on a couch.

"Nobody has eaten, Miri. Food has really become scarce, and expensive when it *is* available. What we grew last summer is almost gone. Our local friends don't even have enough for themselves. But do not fear, help is on the way."

"What do you mean?"

"The Lord showed me this morning in a dream that it's time for some heavenly multiplication." The thin Israeli stood up and headed for a nearby counter. He positioned his smooth hands over several large tin containers and began to pray.

Danny turned to Miri when he finished praying. "Come over and take a look inside."

"Oh, Danny, they're full of cooked fish and bread!"

"To your health!" he proclaimed as he handed her a plate.

The apostles and their helpers spent one year traveling around the globe, preaching repentance and warning about the final judgment to come. They visited Mexico and Brazil before moving on to India, Pakistan, Russia, Nigeria, and Egypt. Miraculous signs followed them wherever they went.

After their year abroad, the believers returned to Jerusalem. The Western Wall plaza had been completely sealed off as work progressed on the World Temple, so the apostles prophesied in the streets of Jerusalem, usually just outside the Old City's bustling Jaffa Gate.

On their return they discovered that the atmosphere had changed dramatically. Although he won reelection easily because of the popular Mideast peace settlement, Yacov Nimrod had stepped down suddenly after suffering a severe heart attack. His rival, Yudah Sephres, had become Israel's premier, and he showed much more tolerance for the emperor's programs.

A majority of Israelis now carried Andre's mark, and few seemed willing to repent or renounce emperor worship. Yet, the emperor had decided not to force the identity chip on the more than half million Orthodox Jews in Israel. He realized most of them would rather die than worship him, and he feared that major rioting would recur if he created more martyrs in the country where his great temple was being built. This would give the lie to his claim to be the herald of peace for Jerusalem.

Yochanan and Natan-el were saddened to learn that many of the Israelis and Palestinians who had earlier given their lives to Yeshua had been put to death. Among them were the two women imprisoned and miraculously released with Sarah—Naomi and Yasmin. Naomi's family had also gone on to be with the Lord.

Sarah Goldman received a shock when she went late one night with Eli to visit her south Jerusalem home.

"What is all that noise?" she asked as she walked up the front walk with her friend.

"You better let me go in first, Sarah. I sense trouble."

A blond Scandinavian woman wearing only a green towel answered the doorbell. "Oh, my, I'll take this one!" she giggled as two other women approached the door.

"Who are you?" demanded Sarah.

A bikini-clad Russian woman answered her. "I'm sorry, honey, we don't do couples."

"This is my home!" Sarah shouted. "Where is my sister, Donna?"

The blond woman looked slightly embarrassed. "She's in the main bedroom, uh . . . with a client."

Eli took Sarah's hand and led her past the three women and through the living room. They noticed Tali's door was shut. As they neared the master bedroom, Eli called Donna's name, and she soon appeared, wearing a cotton robe.

"What in the world have you done to yourself . . . and my home?" Sarah blurted out, trying to control her anger.

"I didn't think you'd be coming back, Sis, and me and my friends needed to make a living somehow." Donna brushed her hair out of her face. "You guys better get out of here. I've got a strong UW soldier in the bedroom."

Eli winced. "You have made your bed, Donna, and you will sleep in its eternal fire forever unless you repent."

"I'm doing just fine, honey. Go back to your flame throwers and leave me alone!"

Sarah sobbed as she followed Eli out the front door. She knew she had lost her sister forever.

One evening Yoseph Steinberg decided to check out a report that a small group of new believers were hiding in a particular building in south Jerusalem. After telling Cindy about his plan, the Beit Yisrael leader took off secretly from the Mount of Olives communal home.

Using the cover of night, Yoseph darted from one building to the next, being careful to stay clear of streetlights and UW foot patrols. After thirty minutes, he reached the apartment building. He dashed up the stairs to the top floor and climbed a metal ladder onto the roof. To his surprise, he discovered sixteen believers huddled together under a black tarp. Several of the believers welcomed Yoseph, recognizing him from the Western Wall plaza.

The learned Israeli stayed for two days and taught the huddled believers from the Scriptures. It was the only "food" they had eaten for a week, although they did have water and powdered chicken broth. The Israelis were extremely grateful for his teaching. Then he made his way back home after dark.

A United World patrol spotted Yoseph as he dashed behind a cypress tree next to an apartment building. "Get him!" one of them yelled from across the street. His two partners immediately aimed their pistols at the tree. "Stop or we'll shoot!"

The Beit Yisrael pastor prayed as he lifted up his hands. A short while later, his body was found by some passersby in a back street alley. He had lost his life in service to his Lord, and his eternal reward would be great.

During his second year in power the European-born emperor further consolidated his iron grip on the world.

He now exerted control over the earth's ten industrial and political giants: the five leading nations of Europe—Germany, France, Great Britain, Italy, and Spain—plus the United States, Japan, Russia, India, and China.

Andre was pleased that his world empire had a solid base of five European countries with a combined population of over three hundred million people. These countries would constitute the iron foot upon which his empire stood. The other foot, the five non-European nations, were not yet solidly in his pocket, but he was certain their allegiance could be counted on nonetheless. To make sure, he appointed devoted lackeys to serve as figurehead leaders in China, India, and Japan. He allowed Vladimir Konstantine to remain as the token leader of Russia, delighted that his vanquished enemy was openly subservient to him.

Andre formed a new body, called the United World Security Council, out of his ten core nations and based it at UW headquarters in Geneva. This council would meet periodically to advise the emperor as he ruled the planet. A revamped Group of Seven economic union was also formed. Finance officials, business leaders, and prominent bankers from the seven nations would meet periodically with Andre's finance minister, Hans Brecht, to set world economic and trade policies. The members included the U.S., Japan, Germany, Britain, France, and Italy. Surging ahead economically in the European Union, Spain replaced ailing Canada as the seventh member.

The universal introduction of the six-day week—four days of work and two of recreation—was extremely popular, giving employees and employers more time off. The emperor's subsequent institution of a fifteen-month year (with a one week "Andre Festival" holiday break between years) logically followed the uniform twenty-four-day months. Appropriately, the three newly created months were named after the emperor and his royal parents—the month of Andre being the first month of each new year. The despot also declared the second year of his rule as year number two of the new universal Andrean Calendar. In doing so, he abolished the various religious-based calendars in use around the globe.

The formation of the new Security Council, on the heels of the devastating world war, brought hope to people everywhere. Most believed Andre's assurances that a new age of prosperity and brotherhood was dawning. However, by the end of his second year on the throne, disaffection with his rule had begun to sprout. Despite the worldwide use of the Euro currency, inflation eroded salaries everywhere. Although world trade in precious commodities like gold, silver, pearls, silk, wine, and olive oil was reaching new peaks, the price of staples had skyrocketed due to radically altered weather patterns and droughts attributed to the Asian nuclear exchanges.

In addition, Andre's AIDS vaccine had produced mutated forms of the virus that were spreading like gangrene under the emperor's licentious sexual policies. Sexually transmitted diseases were now reaching epidemic proportions as a result of the orgies held in front of Andre's nude images. As unprecedented promiscuity swept the planet, doctors discovered that penicillin and other wonder drugs were increasingly ineffective. Consequently, pneumonic plague, diphtheria, tuberculosis, measles, smallpox, malaria, and many flu strains were killing millions across the planet.

The worldwide divorce rate soared as did unwanted pregnancies and abortions. Many politicians and business leaders openly declared themselves homosexuals. The United World Media Center in Geneva began to produce explicit television programs promoting homosexual activity as a solution to overpopulation. Andre himself set the standard.

Natural disasters were wreaking havoc everywhere. Thirteen major earthquakes rocked the globe during the emperor's second year, killing millions of people. Three hurricanes swept over America's south and east coasts. Tornadoes tore through homes and stirred up dust storms. Wildfires blackened half of Australia and northern Brazil. Hordes of grasshoppers and locusts ate up crops everywhere. Massive tidal waves and freak floods caused major oil spills on the world's oceans, resulting in unparalleled ecological disasters. As smoke and dust mixed in the atmosphere with volcanic ash from several major eruptions, unprecedented cold spells gripped northern Europe, Russia, and Canada. Record snowfalls were recorded and crops lost as freezing air moved southward. Gaping holes in the ozone layer appeared over most continents, leading to a sharp rise in skin cancer and eye diseases.

Growing numbers of people turned to drugs and alcohol to forget their problems. Andre legalized marijuana and eased restrictions on cocaine. Great quantities of subsidized European wine flooded the world market, making wine cheaper than milk in most places. But heavy drinking and drug use only added to people's problems. Lawlessness abounded. City dwellers became afraid to venture out of their homes even in the daytime. Gangs of Androids ruled the streets, openly selling drugs and demanding protection money from local businesses. Women and men were attacked and raped.

Tensions between ethnic groups exploded on every continent. Race riots erupted during the latter part of Andre's second year in power, particularly in the United States and South Africa. Suppressed tensions between religious rivals, such as Hindus and Muslims, blew into armed conflicts.

Islamic militants in Asia, North Africa, and the Middle East launched widespread guerrilla attacks against United World forces. After two full years on the throne, the emperor's grip on Algeria, Sudan, and Iran had greatly weakened. Nationalistic groups in China, Russia, North America, and Japan were forming underground movements advocating freedom from the yoke of European imperialism.

As Andre prepared to mark the third anniversary of his ascent to power, the world was on the brink of moral and economic collapse. Still, the demigod kept promising that things would get better, but fewer and fewer people believed him.

30

Abomination of Desolation

"The day of the Lord draws near! It will come as destruction from the Almighty. Fear God, and give Him glory, because the hour of His judgment has come. Fallen, fallen is Babylon the great!"

Sarah sat on the curb not far from where Yochanan thundered forth his prophetic utterances. Feeling weary and dejected, she prayed silently. *How long, Lord, until You avenge the blood of Stacy and Yoseph, of Naomi and Yasmin, and of all the other saints killed by the evil emperor and his false prophet? Lord Yeshua, how long until Your judgment day comes?*

Cindy strolled over to sit down beside her. "You look tired today, Sarah. Are you alright?"

"I'm tired, Cindy, but not just physically. I'm tired of that bloodsucker, Andre, who is enslaving so many." The widow raised her left hand horizontally in front of her nose. "I'm fed up to here with this awful world. I know the Lord's return is close, but I can't help getting weary sometimes, not to mention a little lonely."

Cindy wiped her friend's forehead with a handkerchief. "I know," she replied reassuringly. "It's hard being separated from Yoseph, even for a little while. I want Yeshua to come back so much I can taste it. But, as Yochanan has told us, a few more things must take place first."

"I know it won't be long before the Antichrist seats himself in the temple and proclaims himself god, as Paul wrote in Thessalonians. Then the final war will take place. But when will Yeshua return?"

"The Lord said that even He doesn't know the exact day or hour, only the Father alone. But He did tell us to look for the various signs."

"And we've seen so many," Sarah tilted her head toward Yochanan, "including the ministry of our two friends. A few days ago the media reported that a huge statue of Andre has been moved into the newly completed temple. So the end must be close, right?"

"I think so, Sarah. The image has been set in place for next month's dedication ceremony. Both Daniel and Revelation reveal that God only allows the Antichrist to reign for three and a half years, so it must be nearly time for us to flee Jerusalem."

"That's what I've been thinking, Cindy. We need to ask the apostles about that this evening when we get home."

The golden sun was sinking below the western horizon as the disciples trudged up the Mount of Olives to their home. It had been another fruitful day near Jaffa Gate, with thirty-two people, most of them Orthodox Jews, surrendering their lives to the Messiah. Hot, dry air blew down from the crest of the Mount, carrying with it the sound of children playing. Natan-el coughed as he stopped and turned around to gaze back at the Old City.

"What a superb sight!" he exclaimed as he spotted the temple towering nearly three hundred feet into the air.

"It is a magnificent structure, even if built by the devil himself," Yochanan added as the band of believers drank in the breathtaking view.

"Especially against the orange sky," Sarah sighed aloud.

Natan-el nodded. "And the Lord will redeem it, just as He did after the Hellenists violated our rebuilt temple in the time of the Maccabees."

As the believers neared their home, the fading light around them suddenly brightened. Tali spotted the source. Pink floodlights now bathed the elegant marble temple in a sea of color. "Wow! Look at that!"

"It's magnificent!" Cindy's comment floated gently on the breeze.

"But what a shame that it's for that diabolical Andre," Craig sighed.

Yochanan smiled. "It is for now, Craig. The Lord will have His dedication, His Hanukkah, later. The Antichrist's days are numbered."

"Yochanan, Cindy and I were talking about that very thing this afternoon." The group turned in unison to resume their ascent. "Isn't it about time for us to flee Jerusalem like the Lord told us to do, when we see the Abomination of Desolation standing in the Holy Place?" Sarah held her children's hands so they would not stumble over the rocks.

"That day is very close, Sarah. It's been nearly three and a half years since Andre forged the Mideast peace treaty, allowing him to build his edifice down there on our sacred mount. Late next month, his blasphemous image is scheduled to be unveiled. Jerusalem will then be engulfed in flames, followed by all the world. How blessed are all those believers who remain faithful until the Lord returns!"

Yochanan looked at each of their faces glowing with reflected pink from the Temple Mount floodlights.

"Children, Yeshua's coming is near. Do not be afraid of the pending upheaval. We will give you ample warning before it's time to flee Jerusalem." As the apostle glanced at Eli, he added, "Only a few of you will remain behind with us."

"You mean, you and Natan-el won't be coming with us?" Craig didn't like this prospect.

"No, we have another role to fulfill."

The husky American took a deep breath when he realized what Yochanan meant. "Oh, I almost forgot. I won't be like Peter and try to stop you from fulfilling your preordained role. Still, it's hard to think about you two actually being—killed."

The remark startled Benny. "Yochanan's going to be killed, Mom?"

Sarah picked up her growing son. "It's okay, sweetheart. We'll talk about it tonight."

It was just five weeks later in September when the two witnesses directed the small band of disciples to leave Jerusalem. The evil emperor was about to emulate Antiochus, the ancient Greek-Syrian ruler who had made people worship his idolatrous image inside the Jewish temple. It was time to head for the hills.

Sarah stuffed a few essentials into a backpack. Moshe hoisted Benny over his shoulders. His meager possessions hung from a strap around his waist. Ten minutes later Sarah, Tali, Cindy, Craig, and Ken followed Moshe out the door, heading southeast toward the Judean Desert. Sealed Jewish males throughout Jerusalem were leading other bands of believers in the same direction. Their final destination was the hills east of Hebron.

Streetlights became enemies as the disciples darted down the nearly empty roads. The nightly curfew loomed, so Moshe stepped up his pace. Twice he spotted United

World foot patrols many blocks ahead—his vision being extra keen since his heavenly visit to Mount Zion.

A gray UW jeep suddenly rounded a corner just ten feet in front of the believers. Its bright lights cut the night like a sharp knife. Benny whimpered as Moshe flung his right arm up in the air.

What is he doing? wondered Craig. *That will only attract more attention to us.*

The jeep's three uniformed occupants simultaneously turned their heads in the opposite direction of the believers as they sped past. A nearby explosive sound had caught their attention. Ten minutes later Moshe had led his charges safely out of Jerusalem.

Despite the stifling morning temperature, thousands of Israelis lined the main highway into Jerusalem waving nude statuettes and festive banners in the air. The twenty-two-car motorcade slowly drove up the Judean hills into the holy city.

Prime Minister Yudah Sephres and Foreign Minister Edna Satori met the procession at the western city limits. After a few words of greeting, the Jewish leaders joined the entourage as it proceeded down Jaffa Road toward the ancient walled Old City. Only Religious Affairs Minister Amos Shimshon was noticeably absent.

Wearing his three-tiered jeweled crown, the proud emperor pompously ascended the newly built marble ramp to the refurbished Temple Mount. Distinguished international guests paraded up the ramp after him. Italian marble slabs now covered the worn floor of the ancient holy site. Cedars from Lebanon protruded from newly built flower boxes along the eastern rim of the Mount.

King Dan escorted his son down a long velvet carpet to a diamond-studded throne set up in front of the new temple. Urbane Basillo, dressed in an ivory silk suit and blue tie, escorted Queen Dorothea.

In his welcoming remarks, the prime minister thanked Andre for bringing peace and stability to the Middle East. "Israel has enjoyed unprecedented economic prosperity under the terms of the peace treaty," he proclaimed to the crowd, "and the sense of security has lifted a heavy weight off the lives of all Israelis. We are proud that you selected our small country in which to erect your magnificent temple."

Basillo stood up and almost pranced over to the mahogany table behind the emperor's throne. Like a showman in the center ring, he theatrically lifted a silver breastplate containing twelve precious stones, apparently a reproduction of the one worn by the high priests in the ancient Jewish temples. The lying prophet placed it around his master's bare, bulging chest.

Andre rose before the audience and strutted past the ivory pillars and gold-plated doors of his splendid edifice. The entire entourage followed him into the Holy Place. Television cameras discreetly positioned at various points inside the large, rectangular nave caught shots of the sapphire-studded vaulted ceiling, the interior walls covered with pure gold, the white marble columns and floor.

"God of this world, prince of the air," Basillo's demonic voice boomed throughout the temple's outer chamber. "We call upon you to fill this temple with your power and your glory! We know that your throne is situated above the stars of heaven, but we ask you to dwell with us here on earth. Fill the world with your powerful spirit and help us to be worthy to worship our anointed sovereign, Andre!"

Basillo reached out and pulled on a light blue cord. Instantly, a silk covering tumbled to the floor and a sixty-six-foot, solid gold statue of Andre loomed into view. With diamond eyes and teeth made of the finest pearls, the statue was completely nude, except for an enormous breastplate embedded with huge gems, a replica of the one the emperor himself now wore.

Everyone inside the Holy Place fell on their faces. A malevolent voice proceeded out of the statue's mouth. "A new era of world tranquillity is about to begin!" The powerful words reverberated through the chamber creating a life of their own. Chills ran up everyone's spine. The demon-packed statue continued, "You will be blessed as you listen to and obey my commands!"

The gloating emperor then pivoted on his heels to face the entrance of the Holy of Holies. A television camera placed inside the chamber recorded his every move. He slowly approached the golden throne, decorated on each side with two gold dragons whose wings touched each other directly over the royal seat. Without shame, Andre ceremoniously unzipped his silk slacks and placed them on a velvet stool. His underwear came off next. The viper swelled with pride as he sat down naked on the throne.

The remote-controlled camera zoomed in for a close-up shot. Kings and presidents watched on a large screen in the nave as the Antichrist lifted his arms and head toward heaven. "I am!" he howled with demonic glee. "There is no one besides me! I am the god of the universe, the god of all creation. I and my father, the dragon, are one. Worship me, and live!"

Yochanan and Natan-el tore their rough sackcloth from top to bottom. Although they were not watching Andre's blasphemous display on television, they knew by the Holy Spirit that the Abomination of Desolation had reached its climax.

As they tore their clothes, the heavens burst forth with activity. The archangel Michael quickly prevailed over

Abaddon, the angel of destruction. The fallen angel was hurled out of the sky. Michael's perennial foe rapidly descended to the earth and landed in a desolate section of central Asia.

Although forced out of the heavens, the demon was not at all upset. In fact, he bordered on ecstasy. At last, his time had come. He could turn the key to release the evil hordes bound up for millennia in the bottomless pit.

Abaddon, whose name in Greek was Apollyon, raised the key up over his head. "The pit is open!" he thundered as lightning crashed across the Asian sky.

The earth split apart to leave a gaping one-mile trench. Thick black smoke rose from the abyss. Simultaneously, thousands of locust-like creatures peeled into the darkened sky, flapping their webbed wings and hissing through their sharp teeth. With the tails of scorpions, these hideous creatures stormed through the air leaving a whirlwind of smoke, dust, and sand in their wake.

The order had been clear: They were to hunt down and torment those who did not belong to Yeshua. They were to do this by stinging their victims with their tails. The sting would be like the bite of a scorpion, so miserable that those stung would long to die. Yet death would not come; there would be no release from the pain.

Within an hour of the temple dedication, over one hundred thousand Orthodox Jews had poured into the streets of Jerusalem, joined by sixty thousand Arab Muslims. The outnumbered United World troops used clubs and sticks to herd the rioters back. But the angry crowds would not budge, even when bullets began to fly. For the Jews, the unveiling of the Greek-style pagan idol in the temple, followed by Andre's blasphemous words, was simply the last straw. They preferred to be shot rather than see such desecration on their sacred Temple Mount. The

Muslims were equally distressed that the insolent European had profaned their sacred shrines, situated near his idolatrous temple.

Hosting a sumptuous reception in the temple courtyard, Andre became livid when told the reason for the noisy commotion. "Shoot them!" he bellowed. He also ordered the main road from the Temple Mount closed near Jaffa Gate and instructed Burton Chiles to summon UW forces from the Golan Heights and southern Syria, and from along the borders with Lebanon, Jordan, and Egypt, to be quickly transported to Jerusalem.

Despite the rising death toll, the rioting escalated. The devil's anointed ruler fumed when told that his international guests had to be driven in armored vehicles north around the Old City to get to their west Jerusalem hotel accommodations.

"It's those two rebels, your majesty," Chiles reported. "They keep incinerating our troops who try to move them away from Jaffa Gate. We can't even disperse the large crowd that's gathered around them."

The emperor's body coiled like a serpent ready to strike. "I'll see to that!"

31

Jacob's Troubles

By nightfall, the city of peace had degenerated into a city of chaos. Fires raged out of control. United World forces were firing indiscriminately at the protesters and killing hundreds every hour.

Yudah Sephres was furious that he could not stop Andre's slaughter. His army and police were not strong enough to intervene. They had been severely pared down as a result of the Arab-Israeli Peace Treaty—concocted by the very man now massacring his people.

With a regiment of UW guards surrounding them, Andre and Basillo exited the King David Hotel and marched through the Hinnom Valley to nearby Jaffa Gate, where the two apostles were preaching. The emperor had had enough. Advised by Burton Chiles that a confrontation was about to take place, television cameras began broadcasting live from the scene.

When Yochanan spotted Satan-incarnate, he uttered the prophetic message spoken by the seven peals of thunder many centuries before. The impact of his powerful message blazed like a ring of fire around the globe. Then he looked the beast squarely in the eyes. "Who is the liar but the one who denies that Yeshua is the Messiah? Behold, the Antichrist, the one who denies the Father and the Son! You will be thrust down to Sheol, to the recesses of the pit. Fallen, fallen is the kingdom of Satan! Fallen, fallen is Babylon the great!"

Wearing the cotton toga of a Roman god, the imperial emperor carefully positioned himself so that nearby television cameras could get clear shots of the imminent spectacle. A surge of energy ignited his tanned body. He sneered, "You Jewish sons of a harlot! You serve the dark force who has opposed my father from the beginning of creation. You cannot resist the victory of the great dragon. You will not succeed!"

Andre inched closer. "The dragon has allowed you to continue your troublemaking for nearly three and a half years, but now, your time is up!"

"We have been faithful until death, and now the Lord will give us the crown of life!" Yochanan's powerful voice saturated the airways.

"You can kill our bodies, but you cannot touch our souls!" Natan-el shouted out.

Andre snorted. "And we *shall* kill your bodies!"

The apostles jerked their heads in the direction of the sky over the nearby Mount of Olives. "There He is, in the distant galaxies, coming this way with His holy angels to recompense every man according to His deeds!"

A vile laugh escaped through the emperor's clenched teeth. "You men of darkness are out of your puny little minds!" Instantly, a bayonet of fire shot out of his mouth and skewered both men's stomachs. Eli knelt down next to Yochanan's smoking body, tears pouring down his face.

"Your beauty, O Israel, is slain on your high places," he cried softly. "The mighty have fallen."

At Andre's command, UW forces opened fire on Eli and the other sealed Jews crouched near the dead witnesses. The bullets bounced off the Israeli men like retractions from a steel shield. The phenomenon shocked the emperor, who tried to divert attention back to the slayings.

As Eli and his brothers dragged the apostles' bodies to a nearby curb, Burton Chiles started to clap wildly. Soon the Antichrist's troops began to cheer. The despot acknowledged his soldiers' endorsement and motioned for them to quiet down.

"Moses and Jesus corrupted the true path of the exalted Creative Universal Force. The two rebellious followers of those false prophets, who tormented the earth with their magical powers causing droughts and plagues everywhere, are dead! The era of darkness is over! The eternal age of Aquarius is here! Your god, Emperor Andre, declares a special week-long, worldwide festival to celebrate our great and glorious victory!"

Sarah and Cindy wept as they listened to the 6:00 P.M. evening news on Craig's transistor radio. The BBC reporter almost gloated as he described the scene around the apostles' dead bodies, left on one side of Jaffa Road to rot.

"Israelis, Arabs, visiting tourists, and members of the international press have been coming nonstop over the past three days to gaze at the dead rebels here in Jerusalem," crowed the reporter.

Sarah shut off the radio. "The Bible promises that Yochanan and Natan-el will rise from the dead very soon, but it's still difficult to listen to reports like that. I wonder how Eli is?"

Cindy wiped her puffy eyes. "I'm sure he's okay. Didn't he promise that no harm would come to him?"

"Those were his exact words. You know, I've often wondered what exactly happened when the guys were taken up to heaven and sealed. Do you think they may have actually received their new bodies—a little before the rest of us?"

"The Bible does call them firstfruits to God, the same term used about Yeshua after His death and resurrection. He received His glorified body after He rose from the grave. Haven't you ever asked Eli?"

Sarah crooked her head and smiled. "I have, but he wouldn't answer me. He said it was a very personal subject. What a funny guy! I really love Eli."

"More than Jonathan?"

"Of course not! I love Eli in a different way."

"Well, Yeshua did say there'd be no marriage in heaven. I wonder what our relationships will be like."

"That's one of those remaining mysteries, I suppose. But it won't be long before we find out! Oh, here come the guys."

"Here's some more wood," announced Craig. He and Ken plunked down some dry pine logs near the campfire. "Any news yet?"

"No, just more of the same," replied Sarah as she handed the radio to Craig, who switched it on low.

"Hey, Mom, I'm up here!" shouted Benny from on top of Moshe's shoulders. The big man and his little friend made their way to the others around the fire. The believers quietly discussed the awesome events of the previous days. Their conversation was soon interrupted, however, by another live BBC report from Jaffa Gate. Craig turned up the volume.

"As celebrations continue around the world, we now go live to Peter Horton for a full report on today's activities. Peter, can you describe for our listeners the general situation in Jerusalem right now?"

"John, it's early evening here, following another day of pilgrimage to the place where I am standing just outside of Jaffa Gate. Emperor Andre himself paid a visit here this morning to view the decomposing bodies of the two slain Jewish rebels. A clear plastic sheet has been placed over the bodies so visitors won't be assaulted by the growing stench. His majesty wants the bodies to remain on Jaffa Road until they completely rot, as a reminder of his victory over the forces of darkness."

"Peter, what is the security situation in Jerusalem now? I understand that the rioting has subsided a bit."

"The city, which has been like a war zone for the past three days, is generally quiet now. Reinforced United World troops seem to have finally brought the rioting under control, although at a cost of possibly tens of thousands of lives. Bodies still lie in the streets in many neighborhoods; the raging fires are being brought under control. However, the air is still thick with smoke."

"Nothing new," said Ken as he picked up Craig's radio to turn down the sound.

"John, something very unusual is happening here!" The reporter's voice escalated in pitch, prompting Ken to turn up the sound. "Oh, my God! The bodies of the two rebels are moving! They are getting up on their feet!"

Screams of terror flooded Jaffa Road as hundreds stampeded away from the frightening sight.

"ALU HAINA!"

"John, that was a loud sound coming from the sky. It sounded to me like a voice saying in Hebrew, 'Come up here.'"

The reporter's heart went numb as he watched the two apostles slowly rise into the air. Television cameramen zeroed in as Yochanan and Natan-el rose above the stone walls of the Old City and into the ash-filled sky. The radio reporter stuttered as he tried to describe the scene.

Amid squeals of joy, Sarah and the other disciples leapt to their feet and hugged each other. Their mentors were alive forevermore.

The emperor was enjoying a light supper in his King David suite when a grim faced Basillo burst into his room. "Your majesty, the two rebels have risen from the dead!"

"What?!" railed the enraged ruler as he jumped up to follow him to the large window. "There they are in the air!" exclaimed Andre as he flung open the window and took in the view of the nearby Old City. "Our ancient enemy has struck again!"

"Shall we inquire of the great dragon, your majesty?" The calm in Basillo's voice soothed the growing insanity in the emperor.

"Of course, Urbane. Quickly!"

The two men stopped and silently waited for their master. Before long, a malevolent presence filled the room. It took the shape of a hideous dragon.

"We will crush him!" The dragon spoke without parting its lips. "I command my ministering spirits to go forth to all the world's leaders now and gather the nations to the mountains of Palestine to fight my ancient foe. My throne will remain above the heights of heaven!"

Just then, a demonic spirit, visible to the human eye, flashed out of Andre's half-open mouth. Another one dashed from Basillo's while a third darted from the dragon's. The three powerful spirits flew out through the open window. They were on their way to perform their assigned tasks.

Unknown to the emperor, powerful acts of rebellion against his rule were already in motion in China and Russia.

While Chinese Premier Wu Ting—Andre's handpicked appointee—was at the temple dedication ceremony, an invisible coup was taking place in his giant nation. Deposed military leaders, still enraged over their humiliating defeat at the hands of the European despot, quietly seized power in the new capital, Shanghai. They immediately began implementing a plan to send millions of quickly recruited soldiers west toward the Middle East. They would be joined along the way by volunteer fighters, mostly Muslims from other Asian countries wishing to throw off the yoke of Western imperialist rule. Once the combined Asian force arrived at its Middle East destination, it would meet up with Russian troops and seize control of the world's main oil reserves on the Arabian peninsula.

Vladimir Konstantine had secretly been reconstructing his disbanded army for months, quietly recruiting hundreds of thousands of volunteers and training them in remote locations. When news of the apostles' resurrections reached Moscow, forces loyal to Konstantine launched a coordinated attack on all United World positions around the city, capturing large UW weapons arsenals.

With powerful weapons now once again under his control, Konstantine felt that the time was ripe to dust off his old plans for a large-scale invasion of Israel. The Russian leader had waited a long time to get his revenge against the emperor and Israel. It was essential that he move quickly. UW Mideast forces had been concentrated around Jerusalem. Potential backup forces were tied up around the world putting down mounting rebellions and preventing various regional conflicts from spreading. Andre's world empire was crumbling. The time had come to act.

Konstantine telephoned Ali Akbar Ransani, the popular Iranian religious leader and secret commander of the Islamic Resistance Movement. "I will invade Israel from four directions—from Libya, Egypt, and Sudan in the west and south; from your country in the east; and from Syria in the north. Will you join us? The Muslim republics of our former Soviet Union are ready to do so."

"You have Iran's full support, Vladimir. My volunteer fighters can be ready to move out in a few days' time. I will send them overland through the Kurdish north of Iraq. Can you send some transport planes to Tehran to collect our elite forces?"

"I will send a dozen jets immediately. We will start flying in tonight. I've already begun moving troops by air into Libya and Sudan. We should be ready to invade Israel in ten days. However, I must draw Andre's men into Egypt first."

"With Allah's help, you will."

"Ground troops will set out tomorrow. Chinese and other Asian forces will arrive later to provide backup as we carry our invasion into Saudi Arabia. We must act quickly!"

Konstantine was certain that Andre's Mideast battalions, moving rapidly toward Jerusalem, were not strong enough to block his invasion of Israel. China's westward advance would tie up most of the emperor's Asian forces, while troops in North Africa would be pinned down by seething Muslims, angry over the emperor's desecration of their holy sites on the Temple Mount.

The Russian leader felt confident. Most Islamic nations would support his war to seize the Temple Mount and destroy Israel. With the help of the Asian hordes, he would then go on to gain control over Saudi Arabia's vast oil resources, spreading wealth to his allies and bringing an end to economic depression in his beloved homeland.

Reassured that the dragon had everything under control, the emperor excused Basillo and sat back down to finish his supper. As he picked up his silver goblet, the red wine began to splash over the rim. Half a second later the floors and walls started to shake.

The astounded Antichrist tumbled off his chair onto the carpeted floor.

Across the shallow Hinnom Valley, dozens of people were knocked down to the pavement. It seemed as if the entire planet was in motion. In fact, waves of molten rock in the earth's mantle had begun to pound the outer crust. The planet's core was suddenly heating up to unprecedented temperatures. The earth's plates rubbed violently against each other. Entire continents were shifting as the fierce vibrations cracked the edges of the plates. Across the globe, volcanoes exploded, sending trillions of tons of thick ash into the atmosphere. After seven minutes, the molten lava suddenly cooled, as if by divine decree, and the violent tremors began to subside.

It was the worst earthquake in human history. A tenth of Jerusalem was completely leveled, but the new temple was only slightly damaged. Millions of people around the world had perished, and millions more had been seriously wounded. Fires and tidal waves only intensified the destruction.

Two hours later, the sun looked like someone had placed a huge black tarp over it. Only a faint red glow indicated the full moon in the night skies. The blanket of smoke and ash also obstructed any view of Venus and Mars. The lava cores of the two planets had heated up at exactly the same time as the earth's, causing two tremendous explosions. Venus and Mars were no more.

32

The Day of the Lord

Sitting next to a smoldering fire, Craig studiously mulled over a prophecy found in chapter 12 of the Book of Daniel. He calculated that the Lord would probably appear in just over five weeks. He was especially encouraged by Yochanan's dying words revealing that he could see Yeshua coming toward earth, even if the Messiah was still in a distant galaxy when the apostle miraculously spotted Him.

Moshe sat beside Craig on a large rock. "But Yeshua said that no one would know in advance the exact day or hour of His return, Craig. He also said that the great tribulation would be cut short for the sake of the elect."

"Jerusalem certainly has been experiencing great tribulation the past few days. We just barely escaped the Antichrist's slaughter, and now the whole planet is shaking." Craig picked up a stick and began to draw figures in the dirt.

"At least we're not in Jerusalem tonight, brother. People trapped in cities must be going through hell following the quake."

"Moshe, I know we cannot calculate the exact day or hour, but if Yeshua came two minutes ago, it wouldn't be soon enough for me. Maybe He'll come tomorrow. After all, it is the first day of the Feast of Tabernacles."

"So it is. I nearly forgot." Moshe's eyes gazed north in the direction of his beloved city. "The holiday actually began this evening at sundown. You know, Craig, this festival is also called the Feast of Trumpets and the Feast of Booths. Maybe the last trumpet mentioned by Paul, and in the Book of Revelation, will sound during the feast!"

"Man, we sure are observing the Feast of Tabernacles this year—sleeping under the stars like the ancient Israelites did in the desert. I only wish we had a booth to stay in like they did."

"And I wish we could see some stars. That volcanic ash has ruined the visibility. Look, you can barely make out the full moon."

"Yeah, it looks blood red. At least the nights are still warm, and it's not raining. I wouldn't have wanted to do this in winter!"

The two men laughed good-naturedly just as Sarah and Benny came over to say goodnight. "Have a good sleep, and we'll see you guys in the morning."

"Thanks, Sarah. Are you feeling any better, Benny?" Moshe patted his little friend on the back.

"I can't stop coughing."

The two men laid hands on Benny and asked the Lord to help him breathe despite the falling ash.

Benny held his mother's hand as they tromped back to their small camp under an olive tree. Tali was already snoring.

"Try to get some sleep tonight," Sarah said while spreading a sweater over her son. "I know it's been a difficult time but don't worry. Yeshua is coming back any day now, and then you won't ever cough or be frightened again."

Satan's anointed leader knew that his powerful enemy was prevailing. Yet, despite his feeling of impending doom, Andre ordered United World forces stationed in southern Europe and Africa to set out for the Middle East. He then went on worldwide radio to shore up his crumbling rule.

"Citizens of planet Earth, the forces of darkness, masquerading as that false prophet, Jesus, are trying to destroy our world. Their power is substantial. They have placed lying signs in the sky and caused worldwide disasters.

"Our spiritual enemies have also taken control of Russia and China and are even now preparing to invade the land of Palestine. But with the help of the great and eternal dragon, we will prevail!"

After finishing his satellite broadcast, Andre flew to Cairo to take personal command of UW forces. Holding on to Egypt was vital to his plan to thwart the expected Russian-led attempt to invade and conquer Israel.

Within minutes of Andre's worldwide speech, chunks of Venus and Mars perforated the Van Allen Belt in the earth's upper atmosphere. The larger meteorites—some up to fifty feet in diameter—shot through the belt and pelted the globe like giant hailstones.

The falling fragments caused havoc everywhere, igniting huge fires in forests and inhabited areas and triggering powerful underground earthquakes. Smoke from the fires and dust thickened the dark screen already blotting out the sun's rays.

The meteors plunging into the world's oceans caused giant tidal waves, which destroyed thousands of ships and devastated coastal areas. The planetary debris poisoned all life in the ocean and also in fresh water rivers and lakes.

When a twenty-foot fragment from Mars impacted the Judean Desert, hundreds of buildings in Jerusalem collapsed, killing thousands. Many frightened Jews ran into the streets and cried out for mercy from the God of Israel. Most now believed the message they had heard so often from the two apostles—Yeshua was Israel's Messiah, and He was returning to Jerusalem to judge Andre and the world and to reign on King David's throne.

Amid the growing chaos, Vladimir Konstantine was certain that his multi-nation invasion would succeed. He believed that the meteor showers, earthquakes, and other natural disasters were actually working in his favor, although some of his soldiers were frightened by the distant appearance of Yeshua in the eastern skies above the earth. He explained the celestial show as a trick by Andre to force a retreat. He noted that worldwide faith in the emperor was evaporating. Muslim nations were now fully ready to revolt against his rule. And the thick clouds of ash, dust, and smoke in the upper atmosphere provided an excellent cover for his troop movements into the Middle East.

Russian and Iranian forces, supported by others from Iraq, Afghanistan, and the Muslim republics of the former Soviet Union and Ukraine, were poised to invade Israel from the north. They had easily overpowered token United World units in the staging areas of southern Syria, south Lebanon, and northwestern Jordan. Russian-commanded Libyan, Algerian, and Sudanese forces rapidly surrounded and cut off Cairo, forcing the frightened emperor to flee back to Israel by helicopter. Only a few hours later, Konstantine's Arab allies charged across the Suez Canal and into the Sinai Desert, heading straight for southern Israel.

Upon hearing the good news, the Russian leader summoned his top generals to his underground bunker in northern Syria. "Gentlemen, we have made tremendous progress so far," he boasted. "Our forces are ready to attack from the Sinai. We are all set here in Syria, as we are in Lebanon and Jordan. We shall launch our coordinated assault on Israel just before dawn."

33

Fire and Rain

Hundreds of thousands of Russian soldiers and their allies poured across the borders of northern, eastern, and southern Israel as the first hazy rays of sunlight touched the tip of Mount Hermon. The invading hordes raced like fast-moving storm clouds across the land. By seven in the morning they had penetrated all the way to the cities of Tiberias and Haifa in the Galilee, crossed the Jordan, and moved into the foothills of Judea and Samaria east of Jerusalem. From the south, they advanced forty miles into the Negev Desert, driving toward Beersheba and Hebron. Their goal was to rapidly surround and cut off Jerusalem.

Yudah Sephres was so distraught that he literally pulled out a small clump of gray hair from his balding scalp. "We're under attack, and yet we can't do a thing to stop it!" he sobbed to those gathered with him in the pool hall bunker. "That heavenly sign still hovers in the sky. Those two old men were right—Yeshua is our promised Messiah and we have forsaken Him! Now the Russians and their allies will destroy us. We are doomed!" The prime minister cradled his head in his folded arms on the table.

"I warned you it was a mistake to dismantle our air force and nuclear weapons!" Defense Minister Hochman was almost shouting.

"It's the end of the Jewish state," moaned Foreign Minister Satori.

Less than three hours after the massive invasion was launched, Konstantine arrived by military helicopter to speak to his jubilant troops north of Tiberias. Surrounded by admiring soldiers, he spoke from a stone wall next to the church on the Mount of Beatitudes at the northwest corner of the Sea of Galilee. He wore a giant grin.

"Comrades, your military prowess is changing the course of history. You are bringing in a new, Russian-led world order by your sweat and blood. Andre is not a god. I am the new Caesar who will rule the world!"

As Konstantine's soldiers fired their rifles into the air amid shouts of triumph, the God of Israel unleashed His final judgments on the earth. Worldwide tremors of unprecedented magnitude caused continents and islands to heave up and down. The Russian leader toppled off his pedestal onto the asphalt pavement below and cracked his skull in two.

The earth's core had heated up once again, causing the planet to shudder like a naked child in a cold rain. Skyscrapers shook violently, heaving large chunks of steel and concrete onto the city streets below. Rice paddies were lifted high into the air and dashed back down again. Cars and trucks were tossed about as if they were toys. Enormous holes devoured Egyptian pyramids and giant redwoods. In less than ten minutes, more than one billion people had perished.

Konstantine's forces panicked. The frightened soldiers began firing indiscriminately on their own comrades. Almost instantly, a hurricane of fire and brimstone poured down from the sky on the surviving forces, annihilating every last soldier and leaving bloodied corpses for a vultures' feast.

The wrath of God did not stop there.

Fiery flames showered the world's waters, transforming both salt and fresh water into blood. Pungent gases in the atmosphere caused malignant sores and boils to break out on anyone possessing Andre's mark. There was no escape.

Eli, Moshe, and the other sealed Jews ministered across Israel like a mighty army, leading their frightened and mournful Jewish brethren to the Lord. The people were clamoring to be led, as if a veil had suddenly been lifted from their eyes.

The surviving remnant now realized that the God of Israel was sparing their tiny country from the worst effects of the divine judgments falling all around them. Synagogues overflowed with thankful men, women, and children. They could see the heavenly sign in the sky. The Messiah was returning to save them. Hearts begged for forgiveness, and thousands repented of the sin of unbelief.

Many tearfully recited portions of Isaiah 53, realizing now that it was a prophecy of their rejected Messiah: "He was despised and forsaken of men . . . and we did not esteem Him. Surely our griefs He Himself bore, and our sorrows He carried. . . . He was pierced through for our transgressions. . . . and by His scourging we are healed."

In a state of demonic fury, the Antichrist ordered UW troops stationed outside Jerusalem to forge a human chain around the city so no one could enter or escape. He instructed his forces to crush an armed internal revolt, which had broken out in Jewish neighborhoods, and to round up those Jews and Arabs without the mark. He also ordered the deaths of Israeli government leaders, whom he suspected of masterminding the revolt.

Familiar with the layout of the main government building, UW commanders led elite forces down the secret stairway leading to the pool hall bunker. Two explosives experts blew open the reinforced steel door. Sephres, Satori, and Hochman cowered in one corner of the conference room. They were lined up against the wall and shot in the head.

Andre's demonized soldiers then went on a rampage throughout Jerusalem. They plundered empty houses and apartment buildings, looted shops, and stole every vehicle they could find. Hundreds of Israeli women were subjected to gang rapes in open daylight as their husbands and children watched helplessly at gunpoint. Drunk with power and wine, the thugs then savagely beat their victims into unconsciousness when it was over.

As the rampage continued, the son of perdition proceeded up to the Temple Mount. Once inside, he and his lying cohort held a two-day orgy with male and female prostitutes in front of his idolatrous image. They stopped only when the emperor received word about the imminent military invasion of the Chinese-led Asian hordes from the east.

During October and November, millions of people from Korea, Vietnam, Cambodia, Indonesia, India, Pakistan, Afghanistan, and Iran had joined the Chinese onslaught advancing toward the Middle East. Reeling from the divine judgments that were striking the earth, they had a new satanically inspired goal—to prevent the hated Yeshua and his angelic hosts from capturing Jerusalem.

The swarming mass of humanity pushed westward despite word about the annihilation of the Russian-led forces. By the time forward army brigades had reached the Euphrates River in Iraq, the massive force had swelled to an astonishing two hundred million people stretching all the way back to Afghanistan.

The forward brigades swarmed across the country of Jordan and soon penetrated Israel's Jordan River border near the town of Beit Shean, fifteen miles south of the Sea of Galilee. Asian generals quickly erected command tents in the adjacent Jezreel Valley, not far from the ancient town of Megiddo.

Within two days, the once luscious Israeli valley, where the prophetess Deborah had led her ancient forces to victory and Gideon had divided his men, was teeming with soldiers. The valley became so pregnant with men and equipment that some units were forced to make their way up the northwestern ridge and camp near Nazareth. Others were positioned up and down the nearby Jordan Valley. Some stayed put in Iraq and Jordan, while others fanned out north into Syria and Lebanon.

Andre quickly sent an envoy to the Chinese command post. The generals, now filled with demonic power, assured him they were not out to attack the emperor's forces. They wanted to wipe out the Jews once and for all. After this, the forces could unite and prevent the return of this Yeshua to earth.

I will accomplish what Hitler could not. The emperor relished the thought as he read the dispatch. *Only a few more days, and those bloodsuckers will be wiped off the earth forever. Long live the dragon! Long live his son, Andre!*

34

THE KINGDOM OF GOD

A tidal wave of panic swept over tiny Israel as the people realized they were surrounded. The pierced Messiah was apparently going to punish them for their centuries of unbelief. Israelis outside Jerusalem had started gathering sophisticated weapons left by the decimated Russian troops, hoping to use the arms to ward off the impending onslaught. But it looked like nothing was going to help them now. Only the God of Abraham could save them, and most doubted that He would.

However, Israel's God was not planning to abandon His people. In fact, He was preparing the most impressive deliverance in history. From the very foundation of the world, the Messiah had longed for this moment. He had wept many times for His Jewish brethren, who had suffered so often over the bitter centuries of exile from their land.

Now in the sky over Jerusalem, Yeshua lifted up His arms like Moses of old. Gently, He began to blow out of

His mouth. A rushing wind settled on the mountains, hills, valleys, and plains of Israel. A spirit of grace and supplication was being poured out on the grieving house of David and on the repentant inhabitants of Jerusalem. Their pierced Messiah would save them.

Working out of the pool hall underground bunker, the demented Andre screamed at his officers to slaughter every last Jew who had not been exiled from Jerusalem. United World troops tried to carry out the command, but the Jews stubbornly and effectively resisted. Their weapons were limited to revolvers and clubs, but they fought like game cocks in a ring. Even the children joined in the struggle, throwing stones at the rampaging forces. It was as if a supernatural surge of energy had suddenly taken over. They were not going to lose their beloved city.

And then it hit—another earthquake of such violent proportions that the wobbling planet's lower atmosphere became electrified with lightning and booming thunder. The few mountains and cities that remained were brought down by the enormous quake.

Around Jerusalem, the earth split in two, creating a deep crevice in the Mount of Olives. Half of the Mount shifted three feet to the north; the other half slid an equal distance to the south. This new gorge provided a miraculous escape route out of the disintegrating city for thousands of Jerusalem residents, who quickly fled to the Judean Desert.

As the world shook with fury, hundreds of stars exploded across the Milky Way galaxy, sending out fiery flames into the darkness of space. The earth's remaining planetary cousins blew up as well, and within hours chunks of Jupiter and Saturn began pummeling the world. Millions were killed by the space debris, including many of the soldiers stationed around Israel.

Still driven by demonic delusion, Asian and United World military leaders ignored the divine judgments and continued their final battle preparations. As they did, Israel's holy Messiah began His prophesied descent to earth. The armies of heaven closely followed behind Him. Still reveling in the afterglow of the magnificent marriage supper, they were rejoicing as Yeshua headed in the direction of the city they loved and cherished so dearly.

Chinese surface-to-air Silkworm missiles were directed from the Jezreel Valley at the descending army. Advanced UW warplanes based in Israel, Lebanon, Jordan, and Syria furiously attacked, but to no avail. The missiles and shells sailed right through the descending throng until the Lord, riding on a majestic white horse and wearing a robe dipped in blood, uttered a powerful word of judgment. Instantly, the projectiles reversed direction and turned back upon their handlers, blowing the forces of Satan to bits.

Frightened demons guiding the international commanders shrieked hysterically. Cries of fury bellowed from Andre's lips as well.

Then the Lord issued another word of judgment. This one shredded the terrorized enemy soldiers into pieces like a sharp two-edged sword. Corpses littered the ground from Iraq to the Mediterranean Sea. Eyes, tongues, and flesh began to rot in the intense heat of the earth's sizzling greenhouse temperatures. A blood swamp saturated the ground for two hundred miles around Jerusalem, stretching from Lebanon and Syria to Egypt and Saudi Arabia, and rotting corpses actually floated in pools of blood in the Israeli Jezreel Valley.

The remnant of Israel cheered victoriously as the Lord of Hosts slowly descended toward the Mount of Olives. All of Yeshua's enemies were now dead except for the man of sin and his evil associate, cowering in the dark inside the Holy of Holies.

The Jerusalem believers bowed low as the Messiah's rapturous descent came to an end. The King of the Jews was not entering the city on a humble gray donkey but on a gleaming white stallion.

As the saints sang out a serene song of worship, Yeshua dismounted in triumph. His nail-scarred feet touched the very spot from which He had ascended after His resurrection. Just as He promised, the Lord of the Universe had returned to rule and reign in the city of the Great King.

The believers continued to prostrate themselves as thousands of saints descended on Jerusalem. Eli, kneeling not far from Yeshua, felt a gentle tap on his shoulder. He turned around and fell into the bear hug of his beloved friend, Jonathan, who then warmly embraced Sarah, Tali and Benny.

Yochanan, Natan-el, and the other returning saints joyously accompanied the Son of David as He walked barefoot toward the Temple Mount, which had risen up above the Mount of Olives during the earth's convulsions. A thick stone wall blocking the Old City's Golden Gate—tightly sealed for many centuries—miraculously dissolved as Yeshua approached it. The Lamb of God then made His way through the gate and proceeded up the steps to the cracked, but still standing, temple.

Two powerfully built angels stood guard near the temple's entrance. When the Son of Man spotted them, He gave the command to seize the beast and his false prophet. The angels marched straight to the inner chamber and happily carried out Yeshua's order.

The vanquished men who brought the world to ruin were whisked out of the temple. The Lion of Judah focused His piercing eyes on them. "You evil beasts will not lie in graves with the kings of the earth!" He roared. "You will not be united with them in burial because you have destroyed the world! I have cut off from Babylon both name and survivors, offspring and posterity!"

The Righteous Judge then commanded His angels to throw the two men alive into the flaming lake of fire. As soon as the order passed His lips, the dragon himself appeared behind Andre and Basillo. The prince of darkness could hide himself no longer, for the Lord of Light had returned to earth.

Another powerful angel swooped down from the sky. He took hold of the ancient serpent and cast him into the great abyss. The earth was the Lord's!

With His enemies firmly under His feet, the Prince of Peace proceeded into the temple, followed by hundreds of angels and saints. Jonathan, Eli, Moshe, and Sarah were among them. It was the first day of Hanukkah, and the sanctuary would be cleansed.

Andre's idolatrous statue had crashed to the floor during the last earthquake. Yeshua pointed His finger at the fractured golden image, and it immediately dissolved.

The Son of God bowed low and prayed to His heavenly Father before entering the Holy of Holies. He walked slowly and alone into the sacred chamber. The Antichrist's two blasphemous dragons, which had also tumbled to the marble floor, vanished from sight.

The King of Kings sat down on the golden throne. Above Him on either side appeared two glowing cherubim. Saints and angels peering through the entrance prostrated themselves before the Lord of Glory, now seated on His radiant throne.

The saintly throng burst forth into shouts of ecstatic praise. The raging birth pangs of the kingdom of God were over. David's Greater Son had returned to rule and reign in Jerusalem.

The enduring curse, which had devoured the earth since Adam, was finally broken. Death was swallowed up in victory. Living waters began to flow out from under the rededicated temple. Half of the water cascaded east down the Kidron Valley and into the Dead Sea, which rose as it became fresh. The waters then rushed past the ancient ruins of Sodom and Gomorrah and down to the Red Sea. They brought instant cleansing to all oceans south and east of the Holy Land. Living waters flowing west of Jerusalem poured down through the Judean hills and into the Mediterranean, transforming the western oceans into sweet water.

Jews around the world who had somehow survived the great tribulation and divine judgments were gathered home to their ancient promised land. Israel's Savior would leave none of them in exile any longer.

As Jacob's descendants made their way up to the eternal city, Yochanan gathered together the little flock that had ministered with him and Natan-el at the end of the age. The redeemed saints danced with delight as their voices blended together.

> Great and marvelous are Thy works,
> O Lord God, the Almighty;
> Righteous and true are Thy ways,
> Thou King of the nations.
> Who will not fear, O Lord, and glorify Thy name?
> For Thou alone art holy;
> For all the nations will come and worship before Thee.

"None of us will have to exert any effort to come up to Jerusalem to worship the King," said the Lord's beloved apostle with joy when the singing ended. "We will all be living here permanently with our Messiah, King Yeshua!"

About the Author

David Dolan is an American-born author and journalist living in Israel since 1980. He covered the 1982 Lebanon war for the Voice of Hope radio, based in southern Lebanon. He reported for CBS News from early 1988 through the year 2000. He also worked for CBN Radio and Television in Jerusalem, and is regularly heard on programs carried by the Moody Radio Network and other outlets in the United States, the United Kingdom and New Zealand.

Dolan is a noted international speaker, and also a writer for many publications. He authored the highly acclaimed history of the Arab/Israeli conflict, *Holy War for the Promised Land* in 1990. A recently updated version of that book, along with his latest work, *Israel in Crisis: What Lies Ahead*, which combines current events with biblical prophecy, can be obtained from his website, www.ddolan.com, or in the North America by dialing toll-free 888-890-6938. You may also sign up for his free e-mail Israel Updates via his web site.